MANAGING SOFTWARE QUALITY AND BUSINESS RISK

MANAGING SOFTWARE QUALITY AND BUSINESS RISK

Martyn A. Ould

Venice Consulting Ltd

JOHN WILEY & SONS, LTD

Chichester • New York • Weinheim • Brisbane • Singapore • Toronto

Published by John Wiley & Sons, Ltd
        Baffins Lane, Chichester,
        West Sussex PO19 1UD, England

        National   01243 779777
        International (+44) 1243 779777
        e-mail (for orders and customer service enquiries):
        cs-books@wiley.co.uk
        Visit our home page   on http://www.wiley.co.uk
                         or http://www.wiley.com

Material from *CMM and ISO 9001* by Martyn A. Ould in *Software Process – Improvement and Practice* (volume 2, pp281-9, 1996) has been reused and adapted for this book with the permission of John Wiley & Sons, Ltd.

Figure 4-12 is adapted from figure 1.1 of Jennifer Stapleton's book *DSDM: the method in practice* with the permission of Pearson Education Limited.

A catalogue record for this book is available from the British Library.

ISBN 0-471-99782-X
Camera ready copy prepared for publication by the author.
Printed and bound in Great Britain by Biddles Ltd, Guildford and King's Lynn.
This book is printed on acid-free paper responsibly manufactured from sustainable forestry, in which at least two trees are planted for each one used for paper production.

CONTENTS

PREFACE

In 1990 I wrote a book entitled *Strategies for Software Engineering*. It described a tried and tested approach to the planning of software development projects, based on work that I had done as Quality & Technical Director at the software engineering company Praxis, and on the technical and quality culture that the company had developed. Since then the book has underpinned a three-day workshop given to all staff at team leader level and above, and the approach has seen further years of use in what has increasingly been a changing environment in software development, with timescales getting shorter and the move towards the integration of major 'enterprise' products such as Oracle and SAP accelerating.

As experience has grown and the world has changed, the time has come for a major revision of that book. The fundamental and simple tenet remains the same: that successful software development means managing quality up and risk down. And the techniques for doing this have survived the test of time. So I have carried forward material that remains valid today and I have added new material that is more relevant as we enter the next millennium, and recent experiences that illustrate the approach in action.

If you are a technician at heart than you will no doubt think that the problem of successful software engineering is a technical problem to be solved by technical means. If you are a manager you will no doubt think that it is a managerial problem to be solved with managerial techniques.

As both technician and manager over the years, I have tried to understand just what makes for a successful software development project: one that produces what the client wanted at the agreed price and date. My conclusion is that, aside from universal management skills such as the ability to motivate, someone managing a software development project must be able to make a technical assessment of the problem to be solved, and to go from that assessment to the plans and standards that are the manager's tools. In this book I describe a _planning process_. It is a process designed to lead the manager through that assessment and on to the preparation of the traditional resource plan that deals with schedules and staff allocations and budgets. The process uses two strategic tools which, ideally, are used in strict sequence, though life somehow never turns out that easy.

The failures of the software development industry are well publicised – media scribblers find easy targets in the failure of others while creating nothing themselves, and their analysis rarely rises above the mockery of technology. The reality is of course far more complex, and development failures are invariably caused by a combination of circumstances – circumstances that are rarely purely technical in origin. Recognising this, the software development industry has increasingly taken notice of the use of risk management in other industries and applied standard risk management practices to software development projects.

The first part of the planning process presented in this book is therefore _risk planning_ – a discipline that requires the project manager to assess the risks in the project and to find ways of reducing them to an acceptable level.

In the past decade, there has been a move within the software industry to smarten up its act, in particular to worry about the quality of its product more than it has traditionally done. There has been some confusion over precisely what _quality_ means for software, and for a software development manager there must be a concern about how they will manage quality into the software that their team finally delivers to the client.

So _quality planning_ is the second concern for the manager. Too often this topic is approached from general notions, and purely managerial actions get suggested. But here again I believe the matter is principally a technical one, and it is only by a technical assessment of the quality requirements on the system that appropriate and effective measures can be chosen by the manager in the plan for the project.

So as not to raise expectations in unwarranted ways, I should also say what this book is not about (and hence what makes it less than 1,000 pages long). It is very much about strategy and planning, and hence, with the exception of a little on the topic of monitoring project progress and the use of measurement, the execution of a project is not covered. There are many aspects to project management that deserve books of their own – people management, client management, contractual aspects and so on – but I leave these to those other books.

This is also not a book about estimating, another large topic that I leave to others. My aim is solely to show where estimating fits within the larger risk and quality planning approach I propose. In particular, I show how the decision making processes I offer the manager lead to a sound basis for the customary resource plan.

Finally, this is not a book about software process improvement *per se*. It is in fact about one software process in particular: planning. But in that sense it directly addresses some key practices in the Capability Maturity Model (CMM, *Capability Maturity Model for Software, Version 1.1*, Software Engineering Institute, Carnegie Mellon University, report CMU/SEI-93-TR-24, 1993) in the following way:

- *Level 2: Software Project Planning*, with a much greater emphasis on risk management but, as noted above, no detailed coverage of estimating
- *Level 2: Software Project Tracking and Oversight*, insofar as the approach produces plans that are the basis for subsequent monitoring
- *Level 2: Software Configuration Management*, in that configuration management is treated here as 'quality preservation' at planning time.

In some places I have provided URLs for relevant sites. These are of course subject to change without notice, but were correct at the time of writing.

On a point of pedantry, I have used *they*, *them* and *their* in their (gender) singular usage in order to avoid the offensive *he*, *him*, *his* and the ugly *he/she*, *s/he*, etc. combinations. It is an old usage that is common in speech. Rushers to dictionaries will find the *Oxford English Dictionary* recognises the usage – 'often used in reference to a singular noun ... applicable to one of either sex' – and gives a quotation from a 1526 publication by Wynkyn de Worde (who took over Caxton's press): 'Yf ... a psalme scape ony persone, or a lesson, or else yet they omyt one verse or twayne'.

Many of the illustrations of the approach at work are adapted from development projects done at Praxis and subsequently at Deloitte Consulting and I am grateful to my colleagues, whose professionalism provided so many good examples to draw on. Praxis was set up in 1983 with the express aim of turning software development from a craft skill into an engineering discipline. With its use of rigorous technical and management processes, it set a new standard, one that has spread through ex-colleagues in the Praxis diaspora. Much of that Praxis culture and approach continues in the hands of Praxis Critical Systems.

Finally, I am always open for discussion at *mao@the-old-school.demon.co.uk*.

Martyn Ould, Hinton Charterhouse, April 1999

1   *Introduction*

Early brain damage

I've started up many projects in thirty years in software engineering and seen many people set off on others, and I can't remember not enjoying the early heady days of each, not least because there is so much to do and so much to be organised and all at once. The client is waiting to get started, you have staff arriving, office space needs to be acquired, the computers and software are arriving soon, your management are demanding plans and forecasts – and you haven't the faintest idea what you're up to. Everyone is looking to you to get this ship out to sea – the right way up. Where do you start?

For the first month or so – let's assume this is a development that is expected to run for a reasonable time, say at least six months – the pressure is immense and you need something to hang on to, something to build on, not least so that you don't forget things. And because there is so much immediate managerial work to be done there is little time to get to grips with the problem to be solved and to understand it sufficiently that you know what you have let yourself in for. Brain damage seems to creep over you and it gets harder and harder to get hold of this snake that is already wriggling out of your grasp.

Managing a software development project – like managing anything – is about understanding what you have to do and retaining that understanding, grabbing the snake and then keeping a firm hold on it. It's my contention that, if you don't understand the problem you've been set to solve, you're more or less doomed unless you are very clever or very lucky. And that means taking enough time out to get that understanding. Which is what this book is about.

Down with risk

Life's a pretty unpredictable venture altogether, with software development one of the black spots. No manager needs to be reminded just how risky a venture writing 500 000 lines of code can be.

About half-way into a project I once discovered that (thanks to a good technical authority and a good team of software engineers, as it happened) I had time in the day to think through a number of scenarios for the rest of the project: what happens if release 3b of the custom hardware doesn't arrive on time? How much testing could we get done with release 3a? Suppose the new discs don't have the performance we've been promised – do I have any escape routes? And so on. Like other project managers I have spoken to since, I found this a pretty unnerving feeling to get during a project. It's one that experienced managers get to be suspicious of in themselves (and in others if they claim to be feeling it): if you've time to think, you're either doing a brilliant job or something terrible is going wrong and you haven't spotted it!

As it turned out, things were indeed steaming along nicely, and the time I had to work over possible disaster scenarios was well spent because it helped me really understand the *dynamics* of my project. In particular, I started to get to know all the downstream risks and I could plan to handle them *today*. Now, a moment's thought will tell you that the greatest number of risks are present at the start of the project. And that's just the moment when you don't have the time to think your way through them.

This book won't tell you how to make time at the start of the project. For that you must either work longer hours or become an expert in one of the many 'how to manage your time' techniques (though I'll recommend a favourite of mine to you: Oncken 1984). I'm going to assume that you have made yourself enough time to carry through the technique I'm going to describe. If you haven't, I can only wish you *bon voyage*.

One major part of the technique is about analysing the problem you have been set in a systematic way so that you can spot the major areas of uncertainty and risk, and can plan to minimise them or even circumvent them downstream. Forewarned is forearmed.

This analysis I shall refer to as *risk planning*. It is something people do all the time if they have the snake under control. It is something we, consciously or not, do in everyday life. What I shall do in this book is to present it to you in an orderly fashion, so that you can do it in a step-wise and orderly fashion too. When you do risk planning, you will make a technical assessment of the risks inherent in the project you are going to undertake, and from that assessment deduce what you are going to do about them. In other words you will be planning about all the things that you *don't* know about.

It is always easier to write down what you know than what you don't know. It's probably to do with the embarrassment of saying 'I don't know' that makes this so. We've always been taught to say what we know – exams are an obvious part of our upbringing which reinforces this: we never seem to be invited by the examiner to discuss what we *don't* know. But the most important thing about planning is precisely writing down what you *don't* know, because what you don't know is what you must find out. And a good plan is one that recognises risks and contains activities downstream that will handle them. You don't have to answer all the problems at the planning stage – you simply have to know they exist and plan for tackling them at some later date.

I have often noticed that people who are late producing their plans at the start of their project are late because they feel they cannot issue the plan until they have solved all the problems the project faces. 'Well, I can't say what training we'll need, until we've decided on the language we're going to use, and I can't decide that until we've done our preliminary analysis of the system.' And as long as the plan doesn't get issued, the project rolls along in no particular direction at all.

So, risk planning is designed to make you find out what you don't know and to plan to handle it in the future. That way you get a project plan out early and you have the snake under control before it slips out of your grip. As the time to tackle those risks comes along, your plan will have the activities there to do it. You have given yourself room to move.

Up with quality

That's half the story. The other half is about making sure – from the outset – that the system you deliver is one that has all the quality attributes your client expects of it. Once again, we want to start thinking about this issue right at the start of the project. The problem here is one of pitching the quality at the right level. No client is going to thank you for gold-plating or for delivering a grisly user interface or a flaky application.

When the system is first specified, we describe it in terms of what it should do (its *functional* quality attributes) and how it should be (its *non-functional* quality attributes). Taken together, these attributes form the specification of the system, and they are our target. Being sure we hit that target with what we deliver is not simply a matter of crossing our fingers and hoping all will be well when the system is put together. It is about making sure that we translate those requirements in the final system into requirements on each of the intermediate things that we produce: the designs at various levels, the code, subsystems and so on. This process of *quality factoring* is generally badly handled, in my experience. Crossing fingers is easier but generally less reliable.

I once managed a project that was building a transaction processing system. In the specification we had performance figures to do with the maximum transit times for transactions under certain loadings. One of the key activities we undertook was a coarse analysis of the paths that would be taken by those transactions and some estimates of the path lengths in number of instructions and number of operating system calls. By doing some experimentation with operating system calls to see how long they took, we were able to come up with some estimates of the time that a transaction would take to traverse the code, and hence to emerge from the system. We could not be absolutely certain that things would be OK on the night, but we knew we were not completely out of court with the design we had.

Achieving the required quality is therefore first about factoring quality requirements into quality requirements on intermediate products. It is then about understanding the sorts of *quality control* that make checking for those requirements possible. And this is something that comes from an understanding of what our methods can do for us – what I call the *verification and validation (V&V) potential* of a method.

But how do we choose the right methods in the first place, methods that will help us to build in the quality we are looking for, methods for *quality achievement*? Again, this is an area where we can ask some quite straightforward questions to find the answer, questions that form another part of the quality planning process. These questions are designed to make us decide what are the essential characteristics of the system we are building and then choose the methods that concentrate on those characteristics. The key feature of a screw is that it has a slot in the top for inserting something with which to turn it. A hammer doesn't fit at all, a coin fits reasonably well, but a screwdriver gives us leverage too. We need to make the same assessment of a system to choose the method that fits and gives us the best leverage.

I have seen good methods used to build quality into a system, good quality control used to ensure that things are right, and the whole thing thrown away by poor *quality preservation*: post-release changes made to code without sufficient regard to their effect. The care and attention to detail that had produced a good product was wasted as the system was 'corrupted' by those who took insufficient care to check that the changes they were making worked with existing code, let alone fitted the overall philosophy and architecture.

I shall refer to these three quality-related topics – *quality achievement* through the choice of methods, *quality control* through the choice of verification and validation, and *quality preservation* through the control of change – under the heading of *quality planning*.

> ## HEADLINE
> Together, risk planning and quality planning will give you all you need to plan your project, to grasp the snake and control it.

Silver bullets

In his paper 'No Silver Bullet' (1987), Fred Brooks said 'we see no silver bullet. There is no single development, in either technology or in management technique, that by itself promises even one order-of-magnitude improvement in productivity, in reliability, in simplicity ... [but] a disciplined, consistent effort to develop, propagate, and exploit [many encouraging] innovations should yield an order-of-magnitude improvement. There is no royal road, but there is a road.' He then distinguished between *essential* difficulties that are inherent in a problem such as software engineering, and *accidental* difficulties that attend the solution of the problem but aren't inherent. For software, essential difficulties stem from the conceptual aspects of the software, while we create accidental difficulties such as awkward languages and poor tools. If conceptual problems are to be efficiently tackled we must look at how we formulate complex conceptual structures, and Brooks addressed a number of 'promising attacks':

- buying a product rather than building bespoke – in other words avoiding the conceptual problem altogether

- refining requirements perhaps through rapid prototyping – that is, concentrating on the most difficult part of the conceptual task

- developing software incrementally rather than all at once – the conceptual leaps involved in growing a system are smaller and easier than those required when building one

- breeding good designers, the people who know the meaning of the phrase *conceptual integrity*.

Other proffered bullets to slay the werewolf of software development such as Ada, object-oriented programming, artificial intelligence, expert systems, 'automatic' programming, and graphical programming will, said Brooks, only give us improvements at the margin as they attack only the accidental difficulties of development. Over a decade later we can add to this list of failed silver bullets.

In his list of promising attacks though, Brooks highlights two crucial features of a successful development project: a successful strategy and successful methods. The strategy is designed to minimise the risks inherent in software development; the methods are designed to solve the conceptual problem that is left. Risk management and appropriate methods are the main topic of this book.

Sharp instruments

So, though there are unlikely to be many silver bullets with which software development managers can load their pistols for guaranteed success, for the manager prepared to treat the topic with the same measure of science that the designer approaches the problems of design, there are a number of sharp instruments that can be wielded to good effect, and it is these that this book describes. Briefly put, the methods I describe are designed so that you can

- reliably choose the correct strategy for your software development in a way that reduces the project's exposure to technical risk, and hence your ultimate exposure to business risk, to an acceptable level

- reliably choose the development methods and tools that are most appropriate for the system your team will build, and choose them in a way that gives your client the required degree of quality in the system

- reliably choose the verification and validation strategy appropriate for the products your team will construct

- reliably plan your project on the basis of your chosen strategies and methods

- reliably carry through the development in line with those plans, keeping risk and quality to the required levels.

By reading this book you will learn three techniques.

The first – *risk planning* – is a technique designed to lead you, the manager, through the decision-making process that should start every software development project. Risk planning provides you with the information required to choose a development strategy that has as its goal the reduction of technical risk to the project and business risk to the organisation. Its output is a *Risk Plan*.

The second technique covered is that of *quality planning*, which is designed to lead you to choose development methods, a verification strategy and a change management strategy for your development that have as their goal the delivery of the required quality in the system. Its output is a *Quality Plan*.

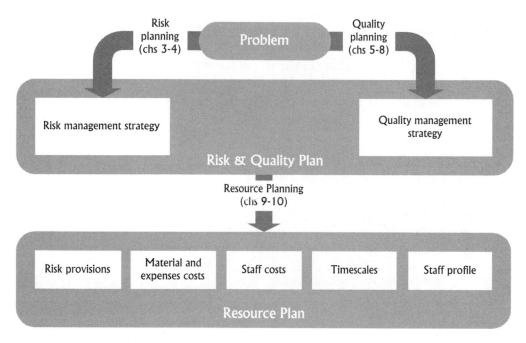

Figure 1-1. The route summarised

The third technique – *resource planning* – takes the outputs of risk planning and quality planning and helps you produce a costed *Resource Plan* for the development, a plan that now takes into account all the risks, uncertainties, the characteristics of the system, the verification requirements and so on. The overall aim is of course to get to a plan that gives you the greatest chance of success. The three techniques and how they fit are summarised in Figure 1-1, and one of the main purposes of the rest of this book is to elaborate this simple picture to the degree that you can get on with such a venture yourself. (If you would like to see more detail right now, take a look at Figure 9-1.)

If you would like a biological analogy let me suggest that a well-functioning and successful project is a lot like a well-functioning and successful human body. It needs three things to be right: the skeleton, the musculature and the nervous system. (OK, I simplify.) Risk planning is going to give us the skeleton of our project; it will make sure that the project itself has an architecture that will not fall down, an architecture that will hold the whole thing together and give something for all the other parts to work on. The methods we choose for quality achievement are the muscles of the project, the mechanisms needed to make the thing move forward and get things done; the muscles/methods provide the power necessary to move the body/project on. Finally, our verification strategy for quality control is the nervous system, the mechanism that is constantly, throughout our life, making sure that all the bits are working and letting us know if things are wrong (pain). And, if I might push the analogy one step further, with our quality preservation we will put in the self-repair mechanisms that always ensure that when things go wrong or need changing the result is still a working human body.

The structure of the book is as follows:
- Chapter 2 provides the next level of detail of the whole planning process.
- Chapter 3 takes apart the concept of *risk* and presents a straightforward process for managing risk during the lifetime of the project.
- Chapter 4 concentrates on planning risk management and on the concept of the *process model* in order to guide you on how to analyse the problem you have been set and how to get the right shape for your project: one that reduces your exposure to risk to an acceptable level.
- Chapter 5 examines the notion of *quality* in software, defining the terms *quality achievement*, *quality control*, *quality preservation* and *quality assurance*, and describes how a Quality Management System can provide the organisational framework in which all this can happen.
- Chapter 6 takes the first step towards building a good system – quality achievement – and gives you a procedure for analysing the system you are building and choosing methods that will give you the best leverage.
- Chapter 7 looks in detail at the question of how to set the right quality levels for each product your project is to produce (including the technique of *quality factoring*), and how to define quality control – veri-

fication and validation – activities to check that they have been achieved.

- Chapter 8 takes us through some of the issues about preserving the quality of our work, in particular through sound *change management* both during and after the development of the system.

- Chapter 9 is the culmination of the processes you will have learnt in earlier chapters: it shows how all the decisions you have now made yield most of the input you require to draw up a full and realistic Resource Plan.

- Chapter 10 presents some straightforward and reliable ways of regularly checking progress and reforecasting outcome, and deals with the knotty problem of measurement.

- In Chapter 11 I tackle a number of blocks that are frequently met by those introducing new software engineering approaches to the work of their teams or their organisations. I suggest practical ways in which you can remove these blocks – for they are real and you should know them.

- Chapter 12 illustrates all these principles through a worked example. In fact, as you read Chapters 2 through 7 you might like to glance at the worked example in Chapter 12 on the fly so that you can see the principles at work.

- Chapter 13 draws together the practical side of the book into a simple step-by-step action list for planning the project.

I hope that, with an understanding of the strategic planning process I describe, you will be able to grasp that snake at the start of the project and have it firmly under control right through to successful delivery of your system to your client.

References

Brooks 1987

No silver bullet: essence and accidents of software engineering. F P Brooks. Computer, **20**, 4, pp10-20, 1987

Oncken 1984

Managing management time. W Oncken Jr. Prentice-Hall, Englewood Cliffs, 1984

2   *Building the boat*

The skeleton: risk planning

Our industry – the software industry – has always been a can-do field … or is it a can-do minefield? The fact that we have pushed our hardware and software to the point where they now infiltrate all of daily life is a tribute to an assured belief that we can make this plastic, highly-shapeable medium of software do anything we want. But that very plasticity can be its downfall too: we say 'yes' too readily, especially if it is something we haven't done before. New is fun.

I have occasionally sat in sessions when a project is being started and the project manager is discussing the plans with the line manager, or when a bid is to be made to a client and the person doing the estimating is discussing the estimates with the salesperson. Software engineers are generally kindly folk, wanting to please (after all, they are in the business of providing bespoke systems to their clients – not unlike tailors), and so often I have heard them let their estimates be talked down to meet the client's or the department's budget. 'Surely we understand how to build this sort of thing well enough that you don't need so long in the design phase?'. 'Our software engineers haven't used Java before but moving from FORTRAN shouldn't be hard – we pay them enough – knock that training out'. 'Surely you can achieve higher productivity figures than those – increase them by 20% and see what the figures look like'. And so on.

Don't misunderstand me – I'm not making a point about salespeople or line managers here. I'm simply reminding us that when push comes to shove compromises have to be made in any commercial venture. The question is: do we know *what* compromises have been made? I believe the only way of ensuring that we do is to start with a plan that has been systematically constructed from the best information, a plan that says 'this is the ideal project shape, duration and cost'. That's the right starting point for compromise.

Now I'm not suggesting my ideal project is one where I can take as long as I like with as many staff as I like. Barry Boehm pointed out many years back (Boehm 1981) that there is an ideal duration and staffing for any project and pushing the various factors to either side of that ideal – and this includes lengthening the project – actually makes it *less* ideal. Obvious really, but when we start to chip away at the budget or the timescale do we keep a note of the risks that we are introducing by moving away from the ideal? I contend that if we start from a plan that has recognised all the uncertainties and all the risks then we shall be clearer in our minds what compromises we are making and hence what extra risks we are – for sound commercial reasons – taking on, and what extra burdens we are therefore asking the project manager and team to shoulder. Tom Gilb neatly sums this up in his *Principle of Risk Exposure*: 'the degree of risk, and its causes, must never be hidden from decision-makers' (Gilb 1988).

Michael Jackson gives the programmer the advice 'don't optimise; but, if you must, do it last' (Jackson 1975). He is saying in effect that we should get the design right first, and then introduce risks by trying to make it run faster. The same advice holds for project managers: 'don't compromise on the ideal plan; but, if you must, do it last' – get the plan right first, then take on risks to get the 'right' answer.

Risk planning is about getting the plan right first.

Software engineers are optimists

What sort of risks and uncertainties are there in the average software development project? Here are a few that might ring a bell:

- what sort of screen layouts will the users want?

- what sort of performance will the database management system give us?

- will the development server provide us with sufficient power to do stress testing of the system?

- will we be able to use the facilities in the new language we have adopted?

- how will the first functions we deliver to the users affect their view of what the subsequent facilities should look like?

- will our design deliver the real-time performance required?

- how does this configuration management tool that we have just bought work?

Some sample answers to these might be 'the first ones we give them', 'enough', 'probably', 'no doubt', 'not enough to worry about' and so on.

Yes, we've all done it. And worse, we might have done it unknowingly. We *assumed* the users would be happy – grateful even – for what they got; that the DBMS would run terrifically fast; that we could start using that new tool tomorrow. We never even thought that there might be some uncertainties here. And as a result we ignored the accompanying risks.

As well as being kindly, software engineers are known for their remarkable optimism (speaking charitably – some would call it foolhardiness). Things go wrong and it's a surprise. For an industry well versed in the corollaries of Murphy's Law, we are notable for our ability to pretend that it has been temporarily suspended on our projects. My advice to project managers is always 'plan for the worst, hope and work for the best'. That way you have some chance of being pleasantly surprised. Of course, it might be simply that we don't like to admit that there could be problems in the development ahead which, right now, we're not sure how we're going to solve. So our plans take no special heed of them.

Risk planning is about taking heed of potential problems.

Bringing realism to our plans

By now it should be clear that I am concerned with discovering at the outset of the project what is hard about it and what is uncertain about it, and then planning it in a way that tackles those hard bits head-on and explicitly deals with those uncertainties. This process of analysis of the problem and the synthesis of the plan is what I shall call *risk planning*. It is above all a *technical* matter because it looks at the technical attributes of the problem.

HEADLINE

Risk planning asks the question 'what are the uncertainties in the problem we have to solve, and what do we need to do during the project to resolve them?'

Before we can get to answers to this question, we shall spend some time in Chapter 3 getting a better understanding of just what risk looks like in software development, how cause and effect can be dealt with separately, the different sorts of *risk reduction measures* that are open to us, and the knotty problem of making some sort of provision in the finances and the schedule for the risks left in our project.

With this understanding in hand we shall see how answers to the question will lead to decisions about the overall shape of your project, what you will commit to and when, what major decision points there will be and when, what iterations you will allow for and when, and so on. They will lead to your choosing what is called a *process model*, or what was once called a *lifecycle*. The term *lifecycle* really isn't very helpful since it presupposes that there is indeed a cycle and this is not always so. The term *process model* is much more precise: it says that we have a model of the process, in our case the software development process. We must start our project planning with a process model of the development that we are going to undertake, in just the same way that we start the planning of a ship, say, with a model of its overall shape: a hull (or several), sails or engines for propulsion, appropriate holds and decking for the planned cargoes, lifting gear, and navigation systems. These major parameters will be determined from consideration of the principal properties we want from the ship. In the same way, the process model of our project will reflect the main parameters of the project: in particular its risks and uncertainties. The model will differ from project to project since the risks and uncertainties differ from project to project.

I shall step out of my boat metaphor for a moment. If we think of our project as a organism trying to reach a goal we can expect that it will need a skeleton to stop it collapsing into an undifferentiated pile; it will need muscles that will give movement towards the goal; and it will need a nervous system that will allow it to check that all is well around the body. The process model is the skeleton.

HEADLINE

The process model will give the overall shape to the project, a shape that is designed to make the project survive under the pressures it will face.

In general terms we will find that risk reduction measures will introduce structural features into our project:

- an overall process model, e.g. *a three-phase project with two intervening review points*

- single activities, e.g. *measure the interface's speed before committing to a design*

- decision points at which one of a number of alternative paths is chosen, e.g. *if a non-networked relational database will suffice use our current environment, otherwise upgrade to the networked version*

- dependencies between activities, i.e. *logic* for your plan, such as *agree interface definition before specification work.*

In Chapter 4 we look in detail at the sorts of process model that we might choose for our project. Suffice it to say here that the sorts of things that might have a place in such a model will include:

- a division of the project into phases with decision points between them, so that we have commitment to a new phase as it becomes understood during the previous phase

- the inclusion of a prototyping activity to remove uncertainty in some aspect of the problem

- a small number of iterations around an activity that, we believe, we cannot guarantee to get right first time

- the development of the core of the system followed by new functions as the need for them becomes apparent, rather than trying to define them all up front.

You can see from each of these examples that something that worries us about the project at its outset is causing us to elaborate the model in a way that reduces our risks downstream.

To pull this together, let us say that we know our projects are risky affairs, and, rather than sweeping them under the carpet, we are going to recognise the risks and proactively manage them by choosing a process model for the project. Just how much risk we decide to 'manage away' and how much we will leave on the table is a commercial decision that will be informed by our technical judgement and we will need to look carefully at how that informing can be done. And whatever we decide, we will record our choices in a Risk Plan for the project, a plan that can be challenged and reviewed.

So it is the preparation of the Risk Plan that will form one of the main threads of this book.

(From now on I shall refer to the *Risk Plan* as though it is always a document, indeed a separate document. In practice you need not feel obliged to be able to point to an actual paper document with the title *Risk Plan* on the front sheet. In some organisations all the risk planning is recorded in a database or a special-purpose tool. As long as that software is holding all the information that I shall call for, then you have a Risk Plan in my terms. We shall also see how sometimes it is more convenient, even if the Risk Plan is a real document, to combine it with the other plans that we shall look at.)

The muscles: methods planning for quality achievement

Over the past twenty years there has been a growth industry in software engineering methods. In the early 1980s Nick Birrell and I felt that there was such a plethora that the software engineer needed to be able to get some overall view of the methods arena, and we wrote *A Practical Handbook for Software Development* in which we described most of the major runners, described the strengths and weaknesses of each, and showed how they fitted into the overall development process: methods for systems definition, methods for design, methods for programming and so on. A point we were at pains to make was that the choice of the most appropriate methods was one of the most important activities for the software engineer, and that that choice would depend on what the major properties of the system being built were. Some systems are principally about data, its structure, flow and transformations. Other systems are about control, its structure, flow and change. The more the method chosen for the problem in hand concentrated on the central issues, the more leverage it would give to the software engineer.

This is a theme that I shall continue in this book. In particular, I shall give some techniques for analysing the system you have to build and thence for choosing the methods most appropriate to build it. There is nothing magical about it. It is simply a matter of matching technology to problem, and to do that we first have to be able to characterise systems and then know what methods treat which characteristics the best.

I was once system designer on a project building a sonar system. The project involved the development of a great deal of special electronics and the software we were to develop was to carry out the major real-time tracking functions in one of the computers attached to all this equipment. The software had to run in several different modes: live, simulation and replay. There were many options that controlled its operation and it had to be resilient to loss of data from the various sensors to which it was ultimately attached. I remember struggling for weeks trying to come up with an architecture that would support all this variety, as well as running on the machine we had to use, together with its operating system. Finally – and not without help from the excellent team I had – we came up with a scheme by which we effectively partitioned the system into a number of discrete components and then modelled the different ways in which they could be combined and the different interactions that would exist between them – which would trigger which and so on. The scheme worked very well and we built a resilient and very flexible system. Moreover, because we had a model of the dynamics of the system we were going to build before we had actually written the code, we were able to exercise it and see if it would behave in the way we wanted it to.

It was some two years later that I read about Petri Nets and realised that we had invented a Petri Net-based system, even to the point of inventing special 'coloured tokens' with special properties. Petri Nets – if you haven't come across them – are simply a way of modelling concurrent cooperating processes. The basic principles are very simple but very powerful. If only I had known about the method before we had started the project! I would then have been able to determine what was most important about the system we had to build, namely the need to organise around forty loosely coupled processes in a way that was changeable dynamically – and we could then have got on and done it that way. I would also have known of the analysis that you can do on a Petri Net to determine its properties, such as whether or not it can deadlock or reach a state from which it cannot 'move'.

That experience proved to me that a clear characterisation of the nature of the problem being solved was vital to effective planning of the system, and it is one of the reasons that the analysis necessary to get that appreciation forms part of the project planning process.

HEADLINE

Methods planning asks the question 'what are the properties of the system we have to build and what do they tell us about the way we must build it?'

An appropriate answer to this question puts us on the road to building a system that works and has some conceptual integrity. If we join two pieces of wood by hammering a screw through them we shall end up with a poor quality joint, one that does not do the job. If we use a screwdriver and glue the joint first we shall end up with a strong joint, one that has the quality we are looking for, one that is fit for purpose. Now it is this notion of fitness for purpose – of *quality* – that I shall be pursuing later in the book, and because the choice of appropriate method is so important for achieving quality in the first place, for getting things right first time, the way we *plan* to achieve quality will have method selection at its heart. We shall look at all of this in detail in Chapter 6.

To pull this together, we can say that methods planning is about analysing the problem to be solved to find methods that will build in quality at the outset. This is the first part of planning for quality and we will capture it in the quality achievement section of a *Quality Plan* for the project.

From now on I shall refer to the Quality Plan as if it is always a separate document. Exactly what form it takes is entirely up to you and the organisation around you. I provide some templates but they are of course only hints. Also, I shall from now on refer in some places to the *Risk & Quality Plan* as if it were a single document. If you are preparing Risk Plans and Quality Plans separately, that's fine – you will simply need to interpret what I say for two documents.

The nervous system: V&V planning for quality control

Once we have answered the question 'what methods?' we are on the road towards a cost-effective strategy for *quality control*, for verification and validation. If we know we are using a screw to make the joint we can verify that the screw has the right properties before we start (an appropriate length and thickness to take the stresses), and once we have screwed it in we can test that the screw is home and secure. This will be the subject of Chapter 7.

For the past few years I have taught a university course on the subject matter of this book. In parallel with my course, the students also have a group project where, in teams of about eight, they prepare a prototype of a system for which they are given an outline requirement statement. A proportion of the marks awarded are gained from a successful demonstration of the prototype to a marking team. I generally run a workshop with the teams at which we do some risk planning and look at how they will prepare and test the prototypes – they are encouraged to adopt a fast prototyping cycle. The discussion starts to turn on what would be a 'good' prototype, and just how 'good' does it have to be. Does it all have to work? Or would it be 'good enough' if some of it worked, whatever they had managed to get working in the short time available? Could they indeed restrict their demonstration of the prototype to just those bits that do work? Of course, this is all getting rather subversive and perhaps even cynical. But I use the point to demonstrate that the amount of quality they build into their system and check for must be determined by the amount that their customers are looking for. No marks are awarded for a late system, no matter how extensive it is. The customer in this case wants *something* by a particular date.

This discussion immediately says a lot about the degree of testing that they should apply to their prototypes. The answer to the question 'how much?' is 'just enough to have something that works to demonstrate'.

This is a universe away from another project in which I was involved at Praxis. It was a safety-critical system in an environment where people's lives would be put in danger if it went wrong. Practically every form of verification was thrown at that development, including mathematical proofs of areas of the design, mathematical proof of the code, semantic and static analysis of the code, and independent teams located away from the main project team that tested the software to high levels of coverage and checked proofs. The answer to the question 'how much?' is 'everything necessary to close off as many openings for error as possible'. Another very noteworthy feature of this project was the intensity of the checking of *all* the products of the project: not just code, but specifications, designs, test specifications themselves, proofs, everything. (I shall use the term *product* in this book to refer to anything that the project produces, whether or not it is finally delivered to the end-customer.)

I offer these two ends of the spectrum of checking for quality to demonstrate again that there are no absolute definitions of what 'quality' is or what lengths we should go to in checking that the quality that we seek is indeed there – what I shall call our *quality control*. At one end of the spectrum we are seeking a level of quality that can be achieved with very slight quality control on just the final product. At the other end our quality control will consist of rigorous checking of every product from the start of the project to the end, simply because the quality demands of the customer are so great.

> ## HEADLINE
> Planning for quality control answers the question 'how good is good enough, and how much checking must we do?' for each product of the development process.

The lesson for our project planning is clear: the choices we make about what quality control, what verification and validation (terms I shall define later), what testing we shall carry out will have a significant effect on the cost and schedule and success of the project. Too little quality control and we deliver a poor quality system, too much and we deliver a good system but at unnecessary cost and probably taking too long. The set of choices that we make about our quality control form what I shall call our *V&V strategy*.

To pull this together, we can say that V&V planning is about analysing the quality requirements of all the products we shall produce during the project and deciding what is the cost-effective and appropriate level of quality control for each. This is the second part of planning for quality, and we will capture it in the quality control section of the project's Quality Plan.

The immune system: change management planning for quality preservation

So, we picked some excellent methods for specifying, designing and programming this system, reinforced them with some well-chosen quality control activities and things are going well: specifications, designs and code of the required quality are appearing from the team at the appointed time.

Dream on. Hardly had we started but the users thought of something new that the system 'just has to have if it is going to be any use to us'. It was a small addition in their eyes, but our Technical Authority looked at what they wanted and could see a mile off that, that far into the project, the whole architecture made it difficult to achieve what they wanted.

Not long after the architecture had been reviewed and signed off, while specifying a component, one of our designers found that the definition of a set of interfaces ignored a parameter that needed to make its way down to a part of the infrastructure. As it stood the design simply would not work.

And, having been given something simple to code, our newest programmer discovered a bug in the compiler that meant that one of the more esoteric features of the language that we were relying on simply didn't work in the current version of the compiler, and the manufacturer had no plans to fix it for six months.

HEADLINE
Change is the one constant.

Now we're getting to reality.

If only people would leave us alone to get on with it. If only we didn't find faults after we thought we'd got everything right. Unfortunately change is a fact of life, with changes coming from outside – people wanting something different or something new – and from inside as we discover earlier mistakes or things we'd rather have done differently. The problem is of course that when we build software systems we are building some of the most complex things that humans build, and that complexity has a time dimension as well; if we take a snapshot of what is happening in the team at any one moment we find all sorts of things being worked on simultaneously and in different states of completion. All of these things are interrelated: component test specifications are written for components that are coded to meet component specifications which are designed to fit within an overall architecture which is designed to meet the specification for the system, and those components are designed to provide certain interfaces to other components which …

Pull one string and the whole mass moves.

Pull one string and the whole thing falls over. Changes are rarely local in such a situation. The connections are so numerous and complex that if we want to change one thing we'll probably have to change ten, and half of those will be being worked on as we speak. It has been observed that one of the crucial differences between software and other human artefacts is that software components can be connected in so many, often invisible, ways. If I change the loading on this bolt in a bridge the impact can be traced through a simple chain of causality determined by the laws of physics. But if I change the range of values accepted by this component the effect could occur at places in the system that are certainly not immediately visible. This new value causes the component to iterate ten more times for a solution to the equation, which in turn delays the activation of a program which as a result might miss a window during which it must present data to an interface which in turn … You get the idea.

If change is so potentially destructive to quality we must manage change to preserve quality. In our planning process we must decide on (or plan to decide on) what mechanisms we will use to deal with each change as it comes along. In this book I shall concentrate solely on the *administrative* side of 'change management'. This is in fact only half of the matter: the other half is the complex technical question of how the effect of a change to this product can be traced to consequent changes in other products. This is all about architectures, coupling, cohesion, interfaces and so on, and I shall leave it to technical texts.

> **HEADLINE**
>
> Planning for quality preservation answers the question 'how shall we prevent change from jeopardising the quality we have achieved?'

As we examine it in more detail we shall see that *change management* requires three separate but related disciplines to be put in place:

- *identification control*, where we ensure that everything is clearly and uniquely identified with some form of name or identifier and, where appropriate, a version identifier

- *change control*, where we ensure that each change, whether internally or externally generated, is cleanly handled through to completion without reducing the quality of our products

- *configuration control*, where we create *baselines* that are formed by consistent sets of products.

Taken together, these three will give us the means of dealing with all those unavoidable changes that we just know will pop up during the project and that will bring it to the floor if they are not properly managed.

To pull this theme together, we can say that quality preservation planning is about planning mechanisms that will make sure that the quality of what you produce stays there and is not eroded by badly managed change. This is the third part of planning for quality and we will capture it in the quality preservation section of the project's Quality Plan.

When to prepare plans

A constant theme of this book will be that planning is about *decision making* – not about writing plans. You record your decisions in a plan for a number of reasons:

- you want other people, such as your staff, to act on your decisions

- you want other people, such as your management, to know you have made decisions and to prove that you are not jeopardising your department's or your company's well-being

- you want other people, such as the finance department, to take external actions as a result of your decisions

- you want to make it possible for others to make an independent review of your decisions

- you have a bad memory.

While the written plan is the end-product, it's the decision-making process you go through that counts. Nevertheless, at some point you are going to put hand to mouse, so in this section we look at the form a Risk & Quality Plan takes, and how it can be produced without undue labour. But let us first start by looking at the different points in a project's life when we prepare plans so that we can understand what the requirements at the different moments are.

Risk planning is important at three points in the life of your project:

- when the work is initially bid for ('bid time')

- when work is started to develop the software ('project inception')

- during the project while development is taking place.

The context I will assume is that you are in a competitive bidding situation and therefore have to prepare a proposal to your would-be client in order to win the contract. You need to produce a competitive price and timescale for producing a system of the quality that the client requires without taking unacceptable risks. If, however, you are developing software as an internal service the situation will be slightly different but the need is the same: to prepare an estimate of effort and timescale that you are confident with and your (internal) customer can understand.

When you draw up your Resource Plan, you will make estimates of the timescales and the costs of the planned development. For the most part these depend on how the project is tackled at a technical level. The Risk & Quality Plan is therefore the major input to the Resource Plan.

In Chapters 3 and 4 I describe the process of risk planning, during which you examine the risks faced by your project and devise a risk management strategy that reduces them to an acceptable level.

In Chapter 5 I look at the question of what makes 'good' software and what the implications are for how we manage quality.

In Chapters 6, 7 and 8 I describe the process of quality planning and how you should decide on your quality achievement, quality control and quality preservation strategies. Quality planning results in the Quality Plan in which you record your decisions. Your Risk Plan and Quality Plan together define the complete technical strategy that you will adopt for the project.

Once a project is running, the Risk Plan needs review as risks materialise or vaporise – we deal with this in Chapter 10. The Quality Plan can act as a work instruction for the entire project, describing how the system is to be developed – the approach, the methods, the tools – and giving a common framework to the technical side of the project. In general, therefore, it is not disposable and generally needs to be maintained.

In summary, we have a trinity of plans prepared at each of the three moments in the lifetime of the project: the Risk Plan, the Quality Plan and the Resource Plan.

Planning at bid time

At bid time we need to produce a document that contains the information resulting from risk and quality planning. Part of the aim is to identify the technical input to the bid before commercial considerations are brought to bear. Some of the deductions – an outline of our technical strategy and the resulting costs – may find their way into the proposal itself in some form, but we need to record the findings as quickly as possible at bid time so that they can be reviewed, and also so that they can become an input to the planning process when the project itself starts.

I suggest that at bid time the Risk & Quality Plan should be produced as a separate document in all but the smallest of bids. You should decide as early as possible during the bid process whether or not you will produce such a plan, and if you decide to produce one it must be appropriately resourced and timetabled. Later in this chapter, I present a contents list for the document and later in the book you will find templates to help you get going more quickly. But remember that your primary motivation for planning at this stage is not just to increase the likelihood of obtaining the contract – you could do that by bidding a (not too obviously) crazy price – but more to increase the *reliability* of the cost estimates and timescale estimates, i.e. to increase the feasibility and likelihood of success of the project you devise.

At bid time you have two main concerns: producing a good (i.e. reliable) estimate of the costs, and convincing the client to buy from you.

Let's take them in turn.

Estimating development costs reliably

The question of what is a 'good' estimate is an old and knotty problem. A manager's view or a salesperson's view might be – if we pull the hat of cynicism firmly over our eyes – that the only good estimate is a low one. But what the realistic manager and the realistic salesperson really want to know is what is achievable with what level of confidence. In other words they are not interested in *one* number – they are interested in one number *and* some error bars: 'what should we bid if we want to be pretty comfortable that the estimate is achievable?' Once a figure has been agreed with the client it becomes a management goal, a statement of intent. But at this point in the affair the estimate is a prediction, so we need to understand it as a prediction.

We can make the prediction more reliable by:

- ensuring that we have included everything that we shall have to do during the project, and

- we have reduced the variability or uncertainty to an acceptable level.

These two goals are precisely what risk and quality planning are all about. The quality analysis reduces the likelihood that we have forgotten anything. And if we get the risk analysis right we can offer a level of risk that the business finds acceptable.

Two decades ago Barry Boehm devised his COCOMO cost estimating model (Boehm 1981). This identified (inter alia) the following factors that affect development costs and schedule:

- 'required software reliability'

- 'product complexity'

- 'use of modern programming practices'

- 'analyst capability'

- 'programmer capability'

- 'programming language experience'

- 'virtual machine experience'

- 'computer turnaround time'

- 'use of software tools'.

Even though the industry is now twice as old, not much has changed, if we reinterpret these a little: 'virtual machine experience' becomes 'experience with the software environment – OS, packages, ERPs etc.', 'use of modern programming practices' becomes 'use of modern development methods'. It is clear from Boehm's analysis that the technical approach to be taken, the skill levels of the staff, and the availability of a good development environment are major factors to be considered in costing projects. Put another way, this says that getting a reliable estimate is going to be very difficult unless some level of planning is carried out. A Risk & Quality Plan provides a framework that is designed to reduce the chance of overlooking costs and cost factors. In particular, we shall see that quite naturally it makes us look carefully at the following:

- choice of overall approach
- choice of methods
- training in methods
- familiarisation with methods
- choice of tools
- training in tools
- familiarisation with tools, packages, etc.
- development, target and maintenance systems.

(Requirements for development hardware and software are of particular importance. These differ from project to project: in some cases you might buy or acquire the necessary facilities, e.g. via rental or loan from the client, especially for the project; in other cases you might use in-house facilities.)

Presenting a good technical case

It may be that you are bidding for work in a competitive situation and hence need to convince your prospective client that you have a sound technical approach in mind. You will want to get that message across in the proposal you submit. Your Risk & Quality Plan can provide useful input to that case. Clearly you should use caution in proposing too detailed a technical approach, as this may subsequently constrain an implementation. The aim is to offer enough evidence that you have understood the problem and are proposing an effective method of reaching a detailed solution, but not enough that you cannot implement a different solution should you win the job and find that you need to make certain changes.

You might on the other hand be planning work for an internal organisation. Again, your proposed costs and timescales will need to be soundly justified and visibly so, and again your Risk & Quality Plan can help make your case for you.

The Risk & Quality Plan can be used to record the technical issues considered and the decisions made during the bidding process. In one sense it is the technical areas of risk and uncertainty that are the most important as these define work that is still to be done for the proposal and some of the *commercial* risks and uncertainties. Early drafts of the Risk & Quality Plan might therefore contain more questions than answers. Additionally, I recommend that you record any alternatives you considered, together with the reasons why they were discarded.

Finally, it is worth bearing in mind that a high quality Risk & Quality Plan produced at bid time can itself be used as a sales aid and given to the client. It can help to demonstrate the (presumably high) level of thought that you have devoted to the client's problem, and your concern with having the right approach for their problem. An external audience for a Risk & Quality Plan would of course view it with different eyes from an internal audience, so you need to take care to ensure that both the form and contents of a Risk & Quality Plan are appropriate if it is to be given to your client.

When you plan the bidding process you will need to decide:

- whether the Risk & Quality Plan is to be a separate document or part of the proposal

- assuming it is to be a separate document, whether it is to be delivered as such to the client, and

- whether it is to be formally reviewed and by whom.

In an ideal world you would write your Risk & Quality Plan and review it before beginning work on your bid. This is because the Risk & Quality Plan is designed to generate much of the input needed for determining the technical approach you will adopt, and for drawing up the plan and costs. We do not always have this luxury, however, and it might be necessary to prepare the Risk & Quality Plan and the bid in parallel. Ideally, the Risk & Quality Plan should always be 'ahead' of the bid with regard to those areas which the Risk & Quality Plan impacts. In deciding to make this compromise, your bid team needs to be clear of the risks being taken.

If the Risk & Quality Plan is to be delivered in some form to the client then you need to review it from this point of view (e.g. paying special attention to vocabulary, style and layout as well as to the technical issues) and this special review needs to be planned for. Later in this Chapter you will find a section on reviewing Risk & Quality Plans.

Planning at project inception

Let us now suppose your organisation was the successful bidder. The champagne has been drunk, the salesperson has moved on to the next sale, and, as the nominated project manager, you are handed the contract and told to bring the project in. In an ideal world you were involved in the bid and even had a say in the contents – but perhaps this whole thing has simply been dropped on your desk. Having read this book, your first instinct will be to get some plans in place and you will be thinking about three in particular: your Risk, Quality and Resource Plans.

If a Risk & Quality Plan was prepared by the sales team at bid time, your new plan can be a refinement of the earlier one:

- It will be more specific about the activities to be undertaken and the products to be produced. For instance, a statement at bid time that a System Specification would be written using VDM might now be expanded into a detailed description of the form the System Specification will take and how VDM will be used to produce it. Or, if object-oriented design was proposed in the bid, then this might be refined to describe the principles of design that will be used – in other words what precisely is meant by 'object-oriented design' in this project – and to describe the precise form the design will take.

- What were originally statements of intent ('we will train everyone with the Whizzo™theorem prover') are now turned into statements of action ('an in-house course on the Whizzo™theorem prover will be arranged with Pode Systems for week 8').

- Outline requirements for development facilities ('we will need two appropriate servers for the theorem prover') must be turned into actions for acquisition ('the Infrastructure Services team has been requested to make available two Beeswax 1904As with ... for week 18').

Your Risk & Quality Plan can now act as a statement of *technical strategy* for the members of your project team. There are significant dangers, especially with large projects, that junior staff do not have clear understanding of how the development is to be done, and hence how their contribution is to fit in. They end up looking over the shoulders of the technical authority trying to figure out what is going on. The Risk & Quality Plan should be a major way of ensuring your staff know what is going on and what part they will play, what approach is being taken, what methods they are to use and what tools will be available. If it is more appropriate you can transfer selected parts of the plan into other documents such as detailed work instructions.

But one of the principal reasons for reworking the Risk & Quality Plan now is that since the original work was done during the bidding stage it is quite possible that new risks have emerged and old ones have gone away – a reappraisal will be needed to check on this.

In what order should you produce the Risk Plan, the Quality Plan and the Resource Plan? Once again you can start from the ideal situation, which is that you write a Risk Plan, then a Quality Plan and then the Resource Plan. To some extent, of course, the Risk Plan and the Quality Plan interact, and you can therefore expect to produce them in parallel. Delaying the preparation of the Resource Plan until this preparatory work is done can be difficult, as your client in particular might want to receive plans as early as possible. If this is the case, I recommend that you deliver an early 'bootstrap' plan that covers only the production of the full plans. This will allow your client to see that matters are under control, and above all it gives the project breathing space to do good risk planning. If, for totally unavoidable reasons, a Resource Plan for the entire project has to be produced before the Risk & Quality Plan can be prepared, then clearly you are taking a risk and you must recognise this.

Once again, it might be the case that the approach being taken to development is of such importance to the client that the Risk & Quality Plan is to be issued to the client. This would mean that it needs additional reviewing as noted above, and this activity should be planned for.

At project inception a further question has to be answered: will the Risk & Quality Plan be a controlled document, in particular one that is kept up to date? If the decisions made at the start of the project are liable to change or are to be significantly refined during the course of the project, there may be good cause for you to plan to review the Risk & Quality Plan at intervals or at significant points during development. If this is the case, this work will need to be planned for in the Resource Plan. The aim should of course always be to be sensitive throughout the project to the risks that can appear at any stage. Those that are thought of at the outset might happen and they might not. You might manage them, and you might not. But you can be sure that new things will also appear as the project progresses. By this I do not mean non-technical Acts of the Universe, such as loss of your development team from accident at sea, or a change of ownership of your client leading to a re-evaluation of the contract by the new owners. I am thinking more of things such as unexpected features of the DBMS you choose, difficulties with your chosen architecture, problems with the compiler. Being sensitive to these is something we will revisit in Chapter 10. Whether you choose to handle these things in a revision of the Risk & Quality Plan or in, say, your monthly progress report and forecast is a small matter – more important is that you handle it.

There are three ways that you might present the Risk & Quality Plan at project inception, depending on the scale and nature of the project:

- If the scale of the strategy issue demands it – for instance, a complex development process is demanded – then you should produce a separate Risk & Quality Plan document as an input to the definitive Resource Plan. In this situation I recommend the contents list given below.

- On a small development project which does not warrant a freestanding Risk & Quality Plan, you can augment the Resource Plan with the material of a Risk & Quality Plan. In this case, a separate appendix in the Resource Plan might be the appropriate place to record the findings of the risk planning activity. If an appendix is used, it should contain the headings and sections given below.

- If the project does not have a full-blown Resource Plan (perhaps you are using an abbreviated work instruction of some form), then you can record such risk planning as is required in that work instruction. If necessary, provide an appendix with the contents list given below.

Re-planning during the project

I once reviewed a large project installing a major new system. There seemed to be a terrible delay between the start of the project and the issue of the plan. In fact work was well under way before a plan was issued. And even then it was not true to say that it had really been 'issued'. There were a few copies around but most of the staff had not had one. Whenever I returned to the project, even though there had been progress and delays and mid-flight alterations, the plan looked pretty much the same.

By following the approach in this book, I hope you will produce a good – i.e. reliable – plan for your project. But I also hope that you don't stop there. If ever there was a 'living document' on your project it should be your plan. Indeed, it should live not just for you but for all your team. Although the main theme of this book is the planning process, it would be incomplete if I did not cover the process of monitoring your project, and reviewing the plan. Of course, as the project proceeds and the design of the system is elaborated so more detail becomes available to you, allowing you to plan later stages in more detail than you were able to at the outset. The area I shall be most concerned with, though, is the risk management part of the plan, because it is the risks where there will be much change. In Chapter 10 I shall look at this review process and also at the role of measurement: as activities get done so we start to understand better the dynamics of our project and the opportunity arises of putting numbers to that understanding – just how long does it take us to prepare a 200-line component? How long does it take to define 200 test cases for a complex component? How many faults are we finding for every thousand lines of code? Are our code reviews finding more faults than our component testing? And what does it tell us about the relative value of each? These are all different questions and some of the answers can be misleading so I sound some cautionary notes on the topic.

The contents of a Risk & Quality Plan

I recommend the contents list shown in Figure 2-1 for your Risk & Quality Plan. The material breaks down easily into separate plans if you prefer to distribute the thing that way – or perhaps if that is the way that your organisation currently works.

Section 2 can be presented as a Risk Register of the sort that we will construct in Chapter 4. The 'consequent activities' in subsections 3.6, 4.4 and 5.4 will cover activities such as training in new methods, the development and maintenance of development, targets and maintenance environments.

Mapping the output of the Risk & Quality Plan into a Resource Plan

One of the principal purposes of Risk & Quality Planning at project inception is deciding how the system is to be developed, in terms of the overall shape of the project, the products to be produced and the activities that will generate and verify them. The resulting decisions are clearly a major input to the Resource Plan. Below I show how the decisions recorded in the Risk & Quality Plan form the input to the Resource Plan (Risk & Quality Plan section headings are in italics):

2   **Risk management plan**

    2.1   *Risks identified*

        This is the principal input to section *2.2* below.

    2.2   *Chosen risk reduction measures*

        This feeds directly into the Resource Plan by determining the overall shape of the project and hence defining a basic shape for the activity network. It also defines the activities to be carried out and the products they will produce. This might be done in considerable detail.

    2.3   *Residual risk assessment*

The assessment of the residual risks after the necessary risk reduction measures have been chosen and, more importantly, the cost and schedule provisions that should be allowed for those residual risks go directly into the Resource Plan.

3 Quality achievement plan

3.1 Characterisation of system to be developed

This is input to sections 3.3 and 3.4 below.

3.2 Client expectations or requirements on development

These will probably become 'automatic' choices in section 3.3 below. (They are likely to be a consideration only at the bid stage as, by project inception time, the contract should define any standards or practices that are obligatory.)

3.3 Chosen development methods

This section, as well as simply identifying in general terms the methods to be used, might well go into considerable detail as to how the methods will be used, adapted and expanded for the project's particular requirements. Any new activities that come out of this analysis (such as the development of special tools to support a method) are recorded in section 3.6.

3.4 Chosen tool support

Tools not available on your existing development facilities will have to be purchased, and this needs to be timetabled and costed into the Resource Plan, so these choices are an input to section 3.6.

3.5 Chosen target environment

This should have been established at bid time but might still be unresolved at project inception. Either way, plans need to ensure that the target environment is procured and installed, and that installation on it is catered for; the necessary activities are recorded in section 3.6.

3.6 Consequent activities

This is the collecting point for all the additional activities that are identified in the planning for quality achievement and that must be carried forward into the Resource Plan.

4 Quality control plan

4.1 Planned product types

This is input to sections 4.3 and 4.4 below.

4.2 Specifications and standards

Where standards for certain products do *not* exist, activities might be necessary to prepare them and these will go forward into the Resource Plan via section *4.4.*

4.3 Quality control activities

The activities in this section are all input to the Resource Plan.

4.4 Consequent activities

This is the collecting point for all the additional activities that are identified in the planning for quality control and that must be carried forward into the Resource Plan.

5 Quality preservation plan

5.1 Identification control

The plan either prescribes an existing identification control approach or calls for one to be prepared for the project.

5.2 Change control

The plan either prescribes an existing change control approach or calls for one to be prepared for the project.

5.3 Configuration control

The plan either prescribes an existing configuration control approach or calls for one to be prepared for the project.

5.4 Consequent activities

This is the collecting point for all the activities that are identified in the planning for quality preservation and that must be carried forward into the Resource Plan.

HEADLINE

Without doubt, the most important sections in the Risk & Quality Plan are *2.2 Chosen risk reduction measures, 3.3 Chosen development methods* and *4.3 Quality control activities*. These provide the major inputs to your Resource Plan.

1 Introduction

2 Risk management plan

2.1 Risks identified

2.2 Chosen risk reduction measures

2.3 Residual risk assessment

3 Quality achievement plan

3.1 Characterisation of system to be developed

3.2 Client expectation or requirements on development

3.3 Chosen development methods

3.4 Chosen tool support

3.5 Chosen target environment

3.6 Consequent activities

4 Quality control plan

4.1 Planned product types

4.2 Specifications and standards

4.3 Quality control activities

4.4 Consequent activities

5 Quality preservation plan

5.1 Identification control

5.2 Change control

5.3 Configuration control

5.4 Consequent activities

Figure 2-1. Contents list of a Risk & Quality Plan

Reviewing a Risk & Quality Plan

Here is a checklist for reviewing a Risk & Quality Plan. You can use it not only when actually reviewing your Risk & Quality Plan at a Structured Walkthrough or inspection, say, but also while you are in the process of preparing the document. (Some of the questions will be more meaningful as we get further into the planning technique.)

- Does the plan record the rationale behind the choice of development process for the project, in particular demonstrating what risks are managed and how?

- Does the plan record all known, unresolved technical issues and has the resolution of these issues been planned for elsewhere?

- Has the level of understanding of the system been realistically determined and recorded?

- Has the nature of the system been adequately understood and recorded?

- Does the plan record the rationale behind the choice of development methods for the system?

- Have all the client's expectations and requirements on the development process been extracted from the *Invitation to Tender* (or *Request for Quotation*) and other relevant documents?

- Has an appropriate level of staff training been allowed for in the timescales of the project and in its budget?

- Has an appropriate level of familiarisation with the chosen development method and the tools been included in the project costs and timescales?

- Does the plan record the rationale for the tools chosen to support the chosen development methods?

- Have all the software licences to be purchased been itemised and costed?

- Have all the components for the development, target and maintenance environments been identified and costed?

- Has the development environment been reconciled with the proposed maintenance environment?

- If the development involves the installation of hardware on your premises or the use of the in-house computer facilities has the computer facilities team been involved in the review of the plan or consulted in its preparation?

- Does the plan clearly spell out what sort of products will be produced?

- For each product type does it identify whether its quality attributes will be specified in standards or in a specification?

- Is there an adequately sound verification activity defined for each product type that is appropriate to the quality attributes?

Chapter recap

Software development is a risky endeavour that starts with many unknowns and uncertainties. Your choice of strategy for your software development project must therefore be determined by the risks you perceive and what you need to do to leave those risks at an acceptable level. That strategy will take the form of a process model that captures the level of commitment you are prepared to undertake given what you can reasonably predict, the points at which major decisions will be made, the activities that will generate the data you will need to make those decisions, any iterations expected to handle uncertainty, and any other specific activities you will undertake to tackle specific problems or answer specific questions. This is *planning for risk management*.

Your choice of methods for the project is determined by what sort of system you are building and its quality requirements. You must match the strengths of the methods to the essential properties of the problem to be solved. Your choice of tools for the project is determined by your choice of methods and by productivity issues. This is *planning for quality achievement*.

Your choice of V&V strategy for the project is largely determined by the methods you choose. You must match the rigour of the V&V strategy to the quality requirements of the system. This is *planning for quality control*.

Your choice of change management strategy for the project is determined by the structure of the system. You must match the rigour of the change management strategy to the demand for change by the business and the quality requirements of the system. This is *planning for quality preservation*.

Risk and quality planning is a rigorous procedure by which you ask the right questions so that all these choices can be made. Your Risk & Quality Plan records your choices and is the primary input to your Resource Plan.

References

Boehm 1981

Software Engineering Economics. B W Boehm. Prentice-Hall, Englewood Cliffs, 1981

Gilb 1988

Principles of Software Engineering Management. T Gilb. Addison-Wesley, Reading, 1988

Jackson 1975

Principles of Program Design. M A Jackson. Academic Press, New York, 1975

3 Icebergs ahead! Business risk

Software development is not the only pursuit of mankind that is risky. New medical procedures, new buildings, new financial measures – all have inherent risk, or, in plain language, could fail. So we should not be surprised if other disciplines have addressed this question of how to manage risk to reduce the likelihood of failure. And indeed we find in the literature a mass of work that until recently was hardly known, let alone practised, in the software world: the discipline of *risk management*.

However, coming to it later than everyone else we have the advantage of being able to pick up on existing theory and practice that can be adopted pretty much without change, and that is what we shall do in this book.

Later in this chapter we shall be looking at the process of risk management in detail, but we should start with some thoughts about what we mean by the idea of 'a risk to a software development project' and especially about how business considerations should drive our risk management activity.

Why are we here? Cardinal aims

We want to manage our risks because we know that risks threaten the success of our project. But this begs a question: what do we mean by a 'successful' project? And it is here that we must return to the business and to the reasons it had for approving the development of the software in the first place. So our first port of call at the outset of our thinking about risk – indeed of our entire involvement with the project as its manager – must be the *business case* for the system. Assuming such a business case was prepared and prepared well (itself a major assumption!), it will tell us just what the business expected to get from the system and at what cost. We can expect it to contain some form of *investment model* which justified the expense to the business in terms of the benefits that are expected. That investment model might not be explicit but we will have to make it so if our risk management is to be business-focused and not random or driven by what we think we can do easily. Our aim will therefore be to pull out of the business case the *cardinal aims* of the project. These will fall under three headings:

- whole life costs
- system goals
- side effects.

Let's take these in turn.

Whole life costs

> **DEFINITION**
>
> The *whole life costs* of a system are the costs of the initial development or procurement of the system, plus the costs of owning the system during its lifetime.

To a degree, it is the initial development cost that most concerns us when we are planning. But of course, the customer of the system, who will be its eventual owner, will also be interested in the costs associated with that ownership. For instance, annual licence fees might be payable to the supplier of a package that is integrated into the system we deliver; systems require backups to be taken and stored; when a system fails there is a cost to the restoration of the service it provides and a cost to the business while it is without the service; as the information kept by the system accumulates so the demand on storage will increase with a resulting expenditure on more and more primary storage. And so on. We can appreciate at once that decisions we make during the initial development will affect those costs of ownership. We might reduce the development cost of a system by incorporating an off-the-shelf product, but we increase the cost of ownership by the amount of the licence fees and restricting changes we can make to adapt the system to the business. We might reduce the development costs by cutting back on testing and delivering a less well tested system but the cost of ownership will shoot up as the business has to pay for the system failures that occur during its lifetime. So there is a balance to be struck between the amount we spend on a system's initial development and the amount we will have to pay to keep it on the road once it is installed.

And it is here that we come up against a common dilemma. When we bid competitively for the development of a system we are presenting the client with a price *for that development*. Will the client have any way of handling a claim from us that 'yes, we are charging more for the development than our competitors, but you will get a better system that will be cheaper to own, so in the long term you will save money by giving us more now'. That's a hard message to sell, and it requires a quite sophisticated client to buy it. The situation can be made harder if the development costs come from one of the client's budgets and the lifetime ownership costs from another.

System goals

> ### DEFINITION
>
> The *system goals* of a system are the primary business reasons for building it.

Let's take some examples. Suppose we are a financial institution. Suppose we want to introduce a new financial product, perhaps a new equity-related insurance policy. We will need computer systems and associated software to support the product. The system goal here is an enabling goal – without the systems the financial product will simply not be possible. Or suppose we want to offer our account customers web-based facilities for managing their accounts. We know that if we can get systems and software to deal with our customers rather than warm bodies at branches we can get our cost per transaction down. In this case the software has the goal of reducing customer transaction costs. Suppose we are an aero-engine manufacturer and we want to have our new engine run quieter and more efficiently: appropriate software in the engine management system could help us achieve that and thereby make our products more attractive to our airline customers. Suppose we are a defence department, the system goal that we seek from a communications system would be to increase our responsiveness to changing situations on the battlefield.

The system goals are what we will later refine as the system requirements: just what do we want this system to *do* for us?

Do we want it to increase the efficiency of the business, make our products more attractive, increase customer satisfaction, or what? The greater or more ambitious the system goals, the greater the whole life costs are likely to be.

I once interviewed the technical director of a major manufacturer of electronic products which were largely dependent on software for their functionality. We discussed what measurements were most important to them in their software development. Their cardinal aims were meeting the market window for their products and delivering products to market that were of high reliability. Development cost was entirely secondary, as was functionality. To meet the window, quality would not be compromised but functionality would be reduced if necessary. If meeting the window meant spending more, so be it. This highlighted for me the way that different organisations have different priorities.

Side effects

> **DEFINITION**
>
> A *side effect* of a system is something that will go in the cost–benefit scales when we prepare the business plan for the system.

A side effect would never be the single driving reason for acquiring the system. Indeed, it could be beneficial or it could be detrimental. For instance, while the main goal of having a good communications system on the battlefield might be better responsiveness to changing situations, an important and valuable side effect might be improved troop morale.

One important side effect will typically relate to the date when a system is to be delivered. Of course, if the system is to support the introduction of a new financial product on 1st November and the TV advertising slots have all been booked then we may regard the achievement of the delivery date as a business goal. But if that is not the case then it will invariably be a beneficial side effect in that the later it is delivered the less we are pleased, though punctuality is not crucial. And as before, such a beneficial side effect can be traded against a cardinal aim such as whole life costs: by spending more in development we can offer an earlier projected delivery date.

Value and variability

Now, it is not always the *absolute value* of a cardinal aim that will be of interest to the organisation acquiring a system. Certainly, we can expect that the owner of a system will want to keep the whole life costs of a system to the lowest figure possible. But in some cases it is the *variability* of a cardinal aim that we want to reduce – and we might be prepared to accept a higher absolute value to achieve a reduced variability. This is most important for whole life costs and delivery date.

EXAMPLE

Government departments like to be able to budget well into the future: they like to know today how much they will be spending on something year in year out for the next, perhaps, ten years, or even more. So a predictable whole life cost can be as important as a low whole life cost, and they might even be prepared to accept a higher development cost if it allows the ownership cost to be more predictable and hence reliable.

We might want to have a high degree of confidence that a given delivery day will be met, rather than that delivery should be as soon as possible: it is not the absolute value that is of concern to the business, it is the predictability.

EXAMPLE

Praxis built the system that supported the administration of a whole new form of national exams for one of the country's examining boards. One of the primary goals of the system was that the pupils taking exams should get their results on the appointed date the first time the new exams were sat. Now, that date was written into law and so there was absolutely no chance of asking for a two-week extension to the timetable if the going started getting tough. What was important was not how soon the system could produce those marks, but that it could be guaranteed to do so on the appointed day.

Apples and pears

One of the problems in making any business case is that of comparing apples and pears. In essence, we would like to give a value to every cardinal aim of the system, and then to put the positive values on one side of the scales and the negative on the other, and see which way the balance tips. Those who are only capable of making decisions that can be reduced to looking at two numbers and deciding which is the greater always demand that everything be reduced to pounds or dollars or whatever – to money. OK, so what is the monetary value of being able to answer 30% more calls from customers within one minute? What is the monetary value of a 10% reduction in noise from an aero-engine? An ingenious mind could probably trace from the cardinal aim to some figure via some argument but it would be littered with assumptions. For instance, if the user interface on our web-based account management system for our customers is not too good, customer satisfaction will fall, and we could say 'well, let's suppose that it's so bad that 30% of our customers find it less than satisfactory, and 10% of those find it so bad they consider moving their account to another bank and suppose the value of …'. The resulting value would certainly be a value, but what would it be worth in the balance given its poor reliability? Let's try something a little harder: in a war, just what is the value in pounds of getting the troops to the battlefield ten minutes quicker?

For those who have to make judgements between apples and pears but cannot bring themselves to the fiction of purely monetary comparisons there are alternative solutions. One is the formidably named *Analytic Hierarchy Process* or AHP (Saaty 1995). This allows subjective comparisons to be made between apples and pears in a structured way that gives us the yes–no answers we all crave. Tool support is available for it.

Risks as threats to the business case for a system

I am making a song and dance about the cardinal aims of the system because, before too long, we will be making decisions about whether we are going to spend money dealing with risks, and if we are going to make those decisions reliably and meaningfully then we must return to the business case for the system and its development project. Only that can tell us whether any expenditure is worth while. In effect we will need to revisit the business case to see if the scales still tip in the right direction.

You might have noticed that I have been talking about 'risks' without having defined what I mean. In common usage a risk is the chance of loss. But now we can be a little more specific in our context.

DEFINITION

A *risk* is any threat to the achievement of one or more of the cardinal aims of the project.

So a risk might threaten an increase in the whole life costs, or threaten the delivery of a business goal, or threaten the delivery of a beneficial side effect or the avoidance of a detrimental side effect. Let's take some straightforward examples.

EXAMPLES

If the requirements on a system are not well understood, we have a risk. This risk can threaten the whole life costs, since we might be forced to rework the software once it has been produced to make it do what was really wanted but which we failed to define fully at the outset. And almost by definition this risk directly threatens the business goals of the project: if we don't know what we are aiming for we shall surely miss.

If some of our development staff are new to the language that we are proposing to use, we have a risk. This risk will certainly threaten the development part of the whole life costs as their unfamiliarity with the language will be very likely to make them slower at their work than experienced staff and hence increase the development cost. But it could also threaten the cost of ownership part of the whole life costs: their unfamiliarity with the language will almost certainly result in poorer code that will be harder to maintain downstream after the system has been delivered.

If we produce a weak user interface for the web-based account management system, we threaten what might be a desired side effect: increased customer satisfaction with the bank's services. Yes, we might have reduced the development costs by not spending the time we should have on analysing how people might want to use the web site but we have done that perhaps only at the cost of introducing a risk, one that threatens a beneficial side effect.

We shall use the expression 'a risk materialises' to mean that the threat underlying the risk materialises, in other words that the event or situation we had been hoping would not happen has struck. On the other side of fortune, we shall say that 'a risk dissipates' if the threat disappears so that the unpleasant event or situation can no longer occur.

Old hat: the risk management process

Given our understanding of what makes a risk, we can begin to look at how we should go about managing the risks we find on our project.

HEADLINE

A conventional risk management process has four steps

1   risk identification – spot the risks

2   risk analysis – take them apart and think about them

3   risk response planning – decide what to do about them

4   risk resolution and monitoring – do whatever you decided.

Of course risk management is not something that is done once and then forgotten. A good project manager will be repeating this set of four steps at regular intervals. At Praxis a project would revisit its plan each month, and in particular this would mean going through the above process: looking to see what the new set of risks were that faced the project, analysing those and revisiting the old ones, etc.

Risk identification: spot your risks

Anyone who has had any involvement in a software project will be able to reel off a list of 'popular' sources of risk:

- vague requirements
- changing requirements
- a volatile or innovative environment
- the difficulty of time and resource estimation
- performance
- reliance on scarce skills
- reliance on suppliers
- a lack of standards and codes of practice.

But how do we compile a full list of risks that are truly *relevant to this project*?

Finding the risks

The most obvious source that we will look to for risks is our own experience. 'Once bitten, twice shy.' The strongest instinct of the project manager is to protect this project from the risks that racked the last project. And if every team member remembers the big mistakes and unmanaged risks from their last project we shall soon have a long list for our new project. Such a list is a good starting point but every risk must be challenged for its relevance today: we are going to start spending money on managing these risks and we cannot afford to waste our funds on things that simply will not happen. Of course the analysis of the risks is yet to come but it is all too easy to feel good about having produced a really long list of risks, as if listing them is solving them. I once talked to a project manager from a utility company who asked me what software we used for tracking risks. I admitted to being slightly embarrassed that we just kept, well, a list. No tool support needed for that. 'Why do you feel you need tool support?' I innocently asked. 'Well, the project I am looking at has a list of over 100 risks.' I found it hard to believe that, if these were indeed non-trivial risks and not just terrible Acts of the Universe, then I could confidently predict failure as the outcome of this project, risk management or no risk management.

As the project proceeds one of the best sources of knowledge about the risks and how they are growing or disappearing is the staff, the people at the sharp end – the very same people we all too easily pressurise into saying that 'everything is fine, it will be fine, believe me'. But it is these people that we really do need to hear from. We will have to create an atmosphere in which the *constructive* consideration of risks is expected. Note my emphasis on 'constructive': Jeremiahs need not apply. We want people to talk openly and honestly in a non-judgmental way about where they see the potential pitfalls.

Appropriately convened workshops can provide the atmosphere we are looking for. This could mean that we have the junior project staff in their own workshop, separated from the senior stakeholders – the senior user managers, the marketing folk, the IT director. The two groups will see different risks from their different perspectives and it will do no harm to separate them to keep them focused on their areas. In an ideal world we might wish that the whole picture could be shared by a single group but we might need to bow to the local situation to get the result we need. We are drifting here into the political and cultural situation you find yourself in and at this point I duck out. The SEI's *Continuous Risk Management* approach tackles these issues and you should check them out via their web site (http:// www.sei.cmu.edu/products/publications/).

> **HEADLINE**
> The list of risks on the project is compiled from project workshops, past experience and corporate checklists.

I stressed above the need for a *complete* list, one that covers not just technical areas such as requirements definition, but also political issues that might undermine team morale, or company issues that could affect people's desire to work on the project, or a host of other things. If we don't feel confident in the depth of our own experience for finding the risks in today's project then we should be able to turn to some prompt-lists that our organisation has been building up over the years to encapsulate the experience of past projects and to assist future projects in not repeating old errors. ('We learn from our mistakes,' I was told by one project manager. 'We learn from them so well we repeat them every project.' Not quite what I was thinking of.) If you do not have a prompt-list of popular risks in your group, start one now, and at the end of each project add the things that threatened or damaged the project, so that others might benefit from your experience. Try to get the risk sources into some sort of structure.

Taxonomies, checklists, and individual and corporate memory will yield plenty of material. In each case we must ask 'yes, that was a risk for one past project, but is it one that we face?' If it isn't, strike it from the list. We will have plenty enough hard, relevant risks without lots of slight possibilities. And to make our risk identification more relevant still to the task in hand we can do a cause–effect analysis. Start with the effect 'the project failed' and work backwards from there. What could have caused it to fail? In what ways can the cardinal aims be missed? And what would have caused those things to happen *on this project*? And so on backwards until we reach something that represents a risk we can start to address. A workshop can be a very effective way of developing the 'cause–effect tree' that captures this analysis. And it has a further very useful side effect: when we come to plan the management of our risks we will need to separate out how we manage the cause from how we manage the effect.

Let's take a simple example. We are delivering an automated system that will run a big warehouse that is being upgraded to increase its capacity and throughput. The system will accept new stock and move it to its appointed storage point. Knowing the orders that have come in from branches, it will print out the day's 'pick-lists' for smaller items so that the staff can pick those items from the stock faces and place them in bins destined for the stores. The system will move these bins and the larger items to the loading bays at the right moment for the waiting vehicles which will deliver them to the branches. We have chosen the warehouse management product that we will buy as the basis of our system. It will need some customisation for this warehouse and these product lines, and we will need to provide connections to our ordering and financial reporting systems. The warehouse will need to be converted, staff trained in the new practices, the system installed. Let's do a cause–effect analysis.

The cardinal aims of this project are, let us say, to be delivered at a cost of £7.5m, to double our throughput capability at the times of peak demand, to reduce the number of mistakes in what is sent to branches to a third of its current value, and to be ready for the start of the peak demand next year.

In this case, the 'threats to the cardinal aims' might be the following four 'base risks':

1   we exceed the development cost target

2   at peak demand we cannot handle twice the throughput

3   we are not ready for the start of the peak period next year

4   we reduce mistakes but not by two-thirds.

These are of course right at the end of the cause–effect chain so we need to back up a little and seek causes for them and make them the risks that we can tackle. We might identify the following as possible causes of risk 3:

5   the supplier of the warehouse management product fails to deliver the customised version in time for us to complete testing before the peak period

6   the machinery installer fails to get the machinery in place ready for integration with the software in time

7   we fail to get sufficient staff trained in the operation of the system in time

8   key people who will be needed to push through the work are over-loaded.

In turn, we might identify a number of causes that might have risk 5 as an effect:

9   the requirements being pushed by the marketing team are not fully validated

10 we demand more 'knobs and whistles' than can reasonably be incorporated in the time available

11 potential new facilities are being built into the machinery and we feel obliged to exploit these from day one.

And for risk 2 we might believe there are the following causes:

12 the algorithms that control the movement and picking of stock may not be right for the way the warehouse is to be set up

13 staff cannot cope with the new technology.

And so on. By doing this sort of analysis we can quickly get back to 'root causes' that we might actually be able to tackle. By tracing each risk to its constituent causes we give ourselves a chance of conquering it.

Interestingly, as this analysis proceeds backwards so we start to find ourselves naming potential ways of *reducing* the risk. 'This is a new warehouse with new working practices driven by a new system and we run the risk that staff might not manage the technology.' Working backwards we might identify a lack of appropriate and adequate training as a risk – and suddenly we are saying 'if we don't put this risk reduction measure in place then this risk could materialise'. Do not be surprised then if it proves difficult to restrict a risk identification workshop to just the identification of risks – you will quite easily slip into designing risk reduction measures. That's fine as long as you finish the main business, which is to flush out the risks – concentrate on that first rather than on thinking of ways around them.

So, we can feel fairly confident that we will not be short of identified risks on our project. Murphy's Law gives us reason enough to feel this way. But we need some ways of helping the project team to get down to particulars for their project. It is all too easy to come up with platitudes or truisms in place of clearly articulated risks that we can attack and manage directly. Terrible and unforeseeable Acts of the Universe are not risks. Yes, the entire team might be swept away by killer bees, but no we probably don't need to have this on our list of risks to be managed. Nor indeed is it much use to list 'we might get the design wrong' as a risk. It might be true, but we need something more specific to get our teeth into: 'none of us has built a system with this degree of concurrency in it before' would be more precise and a lot easier to tackle directly. That's the real risk that we should record, because we immediately start to think of measures that we might take, such as hiring someone who has done it before or making friends with other warehouse operators in non-competing market-places.

Risk	Risk description	Causes
1	We exceed the development cost target	
2	At peak demand we cannot handle twice the throughput	
3	We are not ready for the start of the peak period next year	
4	We reduce mistakes but not by two-thirds	
5	The supplier of the warehouse management product fails to deliver the customised version in time for us to complete testing before the peak period	3
6	The machinery installer fails to get the machinery in place ready for integration with the software in time	3
7	We fail to get sufficient staff trained in the operation of the system in time	3
8	Key people who will be needed to push through the work are over-loaded	3
9	The requirements being pushed by the marketing team are not fully validated	5
10	We demand more 'knobs and whistles' than can reasonably be incorporated in the time available	5
11	Potential new facilities are being built into the machinery and we feel obliged to exploit these from day one	5
12	The algorithms that control the movement and picking of stock may not be right for the way the warehouse is to be set up	2
13	Staff cannot cope with the new technology	2
	etc., including risks leading to numbers 1 and 4 above	

Figure 3-1. First headings for a simple Risk Register

Building the Risk Register

Spotting the risks is the first step. Writing them up is the second, and to help us track our risk management work we will now put together a *Risk Register*.

If you genuinely have a large project with a long list of risks and feel the urge to have tool support, you will find plenty of suitable products on the market-place for keeping your Risk Register, typically built on some form of database. Many people find a spreadsheet adequate. Just what data a risk management tool will invite you to keep will vary but Figure 3-1 shows the start of a simple table that will serve very well and can easily be set up as a spreadsheet or perhaps a simple relational database if you prefer. The table very simply captures the cause–effect tree in Figure 3-2.

Figure 3-2. A cause-effect tree for Figure 3.1

For now we will be content to list the risks in the *Risk description* column, and to indicate which of the risks are expanded with their causes by putting their numbers in italics, and where a risk causes another in the list we note that fact in the *Causes* column. You might prefer to keep all this as a cause–effect graph on the wall, but for simplicity in this book I shall illustrate the ideas with this table. As ever, an advantage to holding it electronically in some form is that it encourages frequent update, or, at least, doesn't make it hard.

> ### HEADLINE
>
> The Risk Register lists the risks and their cause–effect relationships.

Risk analysis: think about your risks

So far we have built our basic Risk Register listing the risks that we feel are relevant to this project and we have refined them to sufficient detail that they are more than a vague, generic threat. Now we must start to take each one apart to understand it further in order to give ourselves the information necessary to choose an appropriate management approach. We'll look at this analysis in a slightly theoretical way to start with so that we get the foundations in place properly, then we can look at some real examples.

An obvious first step is to recognise the following:

> ### HEADLINE
>
> Every risk can be thought of as a *cause* and an *effect*.
> The cause has a *probability* and the effect has a *size* or *impact*.

Since we have defined a risk as a threat to a cardinal aim we expect normally to express the effect of a risk in terms of the nature and scale of that impact on the cardinal aims.

Let's start with the impact of the risk.

Risk impact

We should now be clear that when we talk about the impact of a risk we are talking about its ultimate impact on the cardinal aims of the project.

If the supplier of the warehouse management product fails to deliver the customised version in time for us to complete testing, the impact will be that we shall miss the cardinal aim of being ready for the start of the peak period next year.

If staff cannot cope with the new technology, the impact will be that we shall not be able to handle twice the throughput.

As ever in this book, I would like to tease the (apparently) simple idea of impact apart a little to help us think more clearly about the problem. I want to consider two different *shapes* that a risk can have – our response to them will be different.

Binary risks

I shall use the term *binary risk* to mean one that materialises fully or not at all. Either it hits us or it doesn't. We suffer the full impact or none. A binary risk cannot partly materialise.

EXAMPLES

We might be uncertain about whether or not (note that phrase) the forthcoming release of the communications software we plan to use supports encryption. This is a binary risk. When the release comes on the market, either encryption is supported or it isn't.

The government might or might not make the currently proposed changes to the tax laws. If they do we shall have to change the specification. If they don't we shall not be affected.

We shall see later that any pre-emptive risk reduction measure we consider will also be binary: it will either eliminate the risk completely or leave it untouched.

Sliding risks

I shall use the term *sliding risk* to mean one that can hit us hard, quite hard, slightly, or not at all. Its impact can vary.

EXAMPLE

Our novice programmers could turn out to be quite good, or very poor, and anywhere in between. The impact of their inexperience can be equally variable: their code can be used without further ado, or need to be rewritten, or anything in between.

Some risks start out sliding but then become binary, typically when some 'breaking point' is reached.

Examples

Achieving the required performance could be an uncertainty. If we need to squeeze a little more out of our system we might be able to simply adjust the timing of some processes. If more is needed we might consider rewriting some time-critical code to be more efficient. The impact on costs and timescale is sliding up as the size of the risk increases. But there will come a point where we simply can do no more and we must suffer a step increase in impact and buy a more powerful processor.

The machinery installer might fail to get the machinery in place ready in time for integration with the software. Perhaps there is no advantage to us of an early delivery, and perhaps if they are even the slightest bit late all is lost – this would be a binary risk. More likely is that they can be a bit late, quite a bit late, or a lot late, and the later they are the greater the impact on our cardinal aims. But we can imagine that a point will come when they are so late that the impact goes through the roof. Perhaps if they are a bit late we suffer somewhat on the cardinal aim of dealing with increased throughput because we have had less time to tune the system. But at some point we shall hit the buffers: the peak order period will arrive and we shall not be ready – branches will place orders against sales but the goods don't reach them in time and the customers simply go elsewhere.

Headline

In summary, we measure the impact of a risk in terms of the scale of its effect on our cardinal aims. That impact may be binary – it hits us or it doesn't – or it can be sliding – it hits us by degrees.

Event uncertainty and estimating uncertainty

Having looked at the impact of a risk, let's now turn to its cause.

A cause will either be due to *event uncertainty* or to *estimating uncertainty*. We must look at these in more detail as our response to them must be different.

> ## HEADLINE
>
> *Event uncertainty* is uncertainty about something in the world, some variability in something in the world.

The company supplying us with the hardware we need for our system might or might not be late in delivering at the agreed date. They might be a little late; they might be a lot late. The event, which is the delivery, has variability attached to it. Typically, the events we are talking about for risks will be events that we don't want to happen. It could happen that we get staff who are not familiar with the language that we plan to use. In general terms, some undesirable event could happen with some *probability*. And if it does, we shall suffer some ill effect, some *impact*; in other words, the threat to one or more of the cardinal aims of the project actually happens and the project is impacted to a greater or lesser degree: the system fails to meet its performance target, or our code is hard to maintain.

> ## EXAMPLES
>
> Let's return to that supplier who might be late in delivering our hardware. We might judge the risk to be that 'there is a 25% probability that they will be four or more weeks late.' Here we are characterising the risk as an event uncertainty: an event (failure to deliver on the agreed date) with a probability (25%) and an impact (lateness of system delivery) of a certain size (four weeks or more). When we look at the final impact of this risk on the cardinal aims of the project we transform this, say, into a knock-on effect on the project's development costs (which is a component of the whole life costs) and the impact on the schedule (which is perhaps a beneficial side effect): 'there is a 10% chance that this risk will increase whole life costs by £25 000 and delay operational deployment by two weeks'.
>
> Suppose we are having to recruit staff to bring the team up to strength. There is a risk that they turn out to be not of the calibre we need. Looking at the quality of the new hires over the last year we might feel that there is every possibility that we will get perhaps a third less productivity from new recruits. The probability for this event uncertainty is 'high', and perhaps we can quantify the impact in terms of the reduced productivity: a quick calculation suggests that an

extra cost of £120K and an extra four weeks on the schedule would not be out of the question.

Suppose we think we might fail to get sufficient warehouse staff trained in the operation of the warehouse management system in time to deal with the peak period. Part of this risk is event uncertainty: we might not get enough candidates responding to the advertisements in the local papers. Given that several other retailers have moved their operations to the area recently we can see this being a real problem with a significant cost if we fail to be ready when the orders start to arrive in quantity.

We see a potential problem in that the requirements that the marketing team is pushing for the warehouse management system might not get fully validated by the business. The event uncertainty is 'will they get validated?'. And the impact is that, if those requirements are more than we can handle before the deadlines, we shall find ourselves sacrificing the cardinal aims for nice-to-haves. Now, the marketing team has its own agenda but we trust it to be realistic. So we might rate this risk as low probability though we recognise that the impact could be expensive if we fail to keep requirements under control.

So much for event uncertainty – the chance that something out there might or might not happen.

On the other side of the coin, we can define *estimating uncertainty* thus:

HEADLINE

Estimating uncertainty reflects our lack of concrete information regarding something, as opposed to its intrinsic variability.

Suppose we are estimating the total development costs of our software system. Even though it may be well specified and well understood, there will be uncertainty in our estimation of the development effort required, simply because estimation cannot be reduced to a reliable formula. We might judge that 'there is a 15% probability that development costs will exceed the planned figure by 10% and that delivery will be one month later than planned'. Or we might judge that 'there is a small chance that the tracking algorithms will not maintain track through a 20% data loss': we can make an estimate of the performance of the algorithms but there is some uncertainty about it. Again, the uncertainty can be expressed as a probability that there is a given variation. And of course the impact of such uncertainty can relate to any of the cardinal aims of the project.

EXAMPLES

Suppose we see a risk that the performance of the software system design will be less than required. From our experience we might judge that it will support 200 transactions per second, but there is uncertainty in that. We might judge that 'there is a 20% probability that the system will support 200 transactions per second'. Our estimating uncertainty here is related to a system goal: performance.

We might see a risk in the fact that we don't know what the performance of our database is. We lack concrete information about it. We might feel that, having talked to our colleagues in another company about their experiences, albeit with a slightly different load mix, there is a small chance that it will not be up to the job – the loads we are looking at are less than theirs and we are using a server that is one up the performance ladder from theirs. But we have a nagging feeling that the transaction sizes will cause us problems. Our estimating uncertainty here is related to our ability to estimate the performance of the database.

The algorithms that control the movement and picking of stock may not be right for the way the warehouse is to be set up. We know what algorithms we think would work, but we don't know for sure that they will – we're short of solid information. The last system we did like this was pretty similar so we don't think the chances are high that we have it wrong but if we do get it wrong it would be an expensive mistake. Our estimating uncertainty here is related to an aspect of the cardinal aim of being able to deal with double the throughput during the peak period.

There's a risk that we fail to get sufficient staff trained in the operation of the system in time. Another part of this risk is the estimating uncertainty around not knowing how long it will take us to train people to an adequate level before they are at the necessary level of competence. We have some experience of training people in this situation but it was with staff coming from a similar operation elsewhere in the country and in this case we shall be starting with fresh faces. So the chances are that we shall need longer than usual. Our

> estimating uncertainty here is related to an aspect of the cardinal aim
> of being ready for the peak order period.

(I have been expressing uncertainties as percentages in some of my examples
so far. Later I shall sound some warning bells about spurious accuracy and
bogus statistical-looking statements.)

I said above that 'every risk has a *risk profile* which consists of some *event
uncertainty* or some *estimating uncertainty*'. We can now restate this by saying
that every risk is either about something 'out there' that is intrinsically variable or uncertain (stuff happens), or about our lack of knowledge about
something which might be constant or determinable (we are not omniscient).
In risk analysis our task is to decide which of these two types each risk falls
under because we will deal with the two types in different ways. I won't say
that this analysis between the two types is easy but it is rewarding – it does
make you think that bit harder about what is really going on, and it will make
your thoughts about risk reduction measures clearer later on, so do persevere.

HEADLINE

Try to phrase the nature of an event uncertainty by forming a sen-
tence that starts 'It may happen that …'.

Estimating uncertainty will take the form 'We are uncertain how
much …'.

Event uncertainty will be best addressed by trying to change the world so
that the variability is reduced or that the likelihood of the risk is reduced: we
are proactive – we chase the supplier in order to make it less likely that they
will deliver late, a 'risk-influencing activity'. Estimating uncertainty will be
best addressed by some form of 'information buying' – we experiment with
the design to see just what it will achieve in performance terms.

An event uncertainty will cause us to *influence* something. An estimating
uncertainty will cause us to *find out* something.

But more of this later, we are getting ahead.

First estimates of the scale of the risks

So far, I have been rather loose about expressing the probability of a risk and the scale of its impact. We will need later to look at this knotty problem in more detail. But in the early phases of risk analysis it is sufficient to use quite coarse scales on which to measure these two characteristics.

For the probability of a risk, we might use a percentage ('there is a 20% chance that the database software will fail to meet its performance targets') or a more qualitative assessment ('it seems very likely that the database software will fail to meet its performance targets'), or some vague ranking such as

- VL: 'very likely, rely on it'

- L: 'likely, but don't bet your shirt'

- U: 'unlikely, but don't chance it'

- VU: 'very unlikely, safe to ignore'.

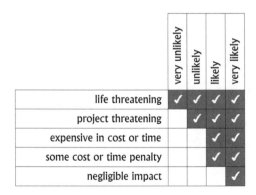

Figure 3-3. The danger slope

For the impact of a risk, we might identify the cardinal aims that are impacted and give a measure of the impact. This might be in direct terms: 'a five-week delivery slippage,' 'an extra £30 000 per year in cost of ownership because of extra licences', 'doubled turnover of data entry staff who are forced to use the system', or a vaguer rating such as:

- L: 'life threatening'

- P: 'project threatening'

- E: 'expensive in cost or time'
- S: 'some cost or time penalty'
- N: 'negligible cost or time penalty'.

These coarse measures will suffice at early workshops. They will help people to concentrate on the 'big' ones. A risk that is unlikely (U) but also project-threatening (P) is worth keeping on the list. One that is unlikely (U) and would cause some cost or time penalty (S) could perhaps be ignored. Again, in very simple terms we can decide that there are some combinations that make us leave the risk unanswered, others that make us look for risk reduction measures. Figure 3-3 suggests how that danger slope looks. Remember that at this stage we are not being statistical about this; we're simply looking for easy ways of getting a handle on the risks and of giving people simple ways to prioritise their effort, whether at the risk analysis workshop or when discussing risk reduction measures.

Updating the Risk Register with the analysis

We can now pull this together in our Risk Register:

1 For each risk in our Risk Register we have decided whether it is caused by event uncertainty or by estimating uncertainty. We mark this in the register.

2 We identify clearly what the uncertainty is ('we are uncertain about the true performance of the database software' or 'it may happen that version 6.4 fails to support concurrency').

3 We add a coarse assessment of the uncertainty concerned.

4 We add a coarse assessment of the impact of the risk.

Our Risk Register now looks like the one in Figure 3-4, where I have left out 'higher level' risks that are the effects of the rest in the list.

Risk response planning: plan for your risks

I used to give the risk management part of a project management course to senior project managers. My session was called, not surprisingly, 'Risk Management'. The lecturer who came after me ran a session which he introduced as 'Certainty Management' – these things *will* happen, so what are you going to do about them? In Chapter 4 we are going to look in detail at the sorts of ways in which we can respond to different risks, but in this chapter we are going to stay with our rather more theoretical view and spend some time teasing apart the generic options open to us when we start to plan what our response will be to risks in the project.

Risk	Risk description	Causes	Source of uncertainty	Nature	Probability	Impact
6	The machinery installer fails to get the machinery in place ready for integration with the software in time	3	event	It may happen that the installer does not have the capability to deal with our requirements and to do the job	U	P
7	We fail to get sufficient staff trained in the operation of the system in time	3	estimate and event	We are uncertain how long it will take to train them. It may happen that we cannot get sufficient candidates to train	L	E
8	Key people who will be needed to push through the work are overloaded	3	estimate	We are uncertain how big the load on them will be and what other commitments they will have at the time	L	S
9	The requirements being pushed by the marketing team are not fully validated	5	event	It may happen that they do not get validated	L	E
10	We demand more 'knobs and whistles' than can reasonably be incorporated in the time available	5	estimate and event	We are uncertain about what it will take to deal with the changes we are looking for. It may happen that we are not prepared to rein in our requirements to meet deadlines	U	E
11	Potential new facilities are being built into the machinery and we feel obliged to exploit these from day one	5	event	It may happen that we are not prepared to rein in our ambitions to meet the deadlines	VU	P
12	The algorithms that control the movement and picking of stock may not be right for the way the warehouse is to be set up	2	estimate	We are uncertain how the flow will look and what the dynamics of the working warehouse will be	U	E
13	Staff cannot cope with the new technology	2	event	It may happen that we do not have the right people with the right training	L	S

etc.

Figure 3-4. Further headings for the Risk Register

I should start perhaps by reminding you that an acceptable response to any risk is 'we will do nothing'. The rest of this chapter will be about doing something, about finding appropriate risk reduction measures, as if we always have to think of something to do. But suppose there is a good chance that the risk will go away soon and that delaying a choice of risk reduction measure would not make it costlier. We would be entirely justified in leaving the risk 'on the table', or, more precisely, in our Risk Register. We can review the position in a week or two, around the time the risk will either dissipate or firm up, and, if it looks as if the risk is more real than apparent, we'll move it into the set of risks we must do something about.

> ### HEADLINE
> Doing nothing yet is always an option as a response to a risk.

So with the 'do nothing' option always in our mind as a possibility, let's look at the range of active risk responses open to us.

Risk reduction measures

We have defined a risk as anything that threatens a cardinal aim of the project. Therefore a risk threatens the cost–benefit model that justified the project – it makes it less likely that the project will be 'successful' in the terms that the business is interested in. Our response to a risk will be to explore what *risk reduction measures* are open to us to remove or reduce the threat, to restore the balance, perhaps only partially.

> ### EXAMPLE
> To take a simple example from the Risk Register above, suppose we are uncertain how many staff can be made available to operate the new system and how long it will take to train them. We will need to look at the projected staffing levels, attrition rates and recruitment plans, and investigate, perhaps through a professional training company or by talking to other companies who have been through the same experience, how long it takes to get people up to the necessary level of competence to work in the new environment.

We should remember that we have two sides of the risk to go for: its probability and its impact – we can take measures that will reduce the probability or we can take measures that will reduce the impact – and a risk reduction measure will generally go for one of these. Of course we might choose two measures: one to reduce the probability and another to reduce the impact should the risk still materialise.

EXAMPLE

Suppose we have some junior staff coming onto the project and they have only recently been trained in Java. This inexperience represents a risk to the project which could lead to poor code. That in turn could lead to reduced quality and increased maintenance costs. We can reduce the *probability* of this happening by giving them some experience in writing software that has already been written well and by supporting them during that work with the services of a guru who can review their work with them. We can also reduce the *impact* of poor code by letting the novices work only on support software or non-critical areas of the system.

Moreover, we will want any risk reduction measure that we choose to be commensurate with the risk. An expensive risk reduction measure that does little to reduce the impact of a small risk will not find its way into our plan for the project, so we will need to look carefully at this question of quantifying risks and candidate risk reduction measures in risk response planning. And of course our analysis will be based on the business case for the system, not on purely technical grounds.

Now let's take risk reduction measures a stage further.

HEADLINE

We can divide risk reduction measures into two sorts: the *pre-emptive risk reduction measure* and the *reactive risk reduction measure*.

Pre-emptive risk reduction measures

With some risks we aren't content to sit on our hands. We decide that we will be proactive.

> ### DEFINITION
>
> A *pre-emptive risk reduction measure* is one that is planned to take effect before the risk materialises.

We have three options open to us:

- an *information-buying activity* or a *process model*
- a *risk-influencing activity*
- *contractual transfer*.

We now take these in turn.

Information-buying activities

> ### HEADLINE
>
> An *information-buying activity* is a risk reduction measure designed to reduce the *cause probability* of a risk (generally an estimating uncertainty).

Some information is needed to remove a risk, an activity is put in hand to get that information, and once it is finished the project can continue in the pre-planned way. An information-buying activity does not lead to a decision which will change the subsequent shape of the project. Let's take a common example.

> ### EXAMPLE
>
> At the start of our project we might be uncertain whether the proposed scheme for navigating the menus will fit the business processes of the system's users (an estimating uncertainty). We reduce the likelihood of this happening by buying information about what would and would not work for the users. To get the information, we plan a study that captures the processes in terms of what the information needs are of people carrying out different roles at different points in the business process, and then compares the resulting process models with the proposed navigation rules. We might also plan a demonstration of the proposed navigation rules in a mock-up of the final system and allow current 'actors' of the business process con-

> cerned to check it against their current needs. We will make the aims
> of the study clear: there is certain information that it must deliver, in-
> formation that will remove the uncertainty that forms the risk con-
> cerned. Once the study is over, the project design team can respond
> to its findings in the design activity. It's very unlikely that any change
> of course will be necessary in the project.

Many information-buying activities involve some form of experimentation:
prototyping, research, modelling, measurement. If we don't know, let's try
something. Doubtful about the performance of those algorithms? Collect
some real data and try them out with it. Unclear what would make a good
user interface? Make a first stab at one and then try it out on the real users
and refine it. Not sure what sort of gearing there should be between the joy-
stick and the motion in the virtual reality system? Prototype a cheap and dirty
version to see how it feels with different values.

Lacking information? Then buy it!

I stress the *buying* part of this transaction because, like all risk reduction
measures, buying information has a price, and an up-front price at that – a
price that we must be confident is worth it, that is commensurate with the
risk. We are going to commit to spending this money in anticipation of a return, or, to be more accurate, the reduction of a negative return.

Risk-influencing activities

> ### HEADLINE
>
> A *risk-influencing activity* is one designed to reduce the *cause probability* of
> a risk (generally an event uncertainty).

There is some variability out there, some chance of things not going the way
we want them to, so we put in place an activity that will influence things to
reduce that variability in the direction we want it. Let's take some straightforward examples.

> ### EXAMPLES
>
> If we believe that the supplier might be late delivering the hardware,
> let's go and make the position over future orders clear to their sales
> director. If we make the position clear enough we might reduce the

risk of late delivery to nothing. But if we have little leverage then such urging could have very little effect on the supplier's performance. The influence can vary enormously. Yet the price to us is probably relatively small – a meeting, a conversation, a weekly phone call.

Earlier we saw a risk that the new staff being recruited to the warehouse management project would not be up to scratch. We can influence this situation by improving the screening that we ask our recruitment agency to use, by being tougher at the interviews, or perhaps by increasing the salaries we are prepared to offer to people with the right skills and the very best track records. The price will probably be bigger invoices from the recruitment agency, more management time spent interviewing and perhaps a bigger salary bill. The influence on productivity and quality could be significant.

We also see a risk that we would demand more 'knobs and whistles' than could reasonably be incorporated in the time available. There is the estimating uncertainty that we are uncertain about what it will take to deal with the changes we are looking for, and there is the event uncertainty that it may happen that we are not prepared to rein in our requirements to meet schedules. We can tackle the second of these by getting the message across to senior management that the whole project – and their reputations   will be jeopardised unless they are firm about keeping requirements demands in check. This is risk-influencing at work – we directly affect the probability of the risk.

Let's look in more detail at those novice software engineers on our project; perhaps they have written in procedural languages in the past, but the object-oriented world is new to them and this system will be written in Java. They represent a risk. The immediate effect of their inexperience might include relative slowness in writing components of code, 'buggy' code, and code that is subsequently hard to maintain because they have not grasped what is needed in an object-oriented world. In cardinal aims terms, the end effect will certainly be increased development costs and very possibly increased costs of ownership, not to mention the possibility that the system will fail to meet a primary system goal because of unreliable operation. The risk involves some event uncertainty – we don't *know* whether they will turn out to be weak programmers – and some estimating uncertainty – we can't be certain what sort of productivity they will achieve. The natural risk-influencing activity in this situation is training. This will reduce the inexperience and hence the cause probability of this risk. And we might well bolster the training with some assistance from our resident Java guru who can work one-on-one with the novices to review their work as they start out.

Imagine that we are integrating a system and that we are acquiring one subsystem from another supplier. We will always regard external suppliers as a potential source of risk, depending on the history of the relationship we have with them. And we will not want to wait until they deliver their subsystem before checking whether it is good enough for our purposes. The risk that we will receive poor work from them, with its consequent effect on timescales and cost to get things right, needs reduction and we will look for a pre-emptive risk reduction measure. Since we do not perhaps want to rely on straight threats (a crude but often used risk-influencing approach) we might instead decide that we will require the supplier to allow us to audit their work as it progresses. This will give us direct visibility of their performance and the opportunity to influence things as they proceed.

Process models

I want to deal now with one class of risk reduction measures that in fact will merit its own chapter shortly: the *process model*.

I've portrayed information-buying activities so far as rather innocuous things – we see some uncertainty due to lack of information, we identify a way of getting the information, we put that in our plan, and when the time comes we just do it, get the information and carry on. Similarly, some risk-influencing activities are straightforward: if the supplier might be late let's go and 'convince' them it is not in their best interests.

Some uncertainties are so big, however, that, until we have the information that is missing, it is very hard, perhaps impossible, to see what might happen on the other side. Perhaps two quite different projects would result. Perhaps, the system would be radically different. Perhaps, we would adopt a quite different approach to its construction – we buy a package rather than building a custom system, or we subcontract a major part instead of doing it ourselves. But things are not always so simple: some risk reduction measures can radically change the overall way the project works, its process model.

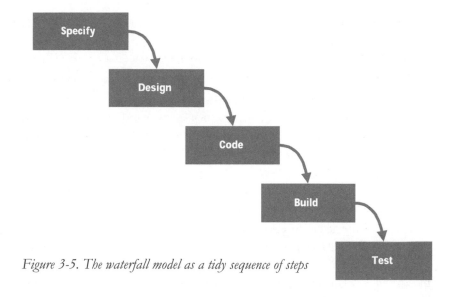

Figure 3-5. The waterfall model as a tidy sequence of steps

Once upon a time the 'standard' shape for a software development project was reckoned to be one that went through a sequence of increasing design detail, followed by a sequence of successive integration of parts into the whole, along the lines of Figure 3-5. (We shall refer to this in the next chapter as the *V Process Model*, a development of the *waterfall model*.) This model of the development process – or *process model* – had the advantage of simplicity. But it also had the disadvantage of assuming that all would be well and a single pass through the phases would suffice. It acquired the name 'the Big Bang approach', suggesting perhaps that anyone using it was surely going to be blown to bits, simply because a rigid application of it allowed risks to go unanswered (and possibly undetected) until the end of the project, at which point terrible delays and cost overruns would appear out of nowhere.

Consequently, a number of alternative process models have been devised in the software industry that address major risks by cutting the project into new phases with new goals and new intermediate decision points.

EXAMPLES

Suppose we have major misgivings about the capability of a new technology proposed for a system – will it do the job or will it not? Our first thought for a risk reduction measure would be to establish the precise capabilities of the technology in a separate, initial study phase before we made any commitment to its use. So a candidate risk reduction measure here would be a process model consisting of an initial study followed perhaps by a phase of project definition and then a further phase for the full development.

Suppose we believe that there is a significant risk that the environment in which our system is designed to work – the people, the organisation structures, the business processes – will themselves change while we are developing the system, so that, when we come to deliver it, the system would no longer 'fit the world' which has meanwhile moved on since we first specified the system. Abandoning the simple Big Bang approach, we might decide that an appropriate risk reduction measure would be to deliver the system in increments, each delivering a bit more functionality to the business, delaying the definition of each increment until the last moment to reduce the potential 'quality gap' induced by the passage of time. Our process model would here consist of a high-level project definition phase followed by a series of development phases each finalising the specification of and delivering an increment of the system.

Both of the above examples reduce the likelihood that the risk will hit the project, in other words its cause probability, by buying information or by influencing the risk. By carrying out that assessment study of the new technology (information buying) early on we make it less likely that we will commit to a design that will not work, and we reduce the probability of getting hit with design problems late in the project. By delivering the system in a sequence of increments and delaying the specification of each increment until the last minute (risk influencing), we reduce the probability of getting hit by finding that the system we have laboured on for so long is no longer appropriate to the business that will use it.

In summary (and there is much more in the next chapter):

DEFINITION

A *process model* is a strategic risk reduction measure that structures the project into phases that are designed to successively reduce risk.

Typically, a process model will break the process up into a number of phases, each of which will be immediately followed by a decision point at which the situation is assessed and the future course of the project is decided. It is this which makes a process model a more strategic form of information-buying or risk-influencing – things could be very different after a decision point.

Contractual transfer

> ### DEFINITION
>
> In *contractual transfer* we take a risky activity and subcontract it to someone else better able to manage that risk.

We will only be prepared to subcontract a risky activity to someone else because they specialise in that sort of work and know the risks and how to deal with them – it is their business and they have the expertise. The subcontract might be on a fixed price so that the entire risk is wrapped up and given to the subcontractor – our exposure is limited to the agreed price. In an ideal world, by paying that price we have completely removed the risk. In the real world, we have certainly passed a sizeable chunk of it, but if our subcontractor fails and we do not get the goods – software, hardware, whatever – our project is again in trouble and the ability to revert to the courts for compensation will not help us get our system to our client.

For these reasons contractual transfer is a contentious option. Badly done it is foolhardy. But many organisations, such as government departments, whose sole job it is to specify and procure systems from suppliers, use contractual transfer as a standard *modus operandi*, and their aim is always to seek out suppliers precisely with the ability to manage the perceived risks. This puts the onus on the procurement agency to make a sound assessment of the risks at the outset, perhaps through a separate study let to a company specialising in just that. Once the risks are understood they can be used as one of the screening mechanisms for potential suppliers.

> ### EXAMPLE
>
> Suppose we need certain specialist equipment for our system. If we decide that our project will develop and provide that equipment itself, we take on the risk associated with any failure to get that equipment to our project on time. If on the other hand we find a subcontractor who is as able, or better able, than us to obtain the equipment, we might decide to transfer the risk to them. In this way we reduce the probability of the risk that hardware delivery turns out to be a

> problem, and we will probably pay for this reduction in a premium that the subcontractor includes in the price to cover the risk as they perceive it.

It is not unknown for a supplier to return risk to the buyer. I was contracted to deliver a system that required us to use some relatively untested hardware which was on a shaky delivery time. We could have taken the risk that the hardware would not perform and/or it would be late. To do that we would have had to put a substantial amount of money and time into our price as financial provision against the risk's materialising. In the event, I 'sold' the risk back to the client on the basis that it would be better for them to hold a provision themselves and pay me for any delays or problems caused than to pay that provision to me. I think this turned out well. There were problems and the client used some of that provision to pay me but they were also, because of their purchasing power, better able to manage the risk by putting pressure on the supplier than I was indirectly on their behalf.

In summary then, contractual transfer transfers a risk to a supplier better able to manage it, thereby reducing the *probability* of the risk materialising, probably in return for a premium in the purchase price.

Reactive risk reduction measures

> **DEFINITION**
>
> A *reactive risk reduction measure* is one that we plan to take effect after a risk materialises.

'OK, so the worst has happened what do we do now?' We have two options: a contingency plan and insurance. It is important to note that even though these risk reduction measures are reactive, our planning for them was entirely proactive, in other words we recognised the risk at the outset and had plan B in place or an insurance policy up our sleeve before the risk got anywhere near materialising.

By definition a reactive risk reduction measure can only reduce the impact of a risk.

Contingency plans

Anyone who has taken a backup on their PC has had a contingency plan: 'if my hard disc fails I can restore the data partially from the backup.' Taking a backup doesn't change the probability of a crash on your hard drive, but it does reduce the impact when it happens – you lose 'only' the work you have done since the last backup, rather than everything. There is a cost to you, namely the lost working time that you are now spending taking the backups and of course the cost of the media that are thereby consumed. But it is a small price to pay against the (certain?) day when that drive decides to fail.

EXAMPLE

Suppose we have subcontracted a subsystem to another supplier who will deliver it on 1st August next year. We have chosen that date because a month after then we expect to be in a position to integrate that subsystem into the body of the system. The early stages of the integration work will of course be checking out interfaces and ensuring that the two things operate correctly at a simple level.

There are two certainties in software projects. The first is that any two things put together will fail. The second is that any dependency on someone else will not be met. So we naturally recognise the supply of the subsystem as a risk to the project and start to think about a 'plan B' which will reduce the impact of a late delivery. The natural thought is to prepare some disposable software that will simulate the operation of the missing subsystem at least to a level that will get us through that early integration work. There will come a point of course where we can go no further without the real subsystem but at least this simulator will buy us some time if we need it.

So, we shall reduce the possible impact (an impact that will principally affect the cardinal aim concerned with delivery of the total system) and we shall stand the cost of preparing and testing the simulation software. In this way a possible impact on the delivery date cardinal aim will be paid for by a definite impact on the whole life costs cardinal aim – we are making a trade-off, one that will need some thought to ensure that the price is one worth paying.

Preparing contingency plans takes time and consumes resources, so we must ensure that the appropriate preparation activities find their way into our plan. For now, we settle for identifying the risk reduction measure. When we come to construct the Work Breakdown Structure that lists *all* the project's activities we will develop in detail the activities necessary.

There is one other thing that we should decide here and now while we are thinking carefully about 'plan B': what will trigger us decide to switch to it? There is no point in having a contingency plan if we do not know what would make us use it. Sometimes the trigger can be a clean 'binary' one: 'if we have not had version 3 from the supplier by the start of integration of the antenna software, adopt the contingency plan to transfer to another supplier'. Unfortunately, there is not always a nice clean date or event that gives the signal: the unpleasant situation we are hoping does not happen might develop gradually – what will make us decide things are bad enough to put the contingency plan into action? There are no general rules that can help here, but a decision must be made.

HEADLINE

If we have chosen a contingency plan as a risk reduction measure for a risk we must record the trigger for it in the Risk Register.

Insurance

Insurance is probably our last line of defence and is uncommon. We pay someone else to take the loss that results from a risk's materialising in return for an up-front premium. As with a contingency plan, a potential impact on a cardinal aim is offset against a definite impact on the whole life costs. It's likely that if we look to an insurer for cover against the risk, they will expect us to put in place some pre-emptive risk reduction measures in addition to handing over the premium, or that the premium will be reduced if we do so.

Matching measures to uncertainties

Before we move on, let's pull some threads together. The table in Figure 3-6 summarises our options. What we see is that contractual transfer looks like the most flexible risk reduction measure, but we have seen how it can be dangerous and is rarely used in practice. Not surprisingly the two styles of reactive risk reduction measure – insurance and contingency planning – only affect the impact of the risk; information-buying reduces the chance that we will get hit because of (estimating) uncertainty that we have, while risk-influencing reduces the chance that we will get hit by a risk that is due to some variability in the world (event uncertainty).

		reactive risk reduction measure			pre-emptive risk reduction measure	
		contingency	insurance	information-buying	risk-influencing	contractual transfer
estimating uncertainty	probability			✓		✓
	impact	✓	✓			✓
event uncertainty	probability				✓	✓
	impact	✓	✓			✓

Figure 3-6. Risks and risk reduction measures

Identifying risk reduction measures is not enough in itself: we must be quite clear about who is responsible for taking action to put the measures in place, and for monitoring the risk, the effect any actions have on it and its out-turn. Some of the actions might need to be taken some way downstream, some might be immediate – make someone responsible. If the project team and its client have agreed to run a joint Risk Register, it becomes even more important to be clear about who is responsible for each risk; it should not be assumed that the project team is dealing with all the risk reduction measures, even where they relate to the client's sphere of influence.

Updating the Risk Register with the chosen risk reduction measures and owners

As elsewhere in life, to make sure a thing happens we give it an owner. So it is with risk reduction measures. In a sense, of course, the project manager is responsible for all the risk management on the project, but it is quite likely that, especially on a large project, we shall want to ensure that responsibility for taking the chosen actions is firmly and clearly delegated to a named person or group. This will be particularly important where the Risk Register and its risks are being jointly managed by the project team and others such as suppliers or the client or a procurement body. Contracts frequently separate these 'collaborators', and any attempt at 'risk sharing' needs the support of agreed processes, and, most probably, agreement over who is taking responsibility for which risks.

#	Risk description	Chosen risk reduction measure(s)	Risk owner
6	The machinery installer fails to get the machinery in place ready for integration with the software in time	Ensure the supplier understands the business criticality for both parties. Increase the visibility of the project in the industry	MAO
7	We fail to get sufficient staff trained in the operation of the system in time	Get some estimates from a training company for the training requirements for the tasks concerned. Find out how long things took at the last major change and scale the figures up. Increase wage levels for trained staff to improve recruitment	GTAM
8	Key people who will be needed to push through the work are overloaded	Inventory other activities currently occupying time of key staff. Negotiate with relevant directors to free more of their time	TJH
9	The requirements being pushed by the marketing team are not fully validated	Get Board agreement that the Board must approve any changes to requirements	SVS
10	We demand more 'knobs and whistles' than can reasonably be incorporated in the time available	Get the supplier to give firm costings quickly. Get Board agreement to stringent change control	CRM
11	Potential new facilities are being built into the machinery and we feel obliged to exploit these from day one	Get Board agreement that the Board must approve any changes to requirements	MH
12	The algorithms that control the movement and picking of stock may not be right for the way the warehouse is to be set up	Prepare simulation of algorithms using consultants recommended by other retailers who had similar requirements	RJB
13	Staff cannot cope with the new technology	Analyse staff skills and move less adaptable staff off key posts	VM

etc.

Figure 3-7. Adding risk reduction measures and owners to the Risk Register

We can now add further columns to the Risk Register entries with our chosen risk reduction measures and risk owners, and we get Figure 3-7.

Residual risk

With both pre-emptive and reactive risk reduction measures we have implicitly recognised that we can never entirely rid ourselves of a risk. As long as we persist with this project there will be risk. The only way of making sure an aircraft does not have an accident in the air is to leave it on the runway. So when we assess candidate risk reduction measures we need to understand just how much protection they give us and how much *residual risk* remains even after we have taken them.

EXAMPLES

We can train our novice programmers very thoroughly in Java, but there will still be a residual risk that they will produce poor code, at least for the first few months.

We can write a simulator to insulate us from the late delivery of a subsystem, but there will come that point when we can proceed no further without the real thing.

We can carry out experiments to establish the likely performance of a database that we intend to build our system on, but in the event it could still prove inadequate when it is faced with the real loadings and patterns of use.

Unfortunately, some risk reduction measures bring their own risks with them and as part of our analysis of a candidate measure we need to see not only what costs it brings but also whether, like a lump in a carpet, we are not just moving the risk around or substituting one for another.

EXAMPLE

We might choose a commercial off-the-shelf (COTS) solution in order to reduce the risk of schedule overrun in initial development. But that package brings with it reliance on a vendor: we might be let down and the move could reduce the flexibility open to our client for future enhancements.

By reining in the ambitions of users to have an all-singing, all-dancing system we may reduce the risk of schedule and cost over-runs, but in turn we might pull back so far that the system doesn't meet their minimum requirements.

When we evaluate a candidate risk reduction measure we must therefore look carefully at whether we are pushing the lump in the carpet around, and judge whether a smaller lump over there is not better than a larger one over here. And if the new lump is big enough we might need to treat it as a new risk that requires its own risk reduction measure, or we might of course decide to 'leave it on the table' as a residual risk.

Definition

A *residual risk* is the risk that remains even after we have taken a risk reduction measure, or a risk that we choose not to manage, or even one that we cannot manage.

So our analysis of a risk will need to examine three things:

- its *probability* and its *impact*

- the *candidate risk reduction measures*: the extent to which they reduce the probability and/or the impact, and the risks they in turn induce

- the *residual risk* for each candidate risk reduction measure: the remaining probability and impact.

Some risk reduction measures will be 'obvious' – little thought and no calculation will be necessary to tell us 'we must do this'. We have untrained staff – we must train them. When we are assessing the cost-effectiveness of a candidate risk reduction measure we can make the same sort of assessment of the residual risk *after* we have applied the risk reduction measure as we applied to the original risk, e.g. using our coarse measures of impact and probability. We can present things in the style suggested by Figure 3-8 where a risk that was both life threatening and likely has been reduced to one that is not likely though still has some cost or time penalty. This sort of picture can work well in a workshop environment and, once more, while not being hugely scientific, can give people a handle on the problem.

But in more complex cases, especially those where the risk reduction measure can be as cheap or as expensive as we like, we will need some ways of determining and perhaps comparing the cost-effectiveness of measures as we plan our responses to the risks we have identified. It is this we now look at.

Quantifying risks, risk reduction measures and residual risk

Perhaps it is because I could never get on with statistics that, when I was looking for simple ways for project managers to evaluate risk reduction measures and residual risk, I was pleased to come across Bob Charette's words: 'Whether the likelihood of a risk takes on a normal or Poisson distribution, or a combination of some others, is not high on most people's list of the things they are knowledgeable about'. I'll vote for that.

So, how do we quantify, put a value to, a risk? How do we give someone an assessment of how likely the risk is to materialise, or of the likely size of its impact?

And how should we express how that assessment is changed by a candidate risk reduction measure, and what the probability and impact of the residual risk is?

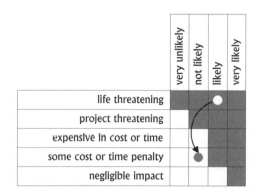

Figure 3-8. Getting under the danger slope

So far, all I have called for in the Risk Register is a coarse assessment, using that danger slope, of the probability and the impact – no numbers were used, our assessments being very much *qualitative*. This was intended to be just enough to get the juices flowing and to allow some quick prioritisation that would separate the risks really needing attention from those that could be dealt with if we had the opportunity. And we could stop there. But there are other reasons for wanting some form of *quantification* of a risk or a residual risk. The question of the 'size' of a (residual) risk is going to play an important part in our costing of the project – so important, in fact, that it is worth a diversion from the main thread at this point.

Risk provisions

When we bid for work, or plan a project for a contract we have won, or forecast the final project costs during the project, we will estimate the 'base cost': the cost of all the activities we know we have to carry out. But we will also want to make some provision for the unforeseen. At bidding time, that provision will give extra financial security, a cushion. Once we are into the project and estimating the final outcome, the provision will give a more prudent or conservative figure for forecasting purposes.

In examples earlier in this chapter I ventured to use phrases like 'There is a 25% probability that the supplier will be four or more weeks late'. I think if someone said this to me I would immediately ask 'Why not 26%? Or 24%?' We use expressions like '25% probability' to give spurious credibility to what we probably mean: 'not very likely.' Equally, '75%' probably (!) means 'pretty likely', '90%' 'as good as certain', '10%' 'I shall be very surprised if it happens'. I wish there were another word than *probability* simply because it suggests so strongly that we are talking statistics or at least something we can do arithmetic on, and I suggest that that is rarely the case. The work *likelihood* has also been grabbed by the statisticians. So I shall persevere with *probability* but you must remember that I do not use it in its statistical sense! (And to really annoy the statisticians I shall use *probability* and *likelihood* interchangeably!)

I might go on to ask the project manager 'What is the probability that the supplier will be ten or more weeks late? Or twenty weeks?'. Clearly what I am trying to do is to get a feel for the *shape* of this risk, not just a single value. This is central to what follows.

The same argument applies to a residual risk: what shape does it have? What is the likelihood that there will now be no delay? What is the likelihood that the delay will be four weeks, ten weeks, twenty weeks?

Just how much risk provision we opt for is a *commercial* decision and it depends on how confident we want to feel in the final number: just how much commercial risk do we want to expose the company to with this bid? Or how prudent do we want to be with our financial forecasts at this point in the project? These are not technical questions but commercial questions, but they will require technical input in the form of some representation of our *confidence*. The more risk provision we decide to add to a bid price, the less the financial exposure, but the less the chance of winning the bid. I was once in a bid review for a large contract. The estimates for the anticipated work to specify, design and build the system had been presented and reviewed and then someone asked 'How much provision should we add?' Someone suggested 15%. I suggested 16%. And then 17%. And then 27%. The point was that we had no rational way of deciding on a figure. In the event the provision was the difference between the base cost and the price we thought we could win the work for, a not uncommon way of solving this problem, but not at all helpful, of course, as it gives the bidder absolutely no idea of how much risk the company is taking on. In the worst case the risk provision is talked down (generally by the salesperson nailing the technician!) until a commercially acceptable number is reached. All that has happened now is that the business has talked itself into the number that it wanted all along to win the sale and has again no idea of the scale of risk that has been taken on.

This single-figure risk provision has another unpleasant aspect. Because it has been equated to the potential profit, it becomes a bucket of money which either gets withheld by senior management who hope to turn it into profit, or is handed over to the project manager who is seen to 'squander' it by using it to cover up non-risk-related problems.

The solution to all these objections is to recognise that:

HEADLINE
Risk provisions must be allocated to specific risks.

First we must know the residual risks in the project (after we have planned for our chosen risk reduction measures) and then we must make a provision *for each of them individually*. The technical input to the question of risk provision is of course the risk analysis that we have done.

But haven't I made things more difficult by saying that our technical assessment of residual risk in particular should be expressed as a *shape*, rather than as a single number? How can we use the shape of the provision in our pricing? At least with a single number – e.g. 15% of the total cost of the planned activities – we could simply add it to that base cost. How do we add a *shape*? Let's look at this question of quantification using the shapes that I described earlier – sliding and binary.

(I want to preface the following remarks with that warning again: although the diagrams that follow look suspiciously like graphs I do not want them to be taken as trying to represent any mathematical functions – just what our insides tell us about a risk and its shape.)

Quantifying a sliding (residual) risk

Suppose we are concerned about a sliding risk: the possible late delivery of some hardware by the supplier. As the delivery gets later so the cost impact gets greater. Let's gauge our confidence in the supplier. Figure 3-9 gives a picture of those feelings. The x-axis represents the potential delay in weeks. The y-axis represents our confidence that the delay will not exceed x. Point A says that we are sure there will be some delay, and point B says that in the worst case delivery could be ten weeks late. How we 'plot' our feelings between these two points gives us the shape of the risk.

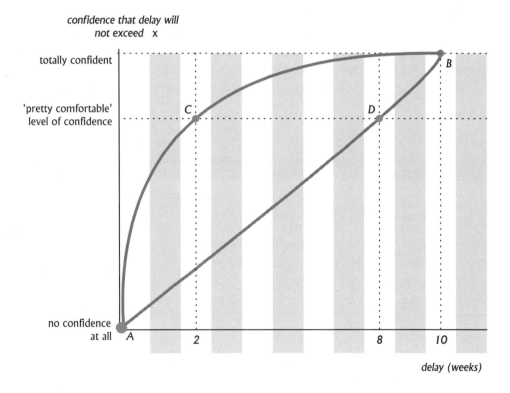

Figure 3-9. Two possible shapes of a risk

In one situation we might be able to go a little further and add point C, which says that we are 'pretty confident' (80%?) that the delay will not be more than two weeks – we start to get the upper curve in the picture.

If on the other hand we were pessimistic and could easily see a delay of eight weeks we would plot point D and start to get something like the lower curve. Essentially we are drawing a crude picture of how likely we feel that we shall take a hit of a given size. The technical input to the choice of provision level is essentially this picture, no matter how crude it is.

Shape ACB says 'it could be anywhere between zero and ten weeks delay, but we feel it's unlikely to be more than two weeks'. Shape ADB says 'it could be anywhere between zero and ten weeks delay, and could easily be at the worse end.' Once we have understood our feelings about the risk, perhaps by privately sketching this sort of picture, we can see what sort of exposure we have at different confidence levels. If we felt like the lower curve in the picture and chose a provision corresponding to a two-week delay we know that there would be a very high probability of blowing that provision – and more. We can check out the exposure we would be taking on for a given choice of provision. As with any good picture, our aim is to have something that focuses our minds and exposes the facts – a basis for rational argument. Let's examine how we can now make use of this understanding in the different situations we find ourselves in.

Firstly, suppose we are using the information as input to the pricing decision. We choose a provision for each residual risk *at a confidence level decided for commercial reasons*. At this point, knowledge of the client's budget, the likely win price, competitors' bids, and so on, come into play, and we can run things backwards: if we choose this bid price what confidence can we have in coming in under it and is that sufficient? This in turn is bound up with larger commercial issues such as our keenness to break into a particular market or account, and the existing risk portfolio across other projects. This only emphasises the need to separate technical risk analysis from commercial provision setting! The technical judgement as to the shape of a risk (one of a number, probably) informs our commercial judgement as to what level of provision and hence what level of risk to expose the company to. Suppose we decide that the risk has the shape of the lower line ADB in Figure 3-9. If we costed on the basis of an eight-week delay we could feel 'pretty comfortable' that that was a safe bet; but if we costed in a two-week delay we could feel pretty comfortable of losing money on that risk.

Secondly, suppose we are using the information at some point during the project. As things unfold, risks materialise or dissipate. As a result, we will 'eat into' the risk provision or we won't, respectively. By tracking risks individually and quantifying them each time we re-assess them, we can tell at any one moment how much risk has materialised (in cost or schedule terms), how much has dissipated, and how much remains in the future. Line management can use this information when forecasting the profitability of the project. We can ensure that the project manager is focused on the unknown as much as on the known.

It's worth noting that a scheme like this, because it provides that basis for rational argument, can help us to operate a development contract on a shared risk and shared reward basis with our client. The contract will involve an agreed price which includes provisions against a set of agreed risks; if we come in below that figure, we share the benefit with the client in some proportion, and if we exceed that figure we share the cost. Such an arrangement – which again calls for a new level of maturity from both parties – can promote a shared desire to make a development work, where a strict division of the parties by the contract can generate dysfunctional behaviour that ensures a sub-optimal solution.

Quantifying a binary (residual) risk

Suppose we are concerned about a binary risk. Let's suppose there is a risk that the next release of the DBMS will not have a security feature that we could really do with and which we plan to use. The feature was promised but we have heard a rumour that the vendor is backing off it for this release. If the feature is not there, we shall have to make some major changes to our software, effectively building in the feature ourselves, and our estimates suggest that this will mean an extra £55K of effort and a two-week slip. There are no curves now. This risk will either cost us £55K or it won't, depending on whether the feature is absent or present. Its impact is fixed. But its probability is variable, and it is the probability that we must get a feel for. Here we are in the position of bookmakers at the racecourse. Each bet is a binary risk – either they pay out or they don't (let's keep it simple and assume they only take bets to win). If I place a bet to win of £10 at 10-1, either I shall collect £110 or nothing. I cannot collect anything in between. The bookmaker cannot make a 'provision' of, say, £50 on that single bet. It doesn't make much sense. What does make sense is adding up the risks across a number of bets (and setting the odds so that overall they make their profit). If we reckon that that security feature is more likely to be in than out, we might reckon a £20K provision 'about right' but if we do we shall either be down £35K or up £20K at the end.

I am getting into this detail simply to emphasise that if we start adding provisions together, the arithmetic will be somewhat suspect for one or two binary risks, but would start to be more meaningful when we have a number of them.

Quantification so far summarised

What I have proposed so far is that our total provision for risk on the project should be the sum of provisions for the individual residual risks, after we have planned our risk reduction measures. Each individual provision is decided on by taking into account the commercial environment and the shape of the risk that our technical judgement has led us to. This will yield three numbers:

- the *least impact* we can suffer (which may well be zero)

- the *chosen level* for the provision

- the *worst impact* that we can suffer (without getting silly).

EXAMPLES

'If one in three of our programming staff are unfamiliar with Java, the minimum impact having trained them will be having to review and rework their work during the first month, which will be equivalent to a 10% increase on their effort. In the worst case (yet possible) we might need to rework all their work in the first month which means a 100% increase on their effort. Knowing the people concerned, I feel pretty confident that a 40% provision will suffice. Converting this into project costs, the three figures are £20K, £80K and £200K.'

'We're planning some simulation studies of the flow algorithms. Once we have the results of that and we have a sound strategy in place, I believe that the worst that can happen is that we have to retune some of the parameters after some trials with the real system and a variety of scenarios. That would be about two weeks' delay. In the best case we will get it right first time and I can imagine that happening. If we want to be pretty comfortable about our provision I think that splitting the difference will be fine. The three figures are therefore no delay, one week's delay and two weeks' delay.'

For a further quantitative view of risk, see Stephen Grey's *Practical Risk Assessment for Project Management* (1995).

Updating the Risk Register with the analysis

Once we have chosen how we want to represent the probability and impact of a risk we can enter the details in our Risk Register. By this time we have analysed the risks, examined the cause and effect, devised candidate risk reduction measures (perhaps pre-emptive and reactive), looked at how each measure changes the risk, made our choice of those that are cost-effective for the level of risk we regard as acceptable, and assessed the residual risk. All of this information can be entered into the Risk Register for use as the project progresses.

Risk	Residual risk	Best case (days)	Chosen case	Worst case
6	The machinery installer fails to get the machinery in place ready for integration with the software in time	0	10	30
7	We fail to get sufficient staff trained in the operation of the system in time	0	5	20
8	Key people who will be needed to push through the work are overloaded	0	0	10
9	The requirements being pushed by the marketing team are not fully validated	0	0	30
10	We demand more 'knobs and whistles' than can reasonably be incorporated in the time available	0	0	20
11	Potential new facilities are being built into the machinery and we feel obliged to exploit these from day one	0	0	0
12	The algorithms that control the movement and picking of stock may not be right for the way the warehouse is to be set up	0	5	20
13	Staff cannot cope with the new technology	10	15	20

Figure 3-10. Adding residual risk quantification to the Risk Register

Given the three points for each of our risks, we might feel inclined to use a statistical spreadsheet which allows distributions (especially triangular distributions) to be used in formulae in cells in order to see what the total effect of the risks will be. Such tools typically use hypercube or Monte Carlo simulation to give a graph of (say) the total cost given these risks. But with some crude assumptions we can get a reasonable figure (i.e. one we can have some faith in) simply by adding up the provisions for the separate risks (ignoring assumptions about independence – I warned you that this was not an exercise in statistics). We might choose to concentrate on schedule impact when we look at the cumulative effect of the residual risks and the total provision that we should make for the level of comfort we are looking for. Our Risk Register now has three more columns, as suggested in Figure 3-10:

Field	Meaning
risk number	A unique identifier for the risk.
risk description	A brief description of the risk in cause–effect terms.
causes risks	A list of the risks that this one itself causes.
source of uncertainty	An indicator saying whether the risk is caused by event and/or estimating uncertainty.
nature of uncertainty	A description of the event and/or estimating uncertainty that is causing the risk.
probability	An assessment of the likelihood that the risk will materialise.
impact	An assessment of the scale of the impact the risk could have if it materialised.
chosen risk reduction measures	A list of the pre-emptive and/or reactive measures chosen to manage the risk.
risk owner	The name of the person(s) delegated with the management of the risk and its monitoring.
residual risk	The nature of the risk that remains once the chosen risk reduction measures have had their full effect.
best case value	An assessment of the scale of the residual risk in terms of its impact on costs and schedule in the best case.
chosen case value	The value chosen as the costs and/or schedule provision for the residual risk.
worst case value	An assessment of the scale of the residual risk in terms of its impact on costs and schedule in the worst case.

Figure 3-11. The full Risk Register entry for a risk

There are other approaches to quantification. Some people propose the use of a triple: 'worst case', 'most likely case' and 'best case'. But I personally find it hard to work with the idea of 'most likely impact'. Perhaps it is points *C* and *D* in the two situations shown in Figure 3-9. I prefer to give my technical judgement in the form of the curve and then have the single figure chosen on commercial grounds.

In some cases, especially where impact cannot be sensibly or easily rendered into cost or schedule terms, other means must be found – we are back at the apples and pears problem.

The full Risk Register entry

We can now pull together the full record for each risk in the Risk Register, as shown in Figure 3-11. How you keep this information is something that you will need to decide. A small number of risks can be dealt with in a simple table or spreadsheet. A larger number might justify a small database. You might go to the extent of using a purpose-built product. As ever, it is the quality of the thinking behind its contents that makes a good Risk Register, not the means by which it is held.

Changing the balance

Earlier on, we were scaling the risks under headings like 'very likely', 'likely', unlikely' and 'very unlikely'.

You might have thought that any risk that is 'very likely', or even just 'likely', should be treated as a certainty. In fact that is more or less what we have done. By deciding to put a risk reduction measure for such a risk into our plan, we have replaced a (very) likely impact by a presumably smaller but definite impact (the cost of the risk reduction measure) plus a much smaller but low probability residual impact. In building our Risk Plan, we aim to have altered the balance in our favour (Figure 3-12).

Opportunities: change the sign for an optimistic view

Everything that I have said so far in this chapter about risks is true for *opportunities* with just a change of sign. Where things were downside, they are now upside; where a risk had an impact that increased the costs or lengthened the schedule, an opportunity can decrease the cost or shorten the schedule.

Turning round our definition of a risk we can say that:

> **DEFINITION**
>
> An *opportunity* is anything that would make more likely the achievement of one or more of the cardinal aims of the project.

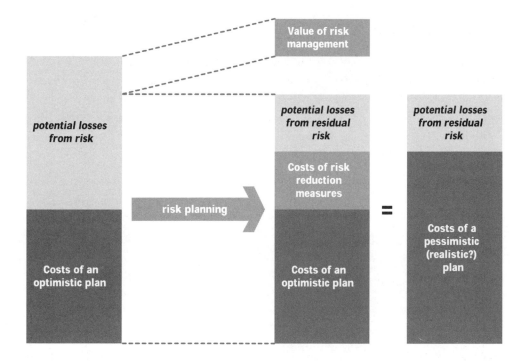

Figure 3-12: Changing the balance of risk

Opportunities arise all the time on projects, but how often do we take seriously the idea of actually *managing* them in as rigorous a way as we consider managing risks? And yet they can have a profound effect on the project as risks. So let's go right back to the idea of the risk management process and think about having an *opportunity management process*:

1 opportunity identification – spot the opportunities

2 opportunity analysis – take them apart and think about them

3 opportunity response planning – decide what to do about them

4 opportunity resolution and monitoring – do whatever you decided.

We can identify things we will do to *increase* the likelihood that an opportunity will materialise, or that will *increase* its impact on the project. We can compare the costs of candidate information-buying and opportunity-influencing activities with the potential gains and decide whether they are worth while. And finally we can make a provision in our costings for the realisation of the opportunity: a best case, a chosen case and a worst case.

> **HEADLINE**
>
> Opportunities should be managed as rigorously as risks.

> **EXAMPLE**
>
> As we start into the design of the system we realise that one of the major components is very similar to a subsystem that we wrote for a recent project. There is an opportunity to reuse that subsystem and save ourselves the design and development of something similar from scratch. In the first instance we need to see how close the match really is so there is some information-buying to be done first, and once we have the facts we can decide what the further cost would be of taking up the opportunity. Those costs could be zero if the fit is very close, or they could be significant if we have to adjust the code to be reused to make it work in our system's environment, or to change our design so that it accommodates the reused software, or of course both of these things.

Finally, to ensure that we really take this whole opportunity thing seriously, we can convert our Risk Register into a Risk and Opportunity Register, something that sounds altogether more balanced!

Yes, we can still take a flyer

Finally, let me conclude this chapter with a warning. The purpose of risk management is not, repeat *not*, to reduce risk to zero or even to minimise risk. It is to reduce risk to *a commercially acceptable level*. When we run a business we take risks but we take just as many as we think commercially sensible. When we bid for a contract by submitting a price we can do one of three things. We can bid a price which we feel confident we will make a profit on – but we risk bidding a price that is higher than our competitors. We can bid a price that our estimates tell us is 'marginal' as far as making a profit is concerned – we are taking a flyer: we might or we might not make a profit but we feel the odds are better than evens that we will and there is not so much new risk to the company as a whole that we do not want the extra risk that winning this work at that price would add. And finally, we can bid a price that we know is less than we think we can do the work for: we can 'buy' the contract, perhaps to ensure getting a first piece of work for a new client and hence getting the opportunity to show what we can do, or to get new experience in a new field that will perhaps open doors to us in the future.

All three options are *business* options and in each case we accept a measure of risk that we believe is commercially justified. Our aim as stressed in Chapter 1 is to base that commercial judgement on sound technical input about what the risks are. The technical judgements *inform* the commercial judgements.

Chapter recap

The business case for any system is made in terms of its cardinal aims. They are expressed in terms of the system's whole life costs, goals and side effects. In some cases we want to reduce the variability of one or more of these as much as defining at what level they should be.

A risk is any threat to any of the cardinal aims of the project.

Risk management follows a four-step procedure, which is iterated through the life of the project:

- risk identification
- risk analysis
- risk response planning
- risk resolution and monitoring.

Risks can be identified at workshops of project staff and stakeholders, and from checklists and experience. They can be analysed into a cause–effect tree showing how one leads to another, finally affecting the cardinal aims of the project.

Each risk can be assessed according to the severity of its impact and the likelihood of its occurring. Some risks are binary and some sliding in their probability.

Risks arise because of event uncertainty or estimating uncertainty.

Risk reduction measures can be pre-emptive or reactive. Pre-emptive risk reduction measures either buy information, or influence the risk, or pass the risk to someone better able to manage it through contractual transfer. Major risk reduction measures can take the form of complete process models for a project, i.e. they provide a complete skeletal structure for the project. Reactive risk reduction measures are contingency plans or insurance.

Each risk has a nominated owner.

A Risk Register is used to capture all the analysis and decisions about the risks on the project.

In order to establish an acceptable level of comfort in the cost or schedule estimate for the project, a provision must be added for the residual risk of each risk identified.

Opportunities can be managed in exactly the same way as risks, with just a change of sign.

> ## Outcome
>
> **A Risk Register**. This lists all the risks, your assessment of them, the risk reduction measures you have chosen to address them, and your assessment of the residual risk. You will use it during the project as a tool for monitoring and managing the residual risks which are not covered in your plan.

The overall benefits of this approach to risk and opportunity management will be that:

- risks are actively managed

- opportunities are actively managed

- provision is intelligently estimated against individual residual risks, rather than being guessed as some gross multiplier on the entire project

- a dialogue can be opened up with the client aimed at reducing the overall risk to the project and thereby increasing client satisfaction.

There is no doubt that moving to such a regime requires an open culture in which risk can be discussed between project and line manager and between company and client, but making this step is one of many necessary to make software development a customer-focused engineering discipline.

It's vital to remember that this risk (and opportunity) process is not a one-off matter. Keeping risks and opportunities under review should be the daily task of the project manager. So in Chapter 10 I shall return to the topic, in particular to look at how we take the Risk Register forward and track the project's progress against the threats and the opportunities that it faces.

Reference

Grey 1995

Practical Risk Assessment for Project Management, S Grey. John Wiley & Sons, Chichester, 1995

Saaty 1995

Decision Making for Leaders, The Analytic Hierarchy Process for Decisions in a Complex World, T L Saaty. RWS Publications, Pittsburgh, 1995

4 *Planning for risk management*

Chapter 3 gave us a vocabulary and some concepts for thinking about risk: cause probability, impact, pre-emptive and reactive risk reduction measures, residual risk and risk quantification. By way of illustration we saw a number of possible risks and possible risk reduction measures. This chapter now puts that vocabulary to work and we look at some very common risks that face many projects and some standard ways in which they can be successfully addressed. In particular we shall concentrate on one of the most important forms of pre-emptive risk reduction measure: the process model.

What is a process model?

I use the term *process model* to refer to what in the past has been called a *lifecycle*. It is a model of the development process, a description of the overall shape of a project, of the route to be taken to getting from the client's requirements to a system in use by the client. A process model is not the same as a method. A project adopts one process model and a number of methods within that process model. Some of the more extensive methods such as Information Engineering and SSADM imply the use of a particular process model, but that is not in general true. First, though, a little history.

In the earlier days of computing, a major birth took place: that of the *stagewise model* of software development, described by Benington (1956). In what was perhaps one of the first steps towards moving the activity onto a more engineering-based footing, a simple formulation of the process was defined that consisted of a sequence of phases through which development was supposed to proceed. The names varied according to the author, but I'm sure the following will be familiar to you:

- analysis of requirements (finding out what the client wants to achieve)

- system specification (specifying what the client will get)

- system design (creating an architecture for the system)

- system construction (building the system)

- system acceptance and delivery (giving it to the user).

The recognition of this simple process really was quite a breakthrough, though we might now look back at it and consider it rather naïve. But it was a model that helped give *structure* to software development, and it still serves its purpose today in many respects. An easy criticism that can be made of it is that it does not explicitly recognise the need for revision, i.e. for returning to earlier phases and reworking things in the light of information obtained during development: information about what the user wants, or how the design might perform, or how the DBMS gets in your way, or whatever.

Thus, we need to accept the possibility that we will iterate during the development, perhaps within a given phase (e.g. reworking a design until we believe that it will give the required performance), or from one phase back to another (e.g. to correct a faulty design decision that, during construction, is exposed by a failure to be able to implement it). The biggest iteration is the one where we complete the development and, when we see what we have produced, we decide we need to start again and redefine the user requirements in the light of what we have produced. Such iterations happen in the real world and we like to capture this in our model. Royce first formulated this idea in what he labelled the *waterfall model* (Royce 1970) (see Figure 4-4).

Another criticism has been that during development we have to make many decisions and those decisions can have a number of possible alternative outcomes. The simple model doesn't recognise this. For instance, depending on the analysis of the client's requirements, we might decide to implement the system from scratch, or to rework an existing one, or to buy a package that supplies most of the functionality required. That single decision can have three very different outcomes.

Put another way, any model of development needs to be able to capture the *sequence* of activities (define *then* design *then* construct), the *iteration* of activities (*do* some prototyping *until* agreement is reached), and *alternative* activities (*if* a package will do *then* buy that *else* build from scratch). Suddenly, we find ourselves wanting to describe software development as if it were a program with the traditional Dijkstra structuring units *sequence, iteration* and *selection*: perhaps a process model is really a program! And to the three constructs for serial processes we will of course want to be able to add *parallelism* in our process models. We will deal with how to represent these features later in this chapter.

Why have process models?

Reducing risk

This business of process models might sound like a notion that would only entertain the software philosopher, but in fact it is vitally important for the software engineer.

> ### HEADLINE
> The purpose of a process model is to give risk-reducing structure to a project.

A project without structure is an unmanageable project. It cannot be planned, it cannot be estimated, it cannot be milestoned, its progress cannot be monitored, and you cannot give your client any promises about its cost or its outcome. A process model offers a structure which is designed to reduce risk, reduce uncertainty and increase manageability.

Different projects have different requirements. If you are developing a new product, the process you go through will, in general, be different from the process you go through to develop a one-off custom-built system. There will be underlying similarities of course, but the differences are great enough to make it worth distinguishing between the two different sorts of development.

When you undertake a software development project you will want to ensure that your exposure to risk is kept to an acceptable level – this will in general be risk of failure of some sort: risk of overrunning the budget, risk of producing the wrong system, risk of producing a system that does not do what was required, risk of producing a system that will never work, and so on. These risks all stem from uncertainty or a lack of knowledge about the system to be developed. The approach taken to software development – the process model – must therefore be designed to take into account the degree of uncertainty that is present at the outset and to give a structure to the project that reduces the risks or costs of failure.

To summarise: the process model used by a project is determined by how much is known and how much is unknown about the required system and what its likely future is. It is designed to reduce exposure to risks in the project.

Boehm's Spiral Model

A significant contribution to the understanding of the importance of risk in software development planning was Barry Boehm's *Spiral Model* of software development and maintenance (Boehm 1986). Boehm first presented the model at the 2nd International Software Process Workshop outside Los Angeles in 1985. At that workshop we heard a great deal of discussion about whether or not we needed *meta-models* – models that would generate models. At the time I found such discussion amusing to me as a one-time mathematician, but rather too esoteric and removed from the reality of project life for me as a project manager. When Clive Roberts and I started working on meta-models ourselves in 1986 as part of the Alvey *IPSE 2.5* project, the importance of a 'driving force' in a model became clearer. In the Spiral Model that driving force is risk and its management.

In the Spiral Model, development and maintenance (which I shall abbreviate to just 'development' here) proceed by repeating a basic five-stage process:

1   determine the objectives, alternatives and constraints

2   evaluate the alternatives; identify and resolve risks

3   develop and verify the next level product

4   plan the next cycle

5   review the outcome of the cycle.

Figure 4-1 suggests the operation of the model: development proceeds by moving clockwise around the origin, passing through the four quadrants that represent stages 1 through 4 above. The length of the radius at any one moment measures the costs we have incurred so far – the cost of a cycle will clearly be determined by the size of the problem being bitten off on that cycle. On each cycle some risks are removed, sufficient to proceed to the next cycle.

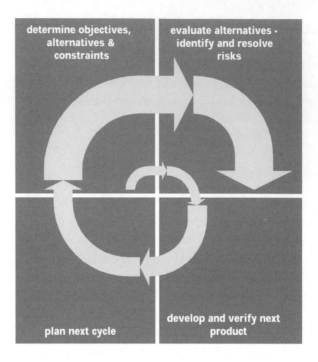

Figure 4-1. The Spiral Model

Notice how the process now becomes *risk driven*, rather than product driven. Boehm gives an example of the model at work in his paper. Gerry Wolff (1989) describes the model in use on an internal development at Praxis. The objective was to develop some form of management information system for the company. Gerry describes the first few phases that took place, and that were driven by the Spiral Model.

In cycle 1, the objectives had been defined concisely as 'to develop an information system to meet the needs of the management' – step 1. To get the ball rolling, a first-cut requirements gathering was carried out; this formed part of the process of defining the objectives and constraints on the project. A number of alternative solutions were then listed – subcontracting to another company, using DBMS *A*, using DBMS *B*, using a database machine *C*, and assembling a set of packages. Criteria for the evaluation were drawn up and the alternatives evaluated against them. As a result a decision was made to continue further with the option of using DBMS *A* and to do some further investigation of the solution using the database machine *C*, which had other attractions.

The second cycle therefore consisted of developing a first version of the system on DBMS A. Since no major problems and/or alternatives were apparent, this cycle could be a fairly standard development: gathering detailed requirements, preparing the system with the 4GLs that came with the chosen DBMS, and evaluation of the result by prospective users.

As a result DBMS A was not found to be a good vehicle: performance was too poor even with the partial system that was put together as the first attempt. Perhaps this could have been seen beforehand as a risk that needed evaluation before the commitment to its use was made. However, the second cycle did produce useful information about requirements, even if the vehicle that supported it was not ideal.

The third cycle was planned to take a further look at the database machine as one way of handling the performance problem, with a new version being developed on it if the evaluation showed it to be a good solution. Unfortunately, other influences external to the project meant that further development could not be funded and the project remained incomplete. However, the experience proved instructive and Gerry Wolff reported a number of observations in his paper:

- Although the Spiral Model moves step by step, with potentially quite short horizons, there may well be longer term objectives that need to be carried through successive cycles – for instance, an objective to use a particular technology once it was sufficiently mature.

- There can quite often be a need for spirals inside spirals – recursion, if you like.

- A cycle might not present a clear set of alternative solutions at the outset, and the aim of a cycle might well be to explore a range of alternatives, e.g. through a prototype.

In a perfect world with clients prepared to proceed in the stepwise fashion implied by the successive cycles of the spiral, committing money in discrete lumps corresponding to the cycles, it would be possible to operate the Spiral Model by making each cycle a separate contract. We shall see that this is indeed what happens in some cases. However, we have to accept, as Boehm does in his paper, that this is not always possible. Very often the development of a software system is just a part of a much larger venture – building a new aircraft, offering new financial services to bank clients, reorganising a government department – ventures that have already been committed to. In such situations, the software development is seen as an 'implementation detail' and not something open to discussion. The contractor who agrees to undertake the work is often asked for a single price for all the work, i.e. for perhaps several, or even an indeterminate number of, turns of the spiral. Such a client wants to be assured of a system for a given price and, while being happy for the contractor to undertake to do the work in several stages, is not prepared to commit to several contracts of as yet unknown price.

EXAMPLE

At Praxis, we prepared a proposal for a client for a system that was, in its final environment, to connect to a number of systems, some of which were not at the time defined. We saw a risk in the integration of our system with these others and, to handle this risk, proposed a fixed price development to include testing our system against simulators of those external systems, plus a T&M (time and materials) contract to cover the integration with the other systems. This was unacceptable to the client, who probably appreciated the risks but wanted a fixed price for the whole development. This particular case points up the importance here of separating commercial imperatives from technical judgements. We did offer a fixed price for the whole development after some rearrangement of contract terms, but knew explicitly the commercial risk we had introduced by letting in the technical difficulties of that final integration.

The naming of parts

Before we launch into the options at our disposal for basic process models, I want to take a small diversion to address a terminological problem that seems to beset even the best of software groups.

I frequently find myself assisting groups with their Quality Management Systems or their software process and coming up against the same confusion. It can be expressed this way. Take the words *user, technical, requirement, system, function, specification, design, definition* and *description*. Select any three, arrange them in a suitable order and use the resulting phrase as the name of the document that defines what the customer wants. Then choose three other words from the list and arrange them and use the result as the name for the document that captures the design of the system. Or at least, that is how it always seems to me when I am told that what the user wants is defined in the *Functional Requirement Definition* or the *User Design Description*, and that the design is recorded in the *System Design Specification* or the *Technical Functional Definition*. Perm any three from nine.

I always offer the following scheme to attempt to help untangle this confusion.

- Users have requirements. Their requirements can be about anything: their business goals, their happiness, the sorts of hardware they like to use, the way they like their software to be written. Anything. When users write down their requirements of a system, they are saying 'whatever you give me must satisfy me in these multifarious ways'. An 'expression' of the users' requirements therefore specifies *a class of systems*: any system in that class, one of which we will build, will satisfy those requirements.

- Systems have attributes. When we specify a system's attributes we are specifying one system – a system we propose to build. And we will have chosen those attributes so that the system will satisfy the requirements that the users have expressed. So a system specification describes *one possible system* in terms of its behaviour and its other properties, and it specifies *a class of possible designs*, one of which we will build.

- A design or architecture is one way of building a system which is to have certain attributes. When we describe a particular architecture we are describing one way in which the desired system attributes can be achieved. So a design or architecture specification specifies one solution, *one of a number of possible designs*.

I believe it is vitally important to separate these concerns if the quality of what we do is to have any chance of getting off to a good start. To repeat: the User Requirements Expression says what(ever) users want from the system; the System Specification defines the attributes of one system that will (we assert) deliver what they want; the System Design defines one implementation of a system with the desired attributes.

I like to talk about users *expressing their requirements* because the word 'expressing' suggests that they are not obliged to be as mathematically rigorous or precise as we will want to be in our specification of the system that we will contract to deliver. I would be perfectly happy if a User Requirements Expression simply said 'Reduce the cost of processing a customer telephone order by 10%'. That's a simple business goal and a simple requirement on the system. The specification of a system that will do this will go into precise detail about *one way of doing this*. But the User Requirements Expression could equally well require that any solution should be based on, say, SAP, or that all code must be written in Ada – strong technical statements both of them, but perfectly valid requirements for the business to have. Similarly a System Specification does not need to be solely a black-box definition of a system: it will, for instance, definitely carry down the attribute that the code should all be in Ada if that is what the customer wants.

I hope this makes clear that the requirements, the specification and the design are very different things, with clearly separated purposes.

At the other end of the spectrum, another question invariably causes confusion: what is a 'module'? Someone somewhere is using the term to mean one or more of the following:

- the contents of a file of source code

- a compilation unit

- a group of compilation units plus their data areas

- an item of software that has a 'module specification'

- a language entity such as a C procedure, or a class method

- a group of procedures

- a recovery unit

- a package

- an abstract data type

- a process, activity or task ('schedulable unit')
- a linked unit.

Most of these things are different from the others in the average environment. A system may be logically decomposed into a number of functional units (sometimes called *subsystems*). The functions of a functional unit might be implemented by different parts of a number of tasks or by code replicated among tasks or shared by tasks. The running system operates as a number of communicating tasks, some replicated dynamically and geographically. Each task is made up of a number of procedures and data structures. The source of these procedures and data structures will come from various source files, and their linkable object code will reside in various libraries.

Typically these different types of units address different problems:

- *Functional* units are about making sure that everything in the System Specification is carried forward into the design and they are chosen to give conceptual integrity to the design (to help development and ease maintenance, inter alia).

- *Schedulable* units are chosen on performance grounds and to achieve the right system dynamics, and they are often constrained by the capabilities of the target operating system.

- *Editable* units are chosen to make the business of maintaining and editing source a manageable task and one within the capabilities of the editor.

- *Compilable* units must be compilable (e.g. must not blow the symbol table) and must be chosen to support the hiding of names.

- *Linkable* units must be linkable (i.e. not blow the linker) and must be chosen to avoid name clashes, to fit in with libraries and so on.

In other words, there will not necessarily be simple one-to-one mappings between functional units, schedulable units, editable units, compilable units and linkable units. We would prefer it if there were, but generally there aren't. In a system consisting of a single program there most likely will be – if we arrange things properly. But in a multi-process and/or multi-processor system there may not be such simple mappings for very good reasons, for instance to do with the fact that we have to build our systems on non-ideal hardware and software using incomplete and/or incompatible development tools with their own idiosyncrasies. (In fact, it's because there isn't a one-to-one mapping that we have complex build mechanisms that transform directories of source files into executable binaries.)

In this book the only 'unit' that I am interested in is 'the smallest thing for which there is a separate specification'. Whatever term I use for this, I shall be 'wrong' in someone's eyes. But the term I shall use is *component*. A design is a statement of an architecture within which a set of components (co)operate in a variety of ways. Also, I shall assume that components are the domain of people whom I shall refer to as *programmers* – people who produce code, in some form or another, that meets that specification for the component.

So now I have the following in my simple world of software development:

- *User Requirements Expression* – an expression of what the users want to get from the system

- *System Specification* – a specification of the attributes of a system that will give the users what they want

- *System Design* – a design for a system that will have the required attributes, in terms of an architecture within which a set of components cooperate

- *Component Specification* – a specification of an individual component and its operation within the system design.

Which process model?

After that diversion, we return to the main thread.

In the same way that a program containing decision points and iterations can execute in many different ways depending on the input data, so the Spiral Model can unwind in different ways depending on the circumstances of the project. We can think of the Spiral Model as a meta-model – a model for models. The Spiral Model can unwind in a number of different ways and each of those ways is a process model itself. And each of those process models can proceed in a different way to give a piece of history so to speak. Although it is possible to use the Spiral Model directly on a project, I feel it is more useful to look at a number of possible unwindings of the spiral that frequently occur in software development. Subsequent sections of this chapter therefore look at a number of 'set-piece' process models, but first here is a quick overview to set the scene.

- If the project is 'well understood' in that it is well specified and a development route can be clearly identified at the outset then a single-pass development will be appropriate: this involves using the *V Process Model*.

- If there are areas of uncertainty about the requirements on the system or its implementation but these are not 'great' then the addition of small-scale prototyping activities to the simple V Process Model will suffice; we then have the *V Process Model with prototyping*, which I shall abbreviate to the *VP Process Model*.

- In the *Evolutionary Delivery Process Model* a sequence of systems is produced. Here each system in the series has full functionality but the aim is to evolve the system over time through a number of versions. The series might or might not terminate depending on whether the system and its environment stabilise with respect to each other.

- If only some of the functionality of the system is required (or clearly perceived and specifiable) initially and the remaining functionality can be delivered over a number of subsequent increments then the *Incremental Delivery Process Model* is appropriate. A sequence of systems is produced. Each is a partial system except the last (if there is one), but all are usable systems.

- If one of the cardinal aims is quick business benefit, or the business environment is changing rapidly, or deployment of the system might be resisted, or ownership by the users might be hard to establish then the *DSDM (Dynamic Systems Development Method) Process Model* is appropriate. Here, a system is built in a highly collaborative way in small increments in tightly constrained 'timeboxes'.

- Finally, if the purpose and nature of the system are very ill-defined then this can be recognised by using the *Exploratory Process Model* on the project.

For each model covered in the following sections you will find discussion under the following headings:

- *The model described*

  We start with a description of the model and summarise it in terms of the *products* that the model produces, a *Work Breakdown Structure* (WBS) fragment that captures the structure and activities of the model, the *major review points*, and finally the *additional costs* of the model seen as a risk reduction measure which, while removing a risk, introduces its own impact on the project's cardinal aims. The WBS fragment will form the basis of your Resource Plan as described in Chapter 9. (If you are not familiar with WBSs quickly read the section on the topic in Chapter 9 before going on.)

- *Where to use the model*

  Knowing the situations where a model is appropriate is clearly key and so each section continues with this.

- *Running a project with this model*

  I have suggested that the purpose of a process model is to provide a project with a structure that makes it manageable. We need to look at the management impact of the different models. We cannot assume that a single management style can be used in all situations; moreover, the process model we choose will have a major bearing on the nature of the contract that can be undertaken with our client. The discussion of each process model therefore contains some guidance on these issues under the sub-heading *Running a project with this model*.

A natural outcome of the analysis of the risks in a project will be some understanding of what commercial risk is involved. In an ideal world we limit our commercial risk to what we can reasonably predict. So, under the sub-heading *Contractual considerations* I describe how the choice of that process model is related to the degree of commercial risk involved.

Warnings

All models are simplifications and should never be interpreted too strictly. Their purpose is to give shape to a project and hence to make it manageable. The need to have a manageable and a successful project always overrides any apparent strictures implied by the process model in use.

There will also be situations where none of the particular models described here for illustration fits the bill well enough. There is clearly no obligation to follow one of the offered models religiously but in such a situation your Risk Plan would describe the model you have invented instead – for instance, some mixture of models – and would outline your reasons for adopting it.

In some cases, your client will wish to impose their own process model on the project. You will need to take this into account when you bid or undertake a project. You might agree to using their model, or prefer to convince them otherwise, or even adjust their model to be more in line with your approaches if you feel that they are preferable.

Finally, you must remember that the process model defines which products should be produced for that style of development, but the format and qualities required of those products are the concern of the project's Quality Plan.

It is with these points in mind that you should read the rest of this chapter.

The V Process Model

Introduction

The V Process Model (Figure 4-2) describes a project in terms of two legs: a specification leg (the left-hand side of the V) and a verification and validation leg (the right-hand side of the V). Down the specification side we have a progression of stages from requirements analysis, through system specification, system design and component specification to individual coded components. The process of compilation or code generation produces executable code which starts us on the V&V side, where we have a progression through component testing and thread or subsystem testing to system testing and on into post-implementation review, where we validate the operation of the system against the original requirements. The model emphasises the fact that the activities in the latter part of the project are all about testing implementations of the specifications produced in the earlier part.

Development in this model proceeds via a sequence of steps that leads to the delivered system. The earlier phases constitute a design process leading from the user's ill-formed notions to code. Each of these early, downward-pointing phases results in a specification, each being derived from the preceding one. There is an implied decomposition from system, through subsystems – however you wish to define the term *subsystem* – to components.

The products from the later, upward-pointing phases are (part-) systems that, through testing, have been shown to satisfy specifications on the other side of the V – see Figure 4-3. Thus, the System in Use, resulting from an Acceptance Testing activity, has been satisfactorily verified against the System Specification. In the process of verification, the Acceptance Test Specification defined the tests that would be carried out. The combination of a specification and the software that satisfies it, together with the specification of the test that established 'satisfaction', is what I term a *development layer*. This is a good moment to look at this in detail as we shall need the concept later on.

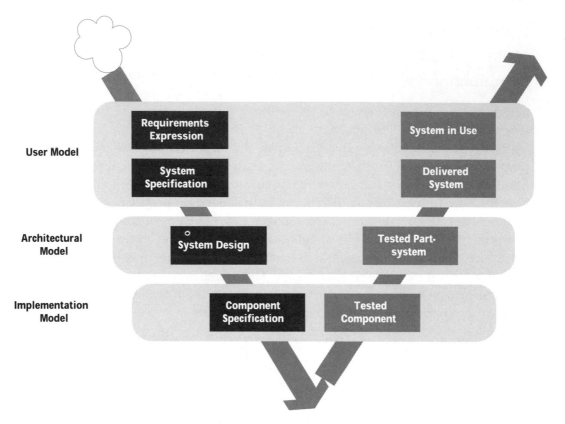

Figure 4-2. The V process model

Development layers

At this point I want to examine the idea of a *development layer* and to describe the following three development layers that we will prepare for a system:

- the *User Layer*
- the *Architecture Layer*
- the *Implementation Layer*.

Figure 4-2 shows the layers. They are 'cuts' across the V Process Model. Let's take them in turn.

The User Layer

The User Layer comes at the system from the users' point of view.

As a minimum, on the specification side of the V Process Model, the User Layer contains a System Specification agreed with the client. In the general case, a preceding Requirements Expression forms part of this development layer.

To recap, the Requirements Expression describes what the user *requires of* a system. This might be to do with organisational, financial or technical matters. It might say 'any system that we buy must generate benefits *X, Y* and *Z*'. It might say 'we actually need a system that provides these specific functions because they are needed if we are to get the benefits we want'. The Requirements Expression specifies a class of systems by describing a need.

The System Specification describes one system that would satisfy the requirement in the Requirements Expression, and in turn specifies a class of implementations of it.

The System Specification must satisfy two criteria:

- it must be a sufficient basis for design and implementation (this is the internal view of the System Specification)

- it must be a sufficient basis for the preparation of an Acceptance Test that the client can agree to as a determining test of the system supplied (this is the external view of the System Specification).

The System Specification will contain three types of statement:

- descriptions of the functionality to be exhibited by the system, i.e. how it will respond to specified stimuli and conditions

- non-functional attributes that the system must possess, such as performance and the various -ilities: portability, maintainability, and so on

- constraints that the system must satisfy, such as use of a given hardware infrastructure (we can think of these as non-functional attributes, as we shall see in Chapter 5).

On the V&V (right-hand) side of the V Process Model – see Figure 4-3 – the User Layer naturally contains the System in Use and the Delivered System, but we will also add the products that are used to verify the Delivered System against the System Specification ('did we users get what we were promised?'), namely the *Acceptance Test Specification*; and to validate the System in Use against the Requirements Expression ('does what we're using achieve what we wanted?'), namely the *Operational Review*.

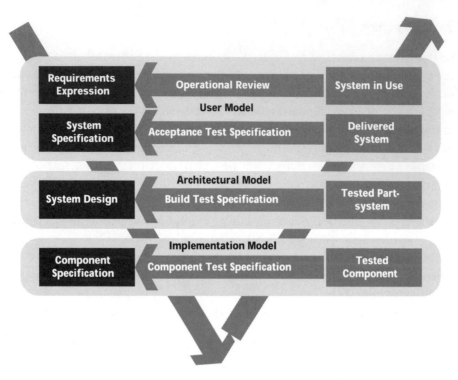

Figure 4-3. Testing and test specifications in the V process model

So, given that the User Layer covers all those aspects of interest to the user (or the client in general), we can expect it to include:

- the Requirements Expression
- the System Specification
- the Acceptance Test Specification
- the Delivered System
- the Operational Review
- the System in Use
- any User Guides, User Manuals, User Training, or other materials required to make the system usable by its users such as scripts for system start-up, process initialisation, and system control, and scripts for the installation of infrastructure components such as communications, the operating system, databases, screens and forms.

The Architecture Layer

On the specification side of the V Process Model, the Architecture Layer captures the software architecture of the system in terms of the structure of its control and its data. It describes how the functional structure of the system is mapped onto the target environment or local infrastructure, be it naked machine or sophisticated transaction processing system or the World Wide Web.

In broad terms we can describe an architecture as mapping one structure to another: the functional structure to the infrastructure. Any non-trivial system will have a number of components identified in its architecture, and we can arrive at the decomposition of the system into those components in a number of ways that vary from method to method. So our discussion of architecture and the choice of methods for the Architecture Layer will centre on *decomposition criteria* and target infrastructure.

A useful way of classifying architectural design methods is to look at the criteria they use for decomposition. This takes us back to the question asked earlier: 'what is a module?'. The question we shall ask here is 'what are the units of decomposition and what characterises them?'. Deciding which method is appropriate becomes a matter of deciding which method uses the most 'natural' criterion for decomposition, i.e. which has 'a style' closest to the world being automated. Some examples arc:

- Units in the architecture might correspond to units in the part of the real world that is being monitored or controlled. This is a criterion at the heart of object-oriented design methods, and methods such as the Model-View-Controller approach, JSD, and JSP.

- Units in the architecture might correspond to security units so that levels of security, security boundaries, authentication, etc. can all be reliably controlled.

- Architectural units may be chosen in a way that reduces communication between them. The *high coherence* and *low coupling* notion introduced by Myers (1975) was an early formulation of this criterion whereby a decomposition is chosen that keeps architectural units (*modules* in Myers' terms) as independent as possible.

It is not unusual for two or more of these criteria to be important in any one system, depending on whether data or control is the most important characteristic of the system, whether dynamic or static structures predominate, and whether time or place is more important. We shall look in much more detail at this in Chapter 6 when we examine the idea of the *computational model*.

What of the target infrastructure? All architectures rely on some provided target infrastructure that supports facilities to do with control structures and data structures. The lowest level infrastructure available will be that provided by the target environment: the hosting operating system together with such things as graphics packages, mailers, DBMSs, communications systems and TP systems. In other words, the target architecture has its own computational model. But it is generally unwise to couch the system architecture directly in terms of the lowest level available. This typically produces designs that have little internal coherence and no central dogma other than the simplest offered by the underlying operating system. So we often define higher-level infrastructures that provide architectural constructs closer to our needs. It is an important function of the Architecture Layer to record what facilities are assumed in the underlying infrastructure. The architecture is then expressed in terms of this higher-level infrastructure.

For example:

- We might produce an architecture for a simple control program in the form of a Finite State Machine. The average operating system does not provide mechanisms for FSMs but our Architecture Layer expresses the architecture in terms of such mechanisms. In the Implementation Layer we will actually describe how those control mechanisms will be implemented in terms of the facilities that are offered by the operating system.

- We might design a concurrent system as a number of processes operating as a Petri Net. Again this will presuppose some mechanism that supports a Petri Net style of operation. The Architecture Layer will give the architecture of the system in terms of a Petri Net and specify the infrastructure necessary to support it.

  This case demonstrates that an important aspect covered by the Architecture Layer is the control aspect and particularly the dynamic control aspect if the system is a concurrent system. Here the system is divided into logical tasks. These are functional units that could operate independently of each other. They communicate data between each other by various means that will be supported by the underlying infrastructure.

  The ideal network is one that maximises the amount of potential concurrency and decoupling between the logical tasks. The potential dynamic structure of the system is thereby captured. Not all this potential might be exploited – exactly how much will be determined in the Implementation Layer.

- We might define an architecture for our system in the form of a set of free-standing programs that operate independently on a database through a database management system (DBMS). Such an architecture thereby presupposes a supporting infrastructure in the form of the facilities provided by the DBMS and the local operating system.

  If we are required to use a particular transaction processing system as part of our target infrastructure, our architecture is going to be very much decided for us, as the authors of such systems generally provide hooks onto which serial code can be hung. Again we take the supporting infrastructure and the implied architecture as givens.

- In an object-oriented architecture each object would be a logical task and the dynamics of message exchange between the object processes would be the basis of the control structure. This architecture could be implemented in a number of ways depending on what mechanisms were available in the target infrastructure, in particular the run-time support that is provided for the language we are using. It is the job of the Implementation Layer to describe that choice.

On the right-hand side of the Architecture Layer we will find part-systems constructed from sets of components. We will subject these to testing that we will define in *Build Test Specifications*.

Summarising, the Architecture Layer will include

- the System Design: an architecture expressed in terms of one or more explicitly defined computational models, based on a specified infrastructure itself based on the supplied infrastructure; this architecture will identify the major components ('subsystems', 'processes', 'activities', etc., according to the decomposition criteria of the computational models), will identify their logical relationships within the terms of the computational models, will (in the case of a concurrent system) show all the necessary concurrency, and will define the logical data structures that support the architecture

- Build Test Specifications that define tests for part-systems against the System Design

- versions of part-systems that have passed tests defined in the Build Test Specifications.

The Implementation Layer

The Implementation Layer captures the way in which the (possibly ideal or logical) architecture is actually implemented. It takes into account the limitations of the target environment (operating system, hardware, database, file system etc.) on which the system must run. It is a record of the 'compromises' made in order to implement the ideal architecture of the Architecture Layer on the less-than-ideal target system. In particular, it covers issues such as:

- which real tasks/activities/processes (schedulable items) will exist to implement the potentially concurrent operation identified in the Architecture Layer; they might for instance be compositions of logical tasks, combined into one physical task for performance reasons

- how each resulting inter-task communication path will be implemented (global data areas, message queues, communications package, service subsystem, operating system services, run-time language support, etc.)

- the structure of each task in terms of compilation (i.e. language specific) units, typically in a component hierarchy

- how data will be passed between units (parameters, messages, global data (not recommended!), etc.)

- how logical data structures will be implemented physically

- which code will be re-entrant and which will be single-thread.

Once these have been established, compilation units can be coded and combined as appropriate into coded components. The tested components form part of the Implementation Layer, being the final 'compromise' of the ideal architecture. The Implementation Layer therefore contains the following items:

- a definition of the physical process structure, its logic and data flow

- a component/component calling hierarchy for each process, showing the data-passing mechanisms

- specification of physical data structures (memory and peripheral based)

- a Component Specification for each component defining its functional and non-functional attributes

- a Component Test Specification for each component

- tested components.

I must emphasise here that the reason for the different development layers is to ensure we recognise the different concerns that we shall have during development, the different issues we will address at different stages of the project. Moreover, it is worth repeating that they are not levels in some form of *decomposition*. They are different views of the same system. Like models in general, each of the development layers concentrates on some aspects and ignores others. The relative rate of development of the different development layers at any one time will depend on the sort of software being developed and the process model that has been adopted.

At one end of the spectrum is the development of a system with little 'speculative' content. In other words, the required functionality can be written down and a solution looks possible; the functionality might be contentious and the solution difficult but progressing from the User Layer into the Implementation Layer and Build Model in one sweep is an appropriate development process –the V Process Model. As we have seen, a frequent (perhaps mandatory) requirement is to establish design constraints imposed by the target infrastructure early on during the project. This will result in some details and/or broad brush material in the Architecture Layer or the Implementation Layer.

At the other end of the spectrum is the exploratory development process typical of AI work. Here, the functionality is only expressible in the most general terms and development takes place by direct experimentation with algorithms and programs, the results being fed back into better understood functionality, an extended architecture and further experiments.

Between these poles is a whole spectrum of development processes involving more or less iteration, more or less experimentation and more or less feedback. The choice of which is to be used depends on where the areas of uncertainty and risk are in the project. But whichever approach is used, a major problem is always that of maintaining the conceptual integrity of functionality, architecture and construction, in other words maintaining a well-structured User Layer, Architecture Layer and Implementation Layer throughout development.

Typically, well-defined systems with low technical risk can be developed in a single pass. The management of their development can make use of traditional planning leading to relatively reliable time and effort predictions. Ill-defined systems with high technical risk require a different form of management that reconciles iteration and experimentation with the need to plan to a schedule. This may require making use of an ability to set functionality to what can be achieved or using techniques of incremental planning, development and delivery so that a potentially unmanageable development is broken down into a sequence of manageable increments.

Interaction between the development layers

In a typical system, getting from one development layer to the 'next' is not necessarily a refinement – it can be a major jump. We have seen that this is principally because there is not necessarily a one-to-one relationship between the units of one development layer and those of the next; there is a 'structure clash'. Thus, the functional structure as perceived by the user will not necessarily bear any relationship to the process structure of the system. This mismatch can make the transition from one development layer to another very difficult, particularly that from User Layer to the Architecture Layer.

In fact, of course, this transition is precisely what we call *design*. And design is the hardest part of any system development simply because it requires this creative leap from one structure to another in a way that preserves all the requirements expressed in the former, yet is feasible in the computational model of the latter. No cook-book technique will ever make this design process mechanical. All methods 'avoid' the problem – most without saying! A good, honest design method will make clear exactly what step is left to the creative skill of the designer.

The difficulty derives from the mismatch between 'function' as expressed in, say, the User Layer and 'function' as expressed in the Architecture Layer. To avoid this difficulty, object-oriented methods have concentrated on producing system architectures that mirror the object structure of the external real-world. With object-oriented definition and object-oriented design we can thereby avoid the mismatch between a system's functional structure and its process structure – the two become the same.

The resulting object-oriented architectures, like all architectures, presuppose some supporting mechanisms for the concepts they use. That support must finally derive from the target infrastructure. If that infrastructure can be supplied through a suitable object-oriented language and its run-time support such as Java, C++, Simula or Smalltalk, then the Implementation Layer can also be in one-to-one correspondence with the Architecture Layer and another structure clash is avoided. If the target infrastructure is, say, COBOL or Visual Basic and a DBMS, then the Implementation Layer will need to 'invert' the architecture in some way so that it can be supported sensibly and efficiently – this is what happens in the latter stages of the design part of JSD.

The fact that we have identified a series of development layers does not imply that there is a corresponding strict ordering of development (or indeed maintenance) activities. Work on any one development layer will require two forms of iteration: *intelligent look-ahead* and *controlled reworking*.

Intelligent look-ahead is what we do when we look ahead to the subsequent development layers to check that what is being proposed is feasible. The distance of look-ahead will be inversely proportional to the degree to which lower levels are under our control. If we intend to use a supplied windows application package or DBMS it is clearly vital that we establish the precise nature of that package (probably by experimentation) before we commit to design based on the package.

The distance of look-ahead will also be determined by the perceived risk in the implementation of the proposed development layer. Technically difficult or innovative solutions will require a greater amount of look-ahead than normal. We have already seen in Chapter 3 that this sort of look-ahead should come out of a consideration of the risks and uncertainties that are in our system or its development. This sort of look-ahead is what underlies the VP Process Model, which we shall investigate in a moment.

Controlled reworking is what we do when we rework earlier development layers in the light of work on a subsequent development layer. It can turn out that the earlier development layer was difficult to implement, did not lead to a 'good' implementation or was actually impossible. This will require adjustment, perhaps under change control.

The V Process Model described

We can now return to the main thread of our description of the V Process Model itself.

The major products

With our new shorthand we can read off the major products of the V Process Model from Figure 4-3:

- The *User Layer* – principally the Requirements Expression, System Specification, Acceptance Test Specification and Delivered System.

- The *Architecture Layer* – principally the System Design, Build Test Specifications and Tested Part-systems.

- The *Implementation Layer* – principally the Component Specifications, Component Test Specifications and Tested Components.

The generic Work Breakdown Structure

The overall shape of the project is of course simple and straightforward:

1000   Produce User Layer

2000   Produce Architecture Layer

3000   Produce Implementation Layer

(But remember that this is not a sequence of activities, simply a list of things we must do.) A simple elaboration with the major products of the layers yields the following:

1000   Produce User Layer

      1100   Produce Requirements Expression

      1200   Produce System Specification

      1300   Produce Acceptance Test Specification

      1400   Produce Delivered System

2000   Prepare Architecture Layer

      2100   Produce System Design

      2200   Produce Build Test Specifications

      2300   Produce Tested Part-systems

3000   Prepare Implementation Layer

      3100   Produce Component Specifications

      3200   Produce Component Test Specifications

      3300   Produce Tested Components

The major review points

The 'oldest' process model is the *waterfall model* (Figure 4-4) to which we return momentarily. This shows a similar progression from inception, through definition, the various stages of design, code, unit testing and integration to final acceptance. The fact that this progression is never smooth and monotonic was acknowledged by drawing the backward arrows suggesting iteration. This model has a number of advantages and disadvantages.

The advantages are that it does give a structure to the whole of a project in the form of a well-defined sequence of phases – well-defined in that we can define clear exit criteria for them. While recognising the need for iteration, this sequence forces a pace through the project. It recognises that there is no perfect solution and that it is not commercially sensible to look for one. It might be commercially preferable to accept a sub-optimal solution in order to make a profit and/or to satisfy the client. As such the model makes a good management tool. The V Process Model preserves this advantage.

The disadvantage is that a compromise can, in the limit, become an error and a project can end up discovering, too late in the day, that it took a wrong turn earlier on. The V Process Model perpetuates this disadvantage. Because there is no explicit admission that there can be risks, their effects are always felt at the last moment rather than anticipated as early as possible.

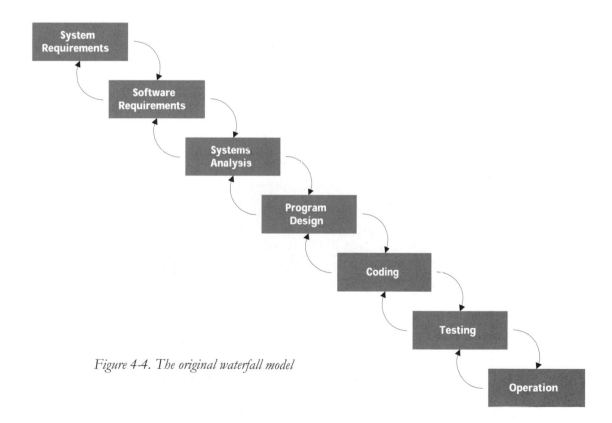

Figure 4-4. The original waterfall model

Also, the simple notion of iteration is generally unsatisfactory. The V Process Model emphasises the full potential of iteration: the fact that, rather than being simply back to the preceding phase, it will more generally be back to the specification activity corresponding to the object in which a problem is found. This failing in the model tells us that it is not appropriate where there is a likelihood of significant iteration – something we return to in a couple of pages.

The obvious review points for the V Process Model are the following:

- review of the System Specification (part of the User Layer) to definitive status – somewhere within *1000 Produce User Layer*

- review of the Acceptance Test Specification to definitive status – also somewhere within *1000 Produce User Layer*

- review of the System Design to definitive status – somewhere within *2000 Produce Architecture Layer*

- review of the Build Test Specifications to definitive status – somewhere within *2000 Produce Architecture Layer*.

The purpose of such reviews is, as always, to ensure that each succeeding stage can proceed on a firm basis and that the work of individuals is coordinated through a common approach and a common understanding.

Where to use the V Process Model

HEADLINE

The V Process Model should be used when there is either a good System Specification and a 'predictable' solution, or a good Requirements Expression and the prospect of a good System Specification and a predictable solution.

Without even a good Requirements Expression it is impossible to choose a process model at all. The judgement about whether a given specification is good and whether there is a technical solution in sight is one that is largely based on experience. So, if there is no major uncertainty as to whether there is a practical solution and there are no major uncertainties over what the system is to do or be like, then the V Process Model is quite appropriate. Figure 4-5 captures this idea that the V Process Model is a 'straight run' from concept to system. Despite the criticism that this simple model has received in the past, it still has its uses.

Figure 4-5. The V Process Model

EXAMPLE

We were implementing a system to act as a communications multiplexer between terminal users and mainframes. The communications protocols to be handled were effectively cast in concrete by manufacturers and international standards, the loadings were not expected to be high, the switching was straightforward, and only the failure conditions gave us any real concern. The development proceeded absolutely classically: a system definition agreed with the client; a design completed before coding started; coding completed before testing and integration started. Since the risks were low we could plan and estimate with confidence and use a simple model for the project.

I don't have any embarrassment admitting that I have used the simple V Process Model but, when I look back, I realise that it was successful simply because the problem and solution domains were so well understood by the team I had working for me! With a different team the situation could have been quite different, and, with the new risks and uncertainties, I would have been wise to have chosen a model that allowed more risk reduction en route.

Running a project with the V Process Model

Contractual considerations

The V Process Model assumes that the system is 'well understood' and that there are no major technical obstacles in view. The development of such a system is relatively risk-free and tolerably reliable estimates can be made of the cost and timescale. Under these conditions a fixed price contract for the entire development is possible.

However, there are often still good reasons for reducing risks as far as possible by splitting such a project into two phases, each being done for a fixed price: a specification phase leading to an implementation phase, as shown in Figure 4-6. The price of the implementation phase can then be one of the outputs of the specification phase and the initial contractual commitment will simply be to the first phase.

This scheme can work to the benefit of both sides. The developer restricts any exposure just to the first phase, which in most situations should be relatively straightforward. The purchaser has the opportunity to steer the specification to the system they want without being constrained by a total contract price, and they can also potentially keep the overall price down since the developer should be able to offer a price with a reduced contingency for the implementation phase once the specification phase has revealed the full extent of the work.

Management considerations

Conceptually the V Process Model is of course very simple and hence it should be equally simple in management terms. However, because its success depends on everything being straightforward, and because life generally isn't, it requires special sensitivity from the project manager to changes in situation. At any stage, assumptions that were true at the outset might become untrue. Suppose your project is started with version 9 of your favourite DBMS, a version whose characteristics you know well, whose performance is understood and whose foibles are appreciated. Midway through the project version 10 is released and you are obliged to use it. Immediately you have an unknown: what bugs have been corrected? What new ones have been introduced? What is the performance now?

Significant changes might need a re-evaluation of the process model you are using. In extreme cases you might find yourself back at the negotiating table because of new risks or uncertainties that the client would like to introduce. This is not a criticism of clients: the system is *their* system and it's their right to want to change it, but such change will invariably mean a renegotiation of contract terms if the scope of the project is to be changed from what was originally negotiated – that is *your* right.

Project managers who have 'come up through the ranks' from being software engineers invariably find the business of asking for a renegotiation of the price a difficult one. When the first change request comes in towards the start of the project – formally or informally – it is all too easy to say 'yes, no problem, we can absorb that'. After all, software engineers are nice people and they want to give their clients the systems their clients want. They want to oblige. Unfortunately, when the second change request comes in and then

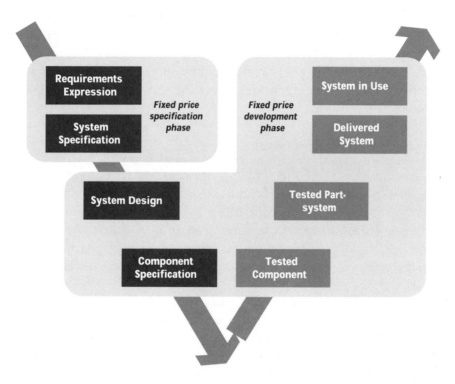

Figure 4-6. The V process model in two phases

the third, a precedent has been set: small changes can be absorbed without extra costs. But the changes get bigger and the project gets further into its budget and timescale and the room for manoeuvre decreases by the day. Finally the time comes when the project manager has to say 'enough is enough – you'll have to pay more', and this can sour a good relationship.

In my experience the best policy by far is to ask for a price increase on the very first change request, no matter how small. The aim is to set a precedent. After all, as project manager, one has a responsibility to one's company and its profitability, as well as to the client. This is a policy I learnt on a fixed price project where we had bid an architecture designed to support certain of the features that the client wanted. Just as we were in the specification phase my client asked for a feature that at first glance looked like the others, but which, on closer examination, proved to be quite impossible with the architecture we had bid. Summoning up my courage I said we had not contracted for that feature and the cost would be another £30 000 for reworking of the specification and the architecture, and possibly renegotiation of the implementation price. There was silence on the other side for a while but, after some discussion and proof of the figures from me, the change was accepted and the project got off to a sound start. (I have colleagues who take an even stronger line and feel that in some cases one should even consider *prompting* for the first change request in order to get the precedent in place. But this is a little too strong for me.)

Subcontracting parts of the process

A frequent adaptation of the simple V Process Model is to split the development into two parts: a specification stage followed by an implementation stage. As we shall see in a moment, this is frequently done in situations where there is considerable uncertainty about what is required, in other words where it is not possible to say at the outset what the system will do with enough precision to make a useful estimate of the total development time and cost.

The first stage can be undertaken as a fixed price contract which delivers the specification, and probably a plan and quotation for the implementation of that specification. The second stage – the implementation – can then also be undertaken as a fixed price contract. This can work well for both parties, as neither side commits to what it cannot reasonably predict.

But there has been a tendency for people to place the second stage contract out to tender, for the simple and understandable reason of wanting to get value for money and of not wanting the supplier's quotation for the second stage to go unchallenged. Unfortunately, it is my experience that, if the second stage contract is placed with a different supplier, the losses can outweigh the gains, for the following reason.

As a development project proceeds, the developers build up an understanding of the client's *application domain*: how their business works, and how the system will work for that business. No matter how conscientious a specifier is, they will never be able to capture all that understanding in the specification. As a result a second supplier receiving that specification as a work instruction for the implementation stage starts at a considerable disadvantage. Application domain knowledge familiar to the specifying supplier will not be known to the implementing supplier; implications of and assumptions in the specification will be unknown to the implementers. They may well have worked in a similar application area in the past but the specific assumptions and characteristics of this one will be new – and unknown.

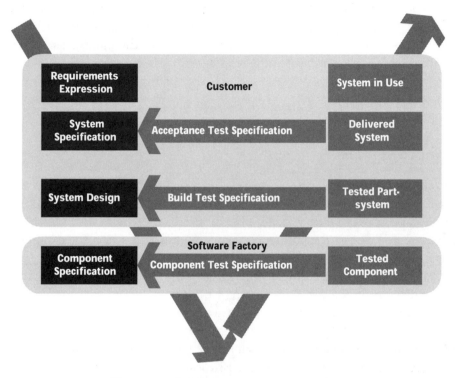

Figure 4-7. Subcontracting component production

It is this break in the flow of domain knowledge that can ruin what was a good idea. A new uncertainty, and hence risk, is introduced into the project and the initial risk of uncertainty in the specification has been replaced by the risk introduced by breaking the flow.

There does not seem a way around this, and I have seen it happen many times. Perhaps the only solution is not to break the project at the specification phase but at the end of the *design* phase. In doing this, we could learn a lesson from the building industry, in which consulting engineers prepare the specifications and the designs and pass these to the construction company, which follows the design and builds what it is told to. The domain knowledge flow has petered out by the time the design is complete and the break at that point represents less of a risk.

We have seen the two-phase – specification then development – approach in Figure 4-6. Figure 4-7 shows the development of the individual components being subcontracted to a 'software factory', who are given Component Specifications and deliver tested components. Figure 4-8 shows a full subcontracting of the entire development; in essence the supplier is given (or has agreed) the System Specification and builds a system which at some point the buyer accepts against an agreed Acceptance Test Specification that is based on the System Specification.

The V Process Model with prototyping: the VP Process Model

Why prototype?

The simple V Process Model works on the assumption that there are no major uncertainties that put the project at risk (particularly in terms of over-running its budget or timescale). However, if there are uncertainties then prototyping is one of the information-buying risk reduction measures we can use to reduce risk and so we introduce the *VP Process Model*.

When we build a prototype we are building something designed to help us establish some feature of a system we ultimately want to build, or, more generally, to get information. That information might be about the exact requirements to be placed on the system, about whether a particular design approach is actually feasible, about what the exact properties of the target infrastructure are or about the nature of a proposed solution.

EXAMPLES

Prototyping a user interface to check its ergonomics and acceptability to the user community.

Prototyping a scheduling algorithm to determine its performance in typical load situations.

Prototyping a heuristic algorithm to check its behaviour against sample real-life data.

Prototyping an entire system to check its viability in terms of performance.

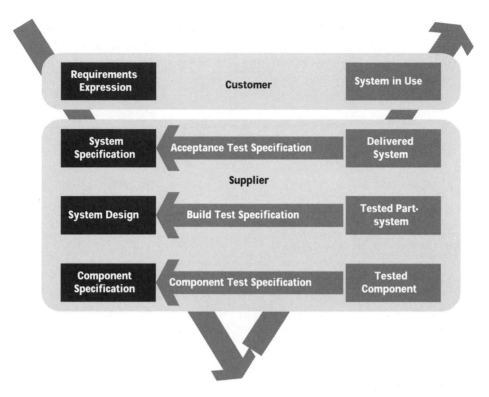

Figure 4-8. Subcontracting the full development of the system

Thus one sort of prototype yields information about some characteristic which is then fed back into the development process. There are many ways of getting such information – simulation, desk calculation, walkthroughs; a prototype is typically used where there are no adequate *analytical* ways of determining the characteristic. You perhaps know the behaviour you want, but you cannot be sure from examining (say) your design whether it will exhibit that behaviour when implemented. A prototype allows you to expose the behaviour of your design so that you can check it.

Another sort of prototype helps in the situation where you are not even sure what behaviour you want – the *ikiwisi* syndrome (I'll know it when I see it). This is the sort of prototype that is built for evaluating user interfaces.

Prototyping is therefore experimentation designed to yield information for the development process. It is worth noting that just as testing cannot prove the absence of bugs, only their presence – because it is a sampling technique – prototyping suffers from the same shortcoming: it cannot prove anything since it requires us to make any general conclusions from the samples we get by using the prototype. Great care has to be taken that the conclusions drawn from the use of a prototype are valid, for instance because the prototype has been exercised in a thorough and systematic fashion and not simply 'played with'.

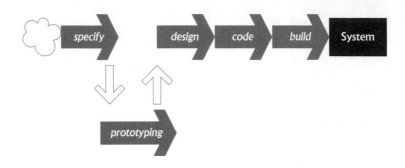

Figure 4-9. The VP Process Model

Figure 4-9 is designed simply to suggest that the simple flow of the V Process Model is broken at some point to accommodate a prototyping activity, an activity which will probably be buying some information for the project to reduce a risk. In the case shown, the prototyping is being done before design, but it could of course take place wherever it is necessary in the process.

Where to use the VP Process Model

HEADLINE
The VP Process Model should be considered when there are risks related to open questions about functionality or feasibility.

The VP Process Model makes sense where there are minor risks that can be resolved with some sort of information-buying or investigative work such as prototyping. For instance, during system specification, it could prove necessary, in order to resolve a feasibility issue, to experiment with a particular design approach; during design it might be necessary to implement a number of alternative codings to determine their relative performance in tandem with the target operating system; or a sample application might need to be built using a DBMS to check the understanding of the workings of the DBMS.

Indeed, prototyping of some form should always be undertaken where the project is to use a piece of software whose properties are not known – even though they might be 'fully' written up in the vendor's manual there is no substitute for actually using the software to find out what it really does and to find out whether the way you intend using it is sensible (or even possible). This is an excellent task for a junior member of the team at a time when it is otherwise difficult to give junior staff useful work. Not only do you get facts to help you avoid future mistakes or to get the design right, etc., but that junior member acquires a new skill and a status in the team that would otherwise be hard to get at this stage.

EXAMPLE

A project for which I was system architect was using a bought-in package to draw on a graphics monitor. One program needed to make a beep on the monitor and nothing more. A designer on the team innocently specified that the package's `ring bell` routine should be called to do this. Unfortunately, at integration this tiny routine dragged in so many supporting library routines that it blew the address space of the program. This taught me that whenever your project is going to use a package as part of the delivered system, you should plan for someone to spend some weeks simply digging to find out what the package *really* does.

The user interface is the commonest subject matter for a prototype. There are two clear reasons for this. Firstly, ease-of-use is a major consideration with any interface with the user, especially with the naïve user or the user not familiar with computers. A poor interface can kill an otherwise good system. Secondly, it's very often the case that what can be communicated across the human–computer interface defines entirely what the system does; the system only does what the user can ask for, so defining the user interface is the same as defining the functionality of the system.

Prototyping in a sense occurs at many levels. There are uncertainties in all projects: it might be said that a project is entirely about the elimination of uncertainties, resulting in the delivered system. But for the most part it is straightforward to estimate for the resolution of such day-to-day problems and the work resulting from the chosen outcome will not vary much from outcome to outcome.

> ## EXAMPLE
>
> During the design of a real-time system, we had the problem of defining an interface for a smart display that was to provide rolling real-time data at the same time as control facilities. This was the first time I had experimented with presenting a client with a look-and-feel simulation of an interface. In little more than two weeks I wrote around 2 000 lines of software in two programs. The first allowed me to interactively create, edit and store a screen. The second allowed me to replay pre-programmed sequences of screens and, to a small extent, mimic inputs and the system's response. I used it to experiment with different screen layouts and to get the client's reactions.
>
> In effect I wrote a screen painter – something common enough these days. It was excellent value. I was able to run sample conversations and show how the real-time update would work too. This was before we had started to design the software that would drive the interface. We had already done some exploratory work to see just what this display could do. So by the time we had finished we could get on with the design confidently.

We can expect therefore that a project could switch from the V to the VP Process Model if a major area of uncertainty arose unexpectedly. In this situation, estimates dependent on the outcome of the resolution of the uncertainty are themselves unreliable, so switching to the VP Process Model can be (correctly) equivalent to a 'no forecast' on future milestones beyond the conclusion of the prototyping activity!

Risks comes in two flavours: those to do with the problem and those to do with the solution. In the first case there is something about the problem itself that we do not fully understand; in the second case we might understand the problem perfectly well but have little idea how we will solve it. I have been involved in situations where there was a large measure of both: we were not clear about the problem that the client wanted us to solve and we certainly weren't clear what sort of solution we might want to apply!

> ## EXAMPLE
>
> In the case of the sonar tracking system, the problem was clear enough: using data coming from some sensors with certain data and failure characteristics, we had to provide track data to certain accuracy under certain conditions. We didn't know of anyone else who knew how to do this and they probably wouldn't tell us how they did it even if they had! We were on our own. Fortunately we had a strong mathematician on the project who came up with some new applications of advanced filtering techniques, which, he decided after some experimentation with them, would do the job. I suspect I didn't realise at the time that there was ever any doubt that his algorithms and logic would work – I was very thankful for his competence – but I remember not being very enthusiastic about the idea that he would experiment with them. Like many a project manager, I wanted something that would work, period!

Let's suppose that you are more enlightened and recognise the need for prototyping and experimentation as an early activity in order to reduce downstream risk. Here is a list of some of the sorts of questions or uncertainties that you might decide you need some form of prototyping to resolve, divided into those two categories.

Here are some examples of uncertainties about the problem:

- If the system has an interface with humans, we will want to check that the syntax and semantics of that interface have the right feel and performance for each of the different types of user. We may be using new devices for the first time, or for the first time with this particular set of users – how will they react to using a tracker ball or a mouse? The only way of answering these questions might be to put the alternatives in front of the users.

- The general issue of performance is a traditional topic that is evaded when it comes to detail. What are the volumes of data involved? What are the response rates required? What is the throughput in numbers of transactions per second? How often must the processes be run? Answering these questions might require some calculations on the part of the customer, calculations that take into account larger requirements such as the quality of service to be offered overall, the communications costs to be incurred by some connected system, or the profile and size of their client base to be supported by their new system.

- What are the error responses of the system to be? How is the system to react to failures of various sorts? What are those failures? What might a hazard analysis reveal?

- Finally, there will always be uncertainty about straightforward functionality – should it do X or Y, or both? How you find out depends on the tools to hand, plus any constraints on the budget.

Here are some examples of uncertainties about the solution:

- The precise functionality of some third-party software is not fully understood. For instance, a DBMS, an operating system, a communications driver, a forms system or an off-the-shelf PC application.

- The performance of some off-the-shelf software might be unknown or unstated by the supplier. For instance, with a DBMS we will want to know the speed with which it returns records for various types of query, for our server, for various configurations of tables, for various volumes of data, for various key structures, and so on.

  For an operating system that will underlie a real-time system we will want to know the speed with which it will perform a context switch. For the run-time package of a language we will want to know the speed with which functions or procedures are called; if the language is object-oriented we will want to know the performance characteristics of the message-passing mechanisms.

- The 'performance' of one of the tools we plan to use might not be known. Typical of this is the compiler – does it produce object code that is fast enough with the sorts of constructs we plan to exploit? Will our configuration control tool support the working of a large team with many thousands of configuration items?

- If we have chosen a particular design strategy for a multi-processing system, we will want to check that under various loading conditions it performs at the right rate.

The major products

We have the same products in the VP Process Model as we had for the V Process Model except that now of course we add the output of any prototyping activity(s) that we decide upon.

The prototype may or may not be a deliverable to the client. There is a strong case to be made against delivering prototypes for actual use. There is too great a danger of preparing the prototype to non-production standards in order to get the fast turnaround one needs. As a result it might be 'lashed up' with poor documentation – not the sort of product one typically wants to have to maintain, let alone deliver!

However, you might deliver prototypes that answer questions for you, simply because they might be needed for the same purpose at some time in the future. A prototype to establish performance will often be useful later in the life of a system when some major change is required that might significantly affect performance. The evaluation of the proposed change could be done with an adaptation of the old prototype quite cheaply. However, such reuse brings with it the requirement that the prototype is documented and developed in a way that makes such reuse both practical and economical, i.e. probably at an increased cost and timescale.

The generic Work Breakdown Structure

The WBS for your complete project will have a decision-making segment in it for each prototyping activity. As we saw in the discussion of the Spiral Model, a prototyping activity might answer a question – resolve an uncertainty – by either exploring a space of possible solutions with a prototype as the means of exploration, or by actually listing alternative solutions and evaluating them against some predefined criteria. The WBS will vary accordingly. In the first case you will have a project fragment of the following shape:

m100   Define the uncertainty

m200   Define a means of exploring solutions (e.g. a prototype, or some experiment)

m300   Carry out the exploration/experiment

m400   Make deductions – i.e. answer the uncertainty

You might need to iterate during the exploration activity – perhaps trying several prototypes, or refining one prototype as you converge on the solution. There will then be a corresponding elaboration of the WBS to reflect this.

In the second case the project fragment will look like this:

n100   Define the uncertainty

n200   Identify alternatives and criteria for choice

n300   Evaluate against those criteria

n400   Choose the best-fit alternative

So we can see four stages in a prototyping activity:

- *The establishment of prototyping objectives.* It is essential to establish why the prototype is being built and what aspects of the proposed system it should reflect. This can be ensured by writing down a list of questions to be answered through the construction of the prototype. It must be possible to decide whether a supposed 'answer' does indeed answer the question so the phrasing of the questions is vital and should be carefully reviewed.

- *Function selection.* A prototype usually covers those aspects of the system from which the required information may be obtained. The selection of the functions to be included in the prototype should be directly influenced by the prototype objectives.

- *Prototype construction.* Fast, low-cost construction is sometimes achieved by adopting less stringent quality standards, except of course where this is in conflict with the objectives. This means that everyone – including the client – must be aware of the fact that the main purpose of the prototype is experimentation and learning rather than long term use. Increasingly though, in the information system arena, industry-standard tools can be used for prototyping so that no reduction in quality is necessary.

- *Evaluation.* This is the most important step and must be planned carefully. The result of the evaluation should either be the information required in the original objectives or a recommendation to produce a further prototype, in other words, to iterate. The purpose of the prototype is to gain information. We must check that that information has indeed been obtained.

The major review points

We will of course have all the review points from the basic V Process Model. Additionally, the completion of any activity that builds a prototype will be a natural place at which to hold some form of review. Since the prototype was intended to answer some question or resolve some uncertainty, our expectation will be that the review will analyse the results of the prototyping activity and supply the necessary answer or resolution. In the WBS fragments above, activities *m400* and *n400* would contain those review points.

The costs of this model as a risk reduction measure

Prototyping will certainly add to development costs and, if the project is in some way 'waiting' on the answer, there could be schedule costs too. In a moment we shall look at how the costs of prototyping – an activity which can easily look like a bottomless pit – can be controlled. Here and with all the other process models, these downside impacts on the project's cost and schedule will always, of course, be what we balance against the perceived risk: its probability and impact on the very same cardinal aims when deciding whether the risk reduction measure is worth while.

Running a project with the VP Process Model

Contractual considerations

In the VP Process Model we recognise that there might be a need for prototyping to remove some uncertainties at certain stages of the project. For instance, some prototyping might be necessary during the system specification to tighten up some area of functionality, or some prototyping might be necessary during architectural work to help decide among alternative designs. The assumption of the model is that some aspect of functionality can be agreed or that a design can be found – it is just a matter of deciding which one – but which one is chosen will have a significant effect on the costs and/or timescales of the project. Here, it is clearly not sensible to undertake the entire project against a fixed price since there is so much uncertainty after a certain point. However, it is possible to undertake fixed price work on the part of the development before the decision is made, perhaps a separately contracted feasibility study that is entirely dedicated to resolving the uncertainty. Once the uncertainty has been resolved and the decision made, a new price can be estimated for the remainder of the project or up to the next major decision point if there is one. Alternatively, estimates can be made of the effect of the different outcomes and, simplistically, the maximum used.

Management considerations

There are of course major implications for the project manager. A prototyping activity needs to be planned into the project and the relevant dependencies of other activities inserted. In the simplest case, the prototyping can be a simple matter – perhaps the use of some Visual Basic to check out the layout and design of some forms – leading to a simple decision. Estimating such an activity is no more difficult than usual and the time limit established can help to guillotine what might otherwise become an endless, subjective debate.

At the other extreme, the building and use of a prototype can be a major project in itself – such as the prototyping of the entire user interface of a system. Here, the project manager must plan for a project within a project: the prototype must be defined, designed, built and used. In particular, it must be defined, otherwise no sensible estimate can be made of the time and effort required even to construct the prototype, and it must not be embarked on without a clear understanding (preferably written down) of what the prototype is designed to achieve.

We are still left with the problem of how to *control* the prototyping activity, especially in the case where the prototype involves the user. In particular, we shall want to be careful to bring the iterative activity *m300 Carry out the exploration/experiment* to a timely conclusion. Take the case where we have decided to use a prototype approach to decide on the structure and appearance of the user interface to our system which has a high degree of user interaction. This is a common situation. Users, being human beings, are capable of indefinitely many views on what is good, what is bad, and what might be better. Let us suppose we decide that we will show our prototype to the prospective users, then take comments on how things should be changed, then update it to accommodate those comments, and then go round again. We could be in for an indefinite amount of iteration. How do we call a halt? How do we say 'enough is enough'?

This is a question that will be answered differently in different situations, depending on the amount of flexibility in the solutions possible, the whims of the users, and so on. An experiment reported by Mayhew *et al.* (1989) showed that where the prototyping activity was controlled by classifying the changes requested and then allocating resources according to a prioritisation scheme. The dangers noted by Mayhew *et al.* are:

- 'In this more flexible environment [where prototyping is being done], the potential number of prototypes and hence the potential amount of iteration is uncertain at the time when the initial project estimation is carried out.

- Prototyping depends on active user involvement to succeed. Development that has such a high degree of participation is inherently less predictable than that which has a more passive level of user involvement.

- Project management are less likely to have experience in the estimation of projects that involve prototyping than those for the more structured approaches.'

In summary, using a prototyping approach may reduce the risk of developing the wrong system, but can introduce plenty of new risks in making the project unmanageable! Their solution is as follows. They define three classes of change that users might ask for in the prototype:

- *Cosmetic* changes that can be made without any effect on the design. These will be cheap and risk-free to make.

- *Local* changes that have a relatively small impact on the rest of the system. The local nature of the changes means that they will cost only a 'moderate' amount and represent a small technical risk.

- *Global* changes that impact other parts of the system. These will be quite likely to require substantial amendment to the design in some way. They will be correspondingly expensive and risky.

From their experience Mayhew *et al.* then propose appropriate ways of dealing with these three categories:

- Cosmetic changes are implemented in the current prototype by the developers without seeking approval (by definition this is possible at low cost).

- Local changes are also implemented directly, but the last version of the prototype is archived against the possibility that the resulting prototype is worse. Since the changes necessary *do* affect the design – albeit in a locally contained way – some form of design review is held to ensure that they are being made correctly.

- A global change can only be incorporated after a design review that looks at all the ramifications and decides how the change should actually be implemented.

With these categories in place, the prototype can be exhibited to the users who, in some way, experiment with it (this is a matter that one cannot pontificate on – it will vary too widely). All the changes the users propose during a session are logged and each is classified at the end of the session. Between sessions, either changes can be made to the existing prototype or a new prototype can be constructed, depending on the classifications of the changes proposed. Project management only get involved in the decisions as to what should happen next.

The benefits of this mechanism were found to be that progress towards the 'right' answer could be monitored; cosmetic changes could be made without management involvement; global changes were only made with management's knowledge and approval, thereby ensuring that any side effects – and hence any impacts on costs and timescale – were sanctioned; and the impact of prototyping on the project as a whole remained visible to management. The technique also offers ways of deciding when prototyping should stop, though such criteria must be locally decided in the context of local budgets and timescales. Mayhew *et al* point out that in their experiment it was not unusual for global changes to appear well into a prototyping session, which probably reflects the fact that there is little correlation between the importance of features to users and the cost of implementing them. However, if only cosmetic changes seem to be coming out of the sessions then a simple guillotine would seem to be appropriate. Stay in control!

Further advice on organising and managing prototyping can be found in Mayhew *et al.* (1990). Some other problems on the human side that have been reported (Livesey 1984) are:

- the difficulty of estimating the resources needed for planning and preparing for prototyping, as well as actually carrying it out

- the way that the existence of a prototype can raise hopes (especially with users) that the system is almost ready

- the frustration that a development team can feel as change after change is requested

- the need for the developer to take on an analyst role to carry out the prototyping.

All of these need careful management and are in part dealt with in the DSDM Process Model, of which more later.

The Evolutionary Delivery Process Model

The Evolutionary Delivery Process Model described

The *Evolutionary Delivery Process Model* can be likened to the VP Process Model in which the prototype is in fact an entire system. A whole sequence of complete systems is developed. Each version is complete in that it provides full functionality to the user, but the versions change as the process unwinds (see Figure 4-10).

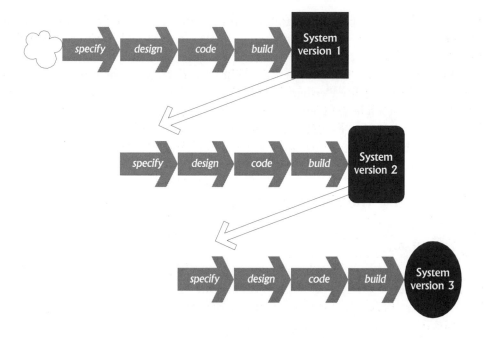

Figure 4-10. The Evolutionary Delivery Process Model

Once a version has been built and used, features of it will be noticed that will require changes to be made. Moreover, once the version is installed and used in its environment, that environment will itself change under the influence of the new version and, to some extent, make it inappropriate – it was after all designed for the old environment! The changes identified are incorporated in the specification for the next version in the series, which is then produced.

The sorts of changes that might be made include changes to functionality, changes in the user interface, changes in non-functional attributes such as reliability, and changes in design, for instance to improve speed or performance.

How we build each version can itself vary; the V or the VP Process Model might be used, for instance. Figure 4-10 shows the simplest possible scheme, where each version in the sequence is developed using the simple V Process Model. Of course, in the average case things are rarely this straightforward. The choice depends on the nature of the changes being incorporated in the new version. It is quite possible that early versions are built using rapid prototyping tools and that at some point during the evolution a decision is made to move to a version that is engineered to higher standards of construction, reliability, performance and so on. However, it is important to remember that every version in the evolving series is of 'production quality', i.e. fit for real use.

You may have realised that the traditional development phase plus what we have always called 'enhancement' together make up one form of the Evolutionary Delivery Process Model. However, by showing it this way we emphasise that changes that turn out to be needed after delivery will often require a return to the definition of the system and its design before the code can be changed.

Where to use the Evolutionary Delivery Process Model

> ### HEADLINE
>
> The Evolutionary Delivery Process Model should be considered when the final form of the system cannot be decided until something has been tried, or the exact relationship between the system and the business is complex or may change.

What sort of risk in the project would lead us to use this model? Clearly, we know enough to build at least the first version of the entire system. But for some reason we believe that when it goes into the field there will be significant changes required. Those reasons could include the possibility that the system will so affect its environment – for instance, the working practices of its users – that it will in some way invalidate itself and thereby need adjustment; or the need for new areas of functionality will become apparent once the system is installed.

(Note that if, at the outset or during development, we identify small areas of functionality that are uncertain we should aim to prototype them there and then rather than leaving them until delivery.)

One place where this model is the natural one is in the development of software products. A product is developed in a fully usable form. Experience with it in the field leads to new functional requirements and amendments to existing functionality, and the vendor chooses which of these will appear in the next release. The product evolves.

The major products

The products are precisely those that are used on the development path, except that there might be a sequence of them. Thus, suppose we used the simple V Process Model for the first system to be developed. All the products we would expect – User Layer, Architecture Layer, etc. – will be produced here. Let us call them *UL1*, *AL1*, and so on. On the second evolution we will produce a new sequence: *UL2*, *AL2*, etc.

The generic Work Breakdown Structure

The WBS will clearly consist of a number of major units:

1000	Plan overall development
2000	Develop version 1
3000	Develop version 2
4000	Develop version 3
...	

Each cycle will be composed of some planning activity, then the production, finishing with some form of review:

n100	Plan this version
n200	Produce this version
n300	Review this version

Note the cyclical similarity with the Spiral Model. The detail within *n200 Produce this version* will of course depend on how you go about it – perhaps with a V Process Model, perhaps with some prototyping or perhaps in a further evolutionary fashion.

The major review points

The major review points are of course after the production of each version, the *n300* activities above. Those activities may need to be long enough to allow the effect of the version on its environment to settle. The sorts of decisions to be made include

- how does the result match user expectations or requirements?

- how is the business different?

- how is the business changing?

- how are expectations or requirements themselves changing as a result of the new version?

- what changes should appear in the next version?

The costs of this model as a risk reduction measure

Every version can be seen as an extra cost, though, by the nature of the risk we are addressing, we had no choice probably but to take it. A more important – and perhaps dangerous – cost is that of the regression testing that must be done on each evolution. It is a universal truth of software development that the best place to look for a fault is where you made the last change. Moreover, a change in one part of a system can have an effect 'miles away' in another part: we add some new fields to this screen form, which affects the locking of the database, which causes certain transactions to time out more frequently, which means that certain backup operations are delayed, which increases the vulnerability of the system to data loss … Whether the next evolution of the system is large or small we shall either need to be very thorough in our regression testing or very convincing about why we are not doing it, and that regression testing is part of this risk reduction measure.

Running a project with the Evolutionary Delivery Process Model

Contractual considerations

If the Evolutionary Delivery Process Model is being used we might guess that the future direction of the system's evolution cannot be determined until something – the first version – is in place and in use. Care should be taken therefore before any contractual commitment is made that extends beyond the production of the first version. Otherwise, managing this model is the same as managing the V or VP Process Model, whichever is used.

An initial version of the system may be delivered to the users very early in development and it is then essential that they are educated to understand the nature of the process: it will not be perfect, some things are going to change, it is a learning exercise in certain respects, and so on. On the positive side users will not be surprised when they see the 'final' version and will also have the opportunity of training on the early versions. The successful use of the model requires that both developer and user are willing to communicate openly during the (possibly long) evolutionary process.

Management considerations

The success of the evolutionary delivery approach rests on the ability of the designer to build modifiability into the system from the start. The steady evolution can fail badly if at some point a change in functionality that is small in externally perceived terms in fact requires a massive restructuring of the software internally. This has implications for the methods chosen to build systems that will undergo evolutionary delivery. Object-oriented development is particularly strong in this area.

The secret is to decide what it is about the system that is unlikely to change and what is likely to change. The system should be founded on structures that are themselves built on those aspects that are least likely to change. Likely-to-change features then need to be implemented in a way that indeed makes them easy to change. A building should not need to have its foundations dug up to accommodate a change in wallpaper, and the same applies to software systems. The assumption in JSD, for instance, is that the entities that are the subject matter of a system are likely to remain constant whereas the functions that the system performs are likely to change. It also assumes that the organisation of the *external* system that the computer is to track is likely to change. For instance, a bank will probably always have clients. This entity type could underlie the system that handles the bank's business. But the information that senior management want about the bank's clients will change frequently, as will the different sorts of accounts. Finding these 'foundation' concepts is crucial and a key question for management as well as for the technicians.

(Ironically, it appears that the technologies we have for the database systems that support organisations are in conflict with the way organisations change! If indeed the entities that are the subject matter of an organisation are the least likely thing to change (assuming the organisation stays in roughly the same business) then they should be at the centre of the system – and indeed if we use a relational database they are: the relational model of those entities is easily captured in the database. Incidentally, that model is also comparatively easy to change, if tedious. On the other hand however, what *does* change in organisations is their logic, that is, how they go about their business – their business rules. And the only tools we have to capture these are the screens, their triggers and all the logic we encode behind those screens in VB, SQL, COBOL, or whatever. And such code is the devil to change! What we desperately need is tools that allow us to capture the business rules of an organisation in a way that makes them easily accessible and easily changed, rather than being buried in code that we cannot change without great pain. Unfortunately, except in very specialised areas this is still a research topic.)

A further major consideration is the control of successive versions. Because we have a sequence of versions we will have a sequence of products: a sequence of User Layers, a sequence of Architecture Layers and so on, as we have seen. As anywhere else in software development, if you've more than one version of anything around, you've potential problems unless you exercise strict control over identification of versions, and their release in baselines. With products you have the worst problem, with perhaps several versions in the field on many sites, perhaps on many different platforms.

Change control and configuration control are key practices that you must exercise, and we shall look at planning for them in Chapter 8.

The Incremental Delivery Process Model

The Incremental Delivery Process Model described

Our next 'standard' process model is the *Incremental Delivery Process Model*. Each delivery to the client is usable but has only partial functionality. Each delivery is the same as the previous one but with some new functionality (see Figure 4-11).

Typically the first delivery consists of a central kernel together with a small amount of functionality. Succeeding increments add further functionality to that kernel.

The success of the Incremental Delivery approach rests on the ability of the designer to create – from the start – an architecture that can support the anticipated final functionality of the system so that there is not a point during the sequence of deliveries where the addition of the next increment of functionality requires a massive re-engineering of the system at the architectural level.

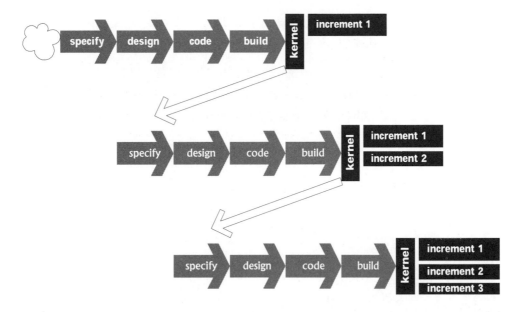

Figure 4-11. The Incremental Delivery Process Model

The major products

The major products are now the initial system or kernel with its partial functionality and a sequence of increments. For each of these there will be new versions of the various development layers, much as with the Evolutionary Delivery Process Model.

The generic Work Breakdown Structure

The overall shape of the project for an incremental delivery naturally breaks down into the initial definition and design work, the implementation of the kernel, and then a sequence of separate developments of the increments. The development of the kernel or of an increment could itself take a number of different forms depending on the outcome of your analysis of the risks and uncertainty of the relevant part of the system. (I should emphasise again the need not to treat these models as in any way special or even normal – they are samples of basic schemes that you should adapt.)

Our WBS will have the following general form:

1000   Plan overall development

2000   Develop kernel and increment 1 (jointly: INC1)

2100   Plan production of INC1

2200   Produce User Layer for INC1

    2210   Produce Requirements Expression for INC1

    2220   Produce System Specification for INC1

    2230   Produce Acceptance Test Specification for INC1

    2240   Produce Delivered INC1

2300   Produce Architecture Layer for INC1

    2310   Produce System Design for INC1

    2320   Produce Build Test Specifications for INC1

    2330   Produce Tested Part-systems for INC1

2400   Produce Implementation Layer for INC1

    2410   Prepare Component Specifications for INC1

    2420   Prepare Component Test Specifications for INC1

    2430   Prepare Tested Components for INC1

3000   Develop increment 2 (INC2)

3100   Plan production of INC2

3200   Produce User Layer for INC2

    3210   Revise Requirements Expression for INC2

    3220   Revise System Specification for INC2

    3230   Produce Acceptance Test Specification for INC2

    3240   Produce Delivered INC2

3300   Produce Architecture Layer for INC2

    3310   Revise Architecture Layer for INC1

    3320   Produce System Design for INC2

    3330   Produce Build Test Specifications for INC2

    3340   Produce Tested Part-systems for INC2

3400   Produce Implementation Layer for INC2

    3410   Revise Implementation Layer for INC1

3420	Prepare Component Specifications for INC2
3430	Prepare Component Test Specifications for INC2
3440	Prepare Tested Components for INC2
3450	Produce Implementation Layer for INC2

4000   Develop increment 3 (INC3)

...

The major review points

In addition to normal review points, note how we need to review and revise development layers for preceding increments, and especially the kernel) as we get into succeeding increments.

The costs of this model as a risk reduction measure

The extra costs that the Incremental Delivery Process Model brings us as a risk reduction measure come from three possible sources:

- reworking of the kernel in order to support the new increment
- reworking of previous increments
- regression testing of previous increments.

An important issue for incremental delivery is the effect that a new increment can have on the kernel that is supporting the entire edifice. When we first built the kernel, perhaps some combination of operating system and DBMS, it was sufficient to support the first two increments. But when the third comes along we find that we need more or different support: a more complex scheduling regime for processes, a security layer that wasn't necessary when the system was not distributed, better data recovery mechanisms now that we are operating on a WAN with its greater unreliability. It is as if the foundations we put down for this two-storey house won't take a third storey and we are faced with having to replace them without bringing the whole building to the ground. This can be an expensive affair, especially if it turns out to be a surprise. In some situations though we can actually plan for it. If time is really tight on the first increment we might decide that we do not have enough time to put in the security layer and it is not necessary anyway, so we plan to leave it out and to do a major rework on the kernel for increment three.

> ## Example
>
> In building a major Oracle database system, the Praxis team found that the first increment had to be on the ground with some minimum functionality very quickly. The final system had to run on a database distributed over five servers, but this first increment only had to provide data loading on a single site. The decision was made to use a kernel which was for a single-site database and to discard it for subsequent increments when the database had to be distributed. This risk reduction measure to deal with the very short timescale for early functionality had the added cost of the development of the discarded kernel but it was fully justified in risk terms.

In general, a new increment will affect earlier increments. This might be at a functional level or an implementation level. If our new increment adds new transactions to support a new financial product, we shall probably have to change the initial enquiry screens for the call centre to additionally provide the call centre person with credit data as well as existing account data. If our new increment offers new reports on the financial database, we shall have to update the existing navigation screens to accommodate it. If our new increment introduces a new process and changes the timing of the software we may need to revisit the scheduling regime across the board. So, either way the new increment is making us rework past increments with all that that entails.

Even if the increment is totally free-standing – perhaps providing some separate reports on an existing database – we are still obliged to think through what possible effect the update could have on existing software and to decide what level of regression testing we shall need to do on past increments.

Where to use the Incremental Delivery Process Model

> ## Headline
>
> The Incremental Delivery Process Model should be considered when:
>
> we can only see part of the functionality at the outset, or
>
> we cannot deliver everything on day one, or
>
> the business could not stand all the change in one go.

Functionality uncertainty

One form of uncertainty that can occur is where a significant amount of the system's functionality is in the form of many similar transactions or other units. The exact number of these might not be known at the outset, so that it is difficult to estimate the amount of work required to develop them. We might therefore choose to deliver the system in (at least) two increments. The first would contain the core of the system. Once we had produced that, we would, we assume, be able to estimate how many of them there will be and how long it will take to develop each. On the other hand, we might know how many there will be but not how long it will take to produce each; this might depend crucially on the architecture of the system chosen during development. In this case a first phase would produce the core of the system plus some small usable subset of all the transactions. From our experiences with that subset we would be able to estimate how long the rest would take and could then commit to delivering subsequent increments with them in.

Perhaps one of the more obvious times when the Incremental Delivery Process Model gets used is in product development. In the product arena there is generally pressure to get something out on the market as quickly as possible, with enhancements in functionality coming along over a number of subsequent releases. The early version will offer a degree of functionality sufficient to get the market-place interested and to sell sufficient licences to get the ball rolling. The product developer could not visualise everything that would be needed, develop it and then try to sell it. The economics and dynamics of the product world do not work that way. The first version will therefore contain basic functionality and – if the developers have been very lucky – will be based on an architecture that will support a number of subsequent enhancements. Unfortunately, those future enhancements cannot be forecast in the early days. As release follows release and the code undergoes further and further change, it gradually 'decays'; in thermodynamical terms the disorder or *entropy* of the system increases.

Finally, as we saw above when thinking about costs, the system can become so disordered that further changes cannot be made without its collapse. The kernel or architecture of the product has served its useful life and here is a case where the foundations have to be replaced to support new parts of the building that were never envisaged at the outset. It is also not unusual for continual enhancement to have a continual deleterious effect on the performance of a system for similar reasons. The original architecture served the originally foreseen functionality, but with successive new layerings it starts to creak, and only a complete overhaul will return the product in its enlarged form to an acceptable level of performance.

Provided we understand product development to have this sort of characteristic we can plan to deal with it: we should at least be ready to spot when entropy has reached unacceptable levels and act accordingly. Unfortunately, commercial considerations can again rule that the system must take 'just one more release' before it is radically restructured for the future. But one release too many can kill the product.

Timescale achievability

The Incremental Delivery Process Model is often used where there is a risk (or even certainty) that the system in its entirety cannot be delivered by the date required by the client, but where the client can make use of a subset of the system at that date and then take larger subsets or the balance at a later date. There are a number of different ways this can appear.

EXAMPLE

Praxis undertook a major project which delivered a whole sequence of partial systems to the client. The final system was a large transaction processing system that lived on a distributed database network. The system was intended to administer a set of national examinations involving hundreds of schools and thousands of students sitting many papers in many subjects. Legal requirements meant that the system had to be in place by a certain date. As is often the case, the client's organisation had a considerable amount of work to do to get itself ready for the transfer to the new automated system from the existing manual system. At various points over the eighteen-month development period, parts of the system were needed for early use – the take-on of basic data for exam syllabuses, the registration of schools, the registration of students for examinations, the registration of people who would mark papers, and so on. At each of these intermediate stages of preparation before the exams were held, a new tranche of transactions was required by the client. By the final date everything had to be in place and the system ready to take the marks and prepare the results.

Time was short and getting that sequence of increments defined was crucial to success. There was no way in which the whole system could be waited for, and so the incremental approach was necessary.

> As increments were developed it would sometimes prove necessary
> to rework old transactions to bring them in line with the new ones.

I have also used the Incremental Delivery Process Model when taking delivery of product from someone else. We were developing a digital framestore for capturing television in real time. The framestore was to be controlled by a microprocessor that itself received commands from a minicomputer. The framestore was custom designed and built, and was being developed in the same timescale as the software. Indeed, the early design of the framestore was done at the same time as the design of the software – the two were intimately related and hence were married at an early age. But we clearly could not wait for the framestore hardware to be completed before we started integrating it with the software on the microprocessor, and the minicomputer with that. There was a major risk that – as at any interface – we had got something wrong in the specification of the hardware and/or the software. We couldn't wait until late in the day to find out whether we had it right.

The solution was to require from the hardware engineers a series of partial framestores – it turned out to be eight. The first hardware delivery was the core: the backplane (bus), the microprocessor, its memory and the I/O ports. As new boards providing new functionality came out of prototype production the framestore was incremented in functionality and the matching control software was blended in. The first version of the hardware – and it makes me blanch to remember it – consisted of around four PCBs in a cardboard box, held apart and vertical by polystyrene packing material, with a power supply taped to the side of the box at one end. Nevertheless it worked perfectly well, though I guess it would not have pleased a safety inspector. The second and third increments added further PCBs, with the fourth version (or thereabouts) going to two 'racks' made out of polystyrene. The major problem at this stage was preventing the whole edifice from collapsing in an untidy heap. Increment five was, I think, in proper metal racking and new versions of the boards – without 'cuts and straps' – started to appear.

That approach proved highly successful – we spotted problems about as early as we possibly could have. We had the continuing problem of bringing software and hardware together at the right times, but the advantage of moving in small steps. It wasn't a brilliantly innovative solution to a risky problem but it was very effective.

Running a project with the Incremental Delivery Process Model

Contractual considerations

The straightforward Incremental Delivery Process Model, by its nature, pre-supposes that at least the first is sufficiently well understood for a commitment to be made on its price and timescale. In the best case, a commitment can be made to a series of increments, particularly if incremental delivery is being used for timescale reasons.

Key to the success of the simple V Process Model is that there is a good specification of the system at the outset that can be agreed by client and developer. In the incremental model, if the specifications of all the increments can be agreed at the outset, the same considerations apply as apply to the V Process Model. But it can be the case that the precise nature of the increments is not known until the time comes to define the next.

In this sort of situation, it becomes necessary to (re)negotiate the contract increment by increment, with each negotiation being preceded by some sort of costing exercise. That exercise might perhaps be based on a preliminary design much as we might undertake in a two-phase development consisting of a fixed price definition phase and a fixed price implementation phase, with one of the outputs from the definition phase being the costs and plan for the second phase.

It needs to be borne in mind, however, that, if the content of all the increments is not known at the outset (and this is probably the most common case), there is a high probability that the underlying architecture that is designed at the beginning does not survive beyond the first few increments. As a result increments after the first will often have part of their cost due to reworking necessary on the architecture. This is something not always considered by developers or understood by customers. But it is a fact of life that if you start out with a ship in mind and later suddenly want it to run on roads you'll be in for some reworking of its chassis.

> ## EXAMPLE
>
> If you are building a system to process transactions coming from automatic bank tellers, early versions of the system might come with basic facilities such as the dispensing of cash and movement of funds between accounts, and future increments might be planned that add additional facilities for the customer. If a new increment is required that, say, handles home banking transactions coming from customers' own PCs, it might not be such a simple matter as adding the odd new transaction process.

Managerial considerations

Clearly, the development of increments can overlap, and there are dangers with this, especially if the increments require concurrent changes to the kernel. In an ideal world such concurrent changes would not be necessary. But our world is not ideal, and the need to compress the delivery schedules of projects often forces project managers to take the pain of such overlaps in order to satisfy commercial requirements. The problem requires as a minimum a strong change management scheme, especially on the kernel.

The DSDM Process Model

The DSDM Process Model described

As the industry attempted to grapple with ever-shortening timescales from customers and the big bang approaches seemed to generate more failures than successes, the Rapid Application Development (RAD) approach emerged as another panacea. It wasn't, of course. Before long it also had a bad name: Rapidly Accelerated Disasters, and variations on that theme. The idea was right – manage timescale and requirements risk by a larger number of shorter steps – but the world lacked a way of managing such situations.

DSDM – the Dynamic Systems Development Method – is an attempt to bring order and discipline to RAD, and for that deserves its own coverage as a process model that you should have in your armoury. Despite its name, it is not a development method as such, more a process model with a set of controls to make it work. It fits neatly into this chapter, and I shall concentrate on just those aspects that touch on our planning interests. (The *DSDM Consortium* is the keeper of the method and publishes the definitive reference manual for members (DSDM 1998); Stapleton (1997) provides practical guidance and case studies. Also, see www.dsdm.org/.)

DSDM calls for frequent delivery of usable software through a combination of the evolutionary and Incremental Delivery Process Models. It emphasises constant quality control with fitness for purpose as its watchword. It uses the five-phase view shown in Figure 4-12.

The *Feasibility Study* is almost an adjunct of risk planning in our sense: it is the step at which the project's situation is assessed to see whether DSDM is the right approach. There are a number of conditions where it can be appropriate but there are also a number of preconditions that must hold for it to be successful. The Feasibility Study looks at both conditions and preconditions (see below).

If the project is suitable DSDM can be applied. The *Business Study* sets the business scene for the work, examining the processes that will be supported. The three cycles shown in Figure 4-12 suggest strongly that iteration will then be the order of the day. The *Functional Model* and the *Design and Build Iteration* both adopt the cycle that we shall see later in Chapter 7:

- say what you will do

- agree how to do it

- do it

- check what you did.

In the *Functional Model Iteration*, analysis leads to prototype which leads to prototype … as the iterations converge on the requirements of the system. Both functional and non-functional attributes of the required system are explored (see Chapter 5).

The prototypes arising from the *Design and Build Iteration* evolve to a *Tested System* that is sufficiently well engineered to be used by the business, what I have referred to as the *Delivered System*.

The *Implementation* phase is when the system is deployed to the business environment and its success monitored. It is shown as another iteration, but this is there solely to handle deployment over time or geography. Once the system is in use, its performance against the needs of the business can be assessed and the result will be either to close the project or to re-enter one of the cycles. Figure 4-12 shows the possible return to the other iterations, or even to the Business Study if necessary.

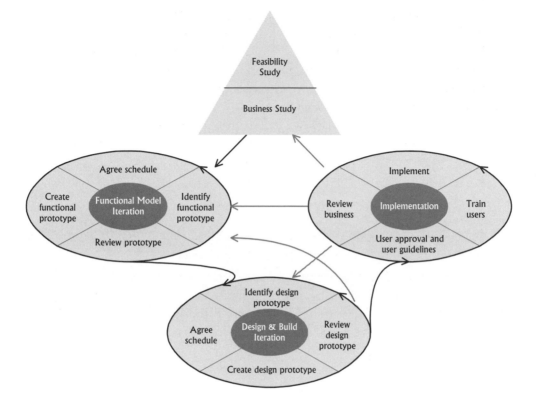

Figure 4-12. Dynamic Systems Development Method

The major products

The *Business Study* prepares the ground by producing

- a *Business Area Definition*, which gives a high-level prioritised view of the processes to be automated

- a *System Architecture Definition*, which acts much as a System Design in my terms

- an *Outline Prototyping Plan*, which sets the scene for planning, including the mechanisms for change management, which, as for our other iterative process models, plays a major part in preserving the quality of the evolving system.

The *Functional Model Iteration* results in particular in:

- a *Functional Model*, which is the functional part of our *System Specification* (though it contains tested software components too)

- a *Risk Analysis*, which informs subsequent work in exactly the same way that our risk planning does.

The *Design and Build Iteration* results in particular in:

- a series of *design prototypes*

- a *Tested System*.

The *Implementation* phase results in particular in:

- a system deployed to the business – what I have referred to as the *System in Use*

- *Project Review Documents*, which assess the degree to which the business requirements have been met by a deployed system and whether there are aspects of the system's construction that should be revisited, perhaps to improve non-functional attributes such as performance or security.

The generic Work Breakdown Structure

The highly iterative nature of the DSDM Process Model makes a generic WBS inappropriate but Figure 4-12 provides the elements that could be used in a particular situation.

The major review points

DSDM has explicit major reviews points as can be seen from Figure 4-12:

- review of functional prototypes during the *Functional Model Iteration*

- review of design prototypes during *Design and Build Iteration*

- review of the success of a deployment to the business in the *Implementation cycle*.

The costs of this model as a risk reduction measure

The DSDM Process Model shows the same apparent costs as the Evolutionary and Incremental Delivery Process Models, in particular the costs of reworking or revisiting past versions or increments. This is largely countered by keeping the increments small and easily reversed, so that the 'wastage' is kept to a minimum. As before if the method is properly applied in the right situations, these costs are far outweighed by the risks inherent in a simpler process model that does not adequately address the timescale risks.

Where to use the DSDM Process Model

The risks that the DSDM Process Model addresses are really just those addressed by the Evolutionary and Incremental Delivery Process Models. The system may be needed quickly, perhaps because the business is changing rapidly, making a protracted definition and construction process inappropriate, or there may be difficulties in deploying the system to the business.

> ## HEADLINE
> The DSDM Process Model should be considered when
> > one of the cardinal aims is quick business benefit, or
> > the business environment is changing rapidly, or
> > deployment of the system might be resisted, or
> > ownership by the users might be hard to establish.

Running a project with the DSDM Process Model

Contractual considerations

By contrast with the other process models we have been looking at, DSDM has a far more collaborative feel about it. The users, indeed all the stakeholders, are actively involved in the prototyping activities and hence in the definition and design of the system. One of DSDM's guiding principles is indeed that the users and developers are jointly empowered to make quick decisions without constantly having to refer to some outside, higher authority such as a traditional Project Control Board above them. It is therefore almost inappropriate to talk in contractual terms. If there are contracts to be struck they will be about the availability of key people from the user community.

Managerial considerations

While the risks in the Headline above might make DSDM an appropriate process model in your situation, your project will need to satisfy several preconditions as well. In summary they are as follows:

- The functionality must be reasonably visible at the user interface. The high involvement of the user community during prototyping makes this essential.

- All the users must be identified. Again, iterative requirements gathering and design demand that all the users are represented if the full picture is to be captured and the system is not to be slanted in one direction.

- Functionality should not be so complex that users cannot be involved in its exploration. Complexity is in the eye of the beholder and varies from application to application and from user community to user community, but if the users cannot handle it then the collaboration will fail.

- If the application is going to be big it needs to be split into smaller functional components. This is simply to make many small increments possible.

- The project must truly be time-constrained. If it isn't the users will not have the commitment required to make a DSDM development successful.

- The requirements should not have been finalised. The assumption behind the iterative functional prototyping is precisely that the requirements have yet to be flushed out in detail.

If the preconditions and conditions are right, your main managerial concern becomes the definition of suitably small increments in the *Functional Model* and *Design and Build* cycles. Every iteration is done using a *timebox*, a discipline that requires careful, even tyrannical management. The aim of a timebox is to produce something. It is an activity lasting between, say, two and six weeks and its end date is inviolable. This is to concentrate minds on the most important aspects of the problem being addressed (Parkinson's Law always applies), to prevent scope creep, and to give the project manager a handle on the estimating.

In Chapter 10 I recommend the use of *work package contracts* as a way of agreeing the aims of a work package with the staff member who is to undertake it – this is an appropriate mechanism for controlling timeboxed activities in DSDM, and Stapleton (1997) offers some pro formas. Each timebox contains its own testing activity, possibly at several levels – quality control is spread throughout the project as we would like it to be. It will be as formal as, say, described in Chapter 7, leaving the same level of evidence. But we will not expect all testing to be defined beforehand – the nature of the prototyping reduces the usefulness of this approach.

Prioritisation is an important tool in the discipline of the timebox. Requirements are placed on the must-have, should-have, could-have and nice-to-have scale. This guides the choice of requirements to be attacked in the next timebox, and together with a functional decomposition of the system into manageable lumps, provides you with the basis for your plan.

Change control is important in DSDM not because the aim is to make change hard but in fact to make it as easy yet as controlled as possible – the iterative nature of the process demands this. The traditional scope creep, which change control aims to stamp out, is prevented through the prioritisation and timeboxing disciplines. DSDM-friendly change control is quick-footed and secure.

The Exploratory Process Model

The Exploratory Process Model described

I include this model simply to show that the Spiral Model can unwind in small turns, with each turn achieving a small amount, and possibly with the whole process not necessarily starting with a clear target in mind. We have to accept that, especially in the more research-oriented environments, this can happen and is often desirable.

The small development steps (each an unwinding) may follow one on another in an apparently unguided fashion. But it is likely that what a step should deal with can only be decided as a result of the previous step: the work is exploring some domain or other.

The major products

In this model our products could be anything, large or small, related or unrelated – we can make no firm prediction. That's the nature of the work!

The generic Work Breakdown Structure

Since the work can only be planned from one small step to another an overall WBS is meaningless, though each development could itself usefully have some structure – it should at least be planned.

The major review points

A similar comment applies here.

Where to use the Exploratory Process Model

> ### HEADLINE
>
> The Exploratory Process Model should be considered when
>
> the goal is very vaguely specified and itself must be discovered, or
>
> the route is very poorly understood and must be found.

Clearly, this model should never be used unless conditions definitely demand it. I would consider it very uncommon outside the research environment. I have found it very useful in controlling a research project without unnecessarily over-constraining it. I feel that even in a research environment– especially if you have a client looking for signs of progress – it helps immensely to set and achieve frequent short-term targets.

> ### EXAMPLE
>
> At Praxis, a colleague, Clive Roberts, and I undertook some research work for a client where we were investigating ways in which we could write formal models of the development process. This was an area where – as far as we could tell – nobody had done any substantial work that we could start from. Additionally, we were but a small part of a much larger collaborative project that was investigating the construction of environments for the support of formal software development, environments that would moreover take an *active* part in development (in contrast to the passive environment of, for instance, UNIX). If we'd known the answer to the problem – just our problem – we could have got on with a normal development. But we only had some ideas about some useful-looking technologies and some

> very broad aims. No question here of agreeing with the client on a price for a delivered piece of software!
>
> Instead we simply worked on a month-by-month timeframe. Each month we would agree with the client a small target of solving one problem, or investigating one topic and making a recommendation, or writing a small prototype, or developing some new idea, or whatever. And we'd concentrate entirely on that, presenting our findings to the client in a report or verbally at the end of the month (or so). After a 'free-ranging discussion' we would set and agree the next parcel of work that we all reckoned would take the topic another step forward (or perhaps recover some ground lost as a result of the previous month's work). The project continued in this way for about four years and, as an outcome, produced results that could never have been predicted or defined at the outset. Progress sometimes felt slow but with research of this sort we should not expect the same rate of delivery as on a 'straightforward' project.

Running a project with the Exploratory Process Model

Contractual considerations

Naturally, on the principle that we should only commit to what we can reasonably predict, no one is going to take a fixed price contract on anything more than the next small unwinding. In a true research environment of course, the client may let a research contract for a period of time, during which a number of developments might or might not take place, according to how things went. But that sort of project is outside the scope of this book.

Management considerations

The Exploratory Process Model assumes that the direction of the project is effectively unknown and unestimatable. A research project of this sort must be run as such, budgets being set according to the price the organisation is prepared to pay for possible results. But naturally those results cannot be guaranteed. The management of the project must be appropriate to research activity, setting goals for but not constraining creativity.

Blending process models

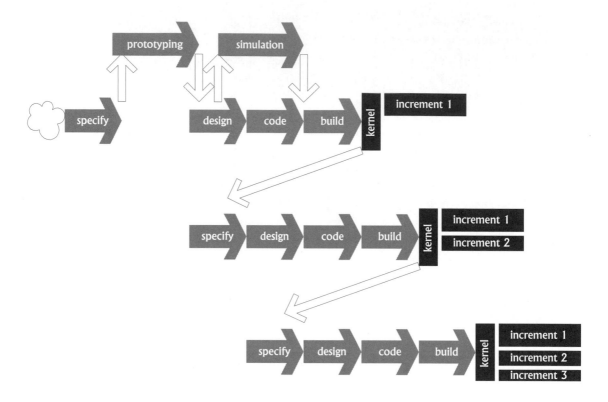

Figure 4-13. A mixed process model

At the beginning of this chapter I stressed that the process models presented above are not the only possible models and they are not to be followed rigidly. They are simply particular examples. I also stressed that, according to the project being undertaken and the areas of risk and uncertainty within it, some blend of process models would be necessary. As a fictitious example, Figure 4-13 suggests a project that is planning to deliver the system in three increments. During the development of the first it expects to carry out a prototyping exercise between the specification and design work and a concurrent simulation activity ready for the build phase. These features of the process model will all have been chosen to address major risks identified for the project. They give the skeleton on which we will hang all the other activities necessary for a successful project, in particular (as we shall see) our qual-ity-related activities.

The WBS for this project will take the following form where the italicised lines are additional to the generic incremental delivery:

1000   Plan overall development

2000   Develop kernel and increment 1 (jointly: INC1)

    2100   Plan production of INC1

    2200   Produce User Layer for INC1

        2210   Produce Requirements Expression for INC1

        2220   Carry out prototyping

            2221   Define the uncertainty

            2222   Define a prototype

            2223   Use the prototype

            2224   Make deductions

        2230   Produce System Specification for INC1

        2240   Produce Acceptance Test Specification for INC1

        2250   Produce Delivered INC1

    2300   Produce Architecture Layer for INC1

        2310   Produce simulator

        2320   Produce System Design for INC1

        2330   Produce Build Test Specifications for INC1

        2340   Produce Tested Part-systems for INC1 *using simulator*

    2400   Produce Implementation Layer for INC1

        2410   Prepare Component Specifications for INC1

        2420   Prepare Component Test Specifications for INC1

        2430   Prepare Tested Components for INC1

3000   Develop increment 2 (INC2)

    3100   Plan production of INC2

    3200   Produce User Layer for INC2

3210   Revise Requirements Expression for INC2

3220   Revise System Specification for INC2

3230   Produce Acceptance Test Specification for INC2

3240   Produce Delivered INC2

3300   Produce Architecture Layer for INC2

3310   Revise Architecture Layer for INC1

3320   Produce System Design for INC2

3330   Produce Build Test Specifications for INC2

3340   Produce Tested Part-systems for INC2

3400   Produce Implementation Layer for INC2

3410   Revise Implementation Layer for INC1

3420   Prepare Component Specifications for INC2

3430   Prepare Component Test Specifications for INC2

3440   Prepare Tested Components for INC2

3450   Produce Implementation Layer for INC2

4000   Develop increment 3 (INC3)

...

EXAMPLE

A major project in Praxis used a combination of the VP and Incremental Delivery Process Models. The first phase of the project did some preliminary experiments – some prototyping – to establish the right overall design, and then proceeded with a series of increments.

I have been fairly informal in the way I represent the process model that we choose for the project. My aim has been solely to capture the overall logic of the project, because when we come to prepare the activity network for the project during resource planning I shall need all that logic to ensure I get the right ordering of activities and the right dependencies between them. So it is enough at this point to make sure that we are recording the shapes and the logic in sufficient detail to make that possible.

The WBS on the other hand is a very precise structure and is the other major output of your risk planning, as you will add more and more detail to it as you proceed through the quality planning for the project.

Incorporating the simple risk reduction measures

So far in this chapter we have looked at major risk reduction measures that take the form of various 'unwindings' of the Spiral Model to address particular classes of risk. But in Chapter 3 we saw that there will often be risk reduction measures that are far less 'structural' in their effect on the project's shape.

For instance, suppose that at some point during development you will have to connect your system to someone else's. Everyone knows that when this is done the combined system won't work. You can be as careful as you like with the specification of the interface, but, as sure as eggs is eggs, something will not be quite right. A lot of time will then be wasted establishing where the fault lies – typically, on which side of the interface the fault lies! Recognising that this risk is a fact of life means that you can plan to manage it before it happens. One possibility is to develop a simulator of the system on the other side of the divide and to use that simulator as a test input generator for your own system before you get to the point of integration. We can then imagine the following *process fragments* that will help you manage this risk:

- design a simulator based on the interface specification *after* the interface has been agreed

- construct the simulator *before* the start of system integration

- test the system against the simulator *before* integration with the other system.

Here we have three simple activities – *design*, *construct* and *test* – together with some logic: *this before that*, or *this after that*. If the interface is complicated or the integration with the other system is likely to be expensive (because they are deeply embedded or remote or whatever) then we can imagine some elaborations. For instance, we might additionally design the simulator to work with real responses from the other system if that already exists. We could capture data from the other system with some additional software and drive the simulator with it so as to test our system with some realistic data, as well as with data concocted from the interface specification. The process fragments would now look as follows:

- once the interface has been agreed, design a simulator based on the interface specification and able to accept recorded live data

- construct the simulator before the start of system integration

- prepare software to capture live data from the other system and collect that data before the start of integration

- test the system against the simulator using recorded data before integration with the other system.

Corresponding activities in the WBS might then be

1320	Design a simulator for the P3 interface
2320	Construct and test the P3 interface simulator
3310	Capture live data from P3 interface
5300	Test P3 interface software with simulator using recorded data

EXAMPLES

Experiment with the database to check out the row locking strategy *before* starting the transaction design.

Train the novice programmers in Java *before* getting them to practice on sample components *before* they start on real components; get their worked reviewed by our Java guru *while* they are programming and *before* their components go for component testing.

Review the specification from the supplier *before* starting the design for Subsystem C (which will be based on it).

Determine the performance of the network *prior to* design sign-off; *if* it is satisfactory *then* proceed *else* plan enhancements and amend the design.

Once it has been coded, measure the efficiency of the search algorithm and tune it *until* it is satisfactory, *before* it is integrated.

To summarise, for each risk in our Risk Register that only requires a simple risk reduction measure (as opposed to a major process model feature), we convert that measure into one or more process fragments designed to manage that risk downstream, where each fragment takes the form of a list of activities together with dependencies that place them in context. That logic will indicate sequencing (typically *before* or *after*), iteration (*repeat until* something is true), or selection (*if* this is true *then* do this *else* do that).

It is good to check each risk reduction measure to see which of the following two groups it falls into:

a information-buying activities whose result will not radically affect the subsequent progress of the project

b information-buying activities for a decision that may lead to significantly different outcomes.

Type *a* activities are fine – they simply add detail to your process model. Type *b* activities are something else: your process model may well need to show alternative processes for the different outcomes of each decision. I have already noted that a process model – like a program – could be expected to contain not just sequence and iteration, but also selection. Such selection is known traditionally as *contingency planning*, and your process model should show how you will handle such contingencies.

Chapter recap

A project without a plan is a ship without a rudder. All projects have risks and it is these that cause projects to go wrong, i.e. to overrun in time and/or budget. The easy part of planning is the bit you understand, but the hard part is knowing what you *don't* know and planning to find out. A central part of your planning process must therefore be the analysis of risks.

Some risks are so major that the overall shape of your project itself can be completely determined by them. Such project shapes – *process models* – are often designed to ensure that (commercial) commitment can be limited to what you can reasonably predict. Typically this means some sort of phasing, with each phase being determined or steered by the previous one. Different process models can be seen as different unwindings of Boehm's *Spiral Model*:

- The V Process Model is a single unwinding in which the whole system is addressed in one go and there are no significant risks to be resolved.

- The VP Process Model is an unwinding in which each prototyping activity is a separate cycle designed to resolve a risk.

- The Evolutionary Delivery Process Model unwinds to allow a reassessment at the end of each cycle of how the system should be changed; as unwindings occur, the system evolves.

- The Incremental Delivery Process Model has an unwinding for each of the increments, which might or might not be known at the outset of development.

- The DSDM Process Model unwinds many times in short, chunked timeboxes to deliver small increments quickly and obtain the buy-in of the business.

- The Exploratory Process Model unwinds in a more or less unpredictable manner, entirely determined by the results of each development.

Other risks are less extensive in their effect on your project's shape. For these you need only devise activities for the chosen risk reduction measures. You must fit these activities into the overall project in such a way that they happen early enough to reduce or remove exposure to the risk. This results in some plan logic saying when in the project they should take place. Each activity together with this piece of logic forms a *process fragment*. In some cases a risk reduction measure can lead to significantly different outcomes, each outcome requiring its own elaboration within the process model: *contingency planning*.

Then comes the point where you must take all of your thinking about your management of the risks on the project and pull together the start of your plan.

In summary:

- you have prepared a Risk Register that identifies the risks and you have made a judgement about the probability and impact of each risk

- you have analysed each risk and sought a cost-effective risk reduction measure that brings the residual risk into your comfort zone

- some of those measures have a 'structural' effect on the project and call for a process model which provides a skeleton Work Breakdown Structure

- other measures lead to process fragments that can be slotted into the overall framework as further activities in the WBS

- the logic of your process – what must be done before or after what, what decisions must be made etc. – will form the basis for your project network during Resource Planning.

> ## OUTCOMES
>
> **A Risk Register**. This lists all the risks, your assessment of them, the risk reduction measures you have chosen to address them, and your assessment of the residual risk. You will use it during the project as a tool for monitoring and managing the residual risks.
>
> **An overall process model**. This captures the logic of the phases, the positioning of activities that form risk reduction measures. You will use it when preparing your activity network during resource planning.
>
> **A skeleton WBS**. You derive this from your chosen process model and your chosen plan fragments. You will add to this framework as you go through the quality planning for your project.

References

Benington 1956

Production of large computer programs. H D Benington. In *Proceedings, Symposium on Advanced Programming Methods for Digital Computers*, pp15-27. Office of Naval Research (ONR Report ACR-15), USA, 1956. (Adapted in *Annals of the History of Computing*, **5**, 4, pp350-361, 1983)

Boehm 1986

A spiral model of software development and enhancement. B W Boehm. In *ACM SIGSOFT Software Engineering Notes*, **11**, 4, pp14-24. ACM, New York, 1986

DSDM 1998

DSDM Manual. DSDM Consortium. 1998

Livesey 1984

Experience with prototyping in a multi national organization. P B Livesey. In *Approaches to prototyping*, pp92-104. Springer-Verlag, Berlin, 1984

Mayhew *et al.* 1989

Control of software prototyping process: change classification approach. P J Mayhew, C J Worsley, and P A Dearnley. In *Information and Software Technology*, **31**, 2, pp59-66

Mayhew *et al.* 1990

Organization and management of systems prototyping. P J Mayhew, P A Dearnley. *Information and Software Technology*, **32**, 4, pp245-252. May 1990

Myers 1975

Reliable Software through Composite Design. G J Myers. Van Nostrand Rhein-hold, New York, 1985

Royce 1970

Managing the development of large software systems: concepts and techniques. W W Royce. In *Proceedings of WESCON 1970*

Stapleton 1997

DSDM. J Stapleton. Addison-Wesley, Harlow, 1997

Wolff 1989

The management of risk in system development: 'Project SP' and the 'New Spiral Model'. J G Wolff. In *Software Engineering Journal,* **4**, 3, pp134-142. May 1989

5 Software quality

Quality? Software?

The problems of the software industry in producing 'quality' software are well touted, if not so well documented (though see Stephen Flowers's *Software Failure: Management Failure* (Flowers 1996)).

The three ways in which systems fail to meet expectations – an adequate definition of 'poor quality' for now – can be easily expressed as: 'too costly', 'too late' and 'not what we wanted'. I've chosen those words carefully.

'The system turned out too costly' is not the same as 'the system turned out more expensive than forecast'. Suppose you are a pharmaceutical company and I agree to build you a document management system to look after the records from the clinical trials that you carry out during the development of a new drug. I tell you it will cost £1m. And suppose I deliver it on the date promised, but the bill is £1.2m. Well, I spent more than I said I would, but your business case for that system said that it would take a week off the time-to-market of each new drug, and since you are bringing three new drugs to market this year and the profits from each are £300K per day you will still be very much in pocket in the first year of use and even better off in subsequent years. Seen from the perspective of the returns you anticipate, the system remains very good value.

But if I had been six months late in delivering it but for the promised £1m, it would be a different story: now you have lost many days of additional profit which could be seen as additional cost on the project and the system's value for money goes into the red. Worse, in the additional six months it took to get the system to you, you made some major changes to the way that you manage clinical trials and now it looks as though you are going to get a system that supports yesterday's business – this is really bad news.

If you are an avionics manufacturer, you might be very happy for me to spend two years developing a safety-critical system that will not fail in many thousands of hours of running. But if you want to get a new PC software package into the market-place you would not thank me for treating the development in exactly the same way: time to market is more important than the mean time between failures (MTBF) of your new virtual reality drawing package for garden designers.

So there is always a complex equation in which cost, timeliness and business relevance – the business case for the system – must all be balanced against each other. This comes home to us when we observe how, if the user community really takes to a new system, any cost and timescale overruns can easily be forgotten as the longer-term benefit to the business is realised. 'It's a great system, it really improves our responsiveness to our customers on the phone and they really appreciate it – it was worth waiting for.'

What this tells us is that a quality system is no more and no less than a system that gets the balance right for the customer. There is no absolute quality. Quality is always relative and always in the eye of the beholder. If you like wood, the boat for you is the one with lots of wood. So when we plan a project to deliver quality we cannot start with some absolute concept of what we will deliver. We must discover what the customer means by 'quality' and all our planning must be informed by that. In our risk management we applied a very similar principle: the economics of the original business case for the project informed our decisions about what risk reduction measures made sense. So too with quality. Our responsibility from the outset must be to ask our customer 'what will make you happy?' and the initial place to record the response is the project's Requirements Expression.

A definition of 'quality'

First, we need a working definition of the notion of *quality* and in this book we shall use the definition of quality given in the international standard ISO 8402:

> **DEFINITION**
>
> *Quality*: the totality of features and characteristics of a product, process or service that bear on its ability to satisfy stated or implied needs.

We are concerned with a *product* and that product is software. So for our purposes, the *quality* we require of our software is simply the sum of whatever features and characteristics we (or our client or customer) wish it to have, and if we want to control quality we must start by finding a way to define each feature and characteristic, what in this book I shall refer to as *quality attributes*.

Quality attributes come in all shapes and forms and we will find it useful for future discussion to think of them as coming in two varieties:

- *Functional quality attributes* – these apply to pieces of software, from the smallest components to entire systems. Examples might be

  - 'when the pressure sensor reading climbs through a pressure level of 3.2 bar, the relief valve control line shall be set to open'

  - 'at the request of the user from a menu, the account status shall be printed with the following data displayed as shown in figure 4.6: …'

  - 'all relevant data shall be secured to disc before any transaction is cleared'

  - 'if x<0 the component shall return the value zero'.

- *Non-functional quality attributes* – these can apply to any product of the development process: specifications, code, manuals, training courses, or the final system itself. Examples might be

  - 'with no other load present the system shall complete any type *B* transaction within 1.5 s, the duration being that time from the operator's pressing the ENTER key to screen acknowledgement'

  - 'the system shall be capable of operation on a computer with 64 Mb of memory'

  - 'the system shall give uninterrupted service despite any power outages of up to 2 s in duration'

- 'each component specification shall define the input variables, the valid range for each, ...'

- 'the system will be ready for use by 23rd August next year'

- 'the system shall have a failure rate not exceeding one in 10^4 demands under all conditions'

- 'a warehouse employee shall be able to use the system confidently after two hours' tuition'

- 'every test report shall state the version of each component used in the test, ...'

- 'the system shall be designed so that the addition of a new type A transaction does not require changes to existing software'

- 'the system will cost less than £1.4m to develop'

- 'the training course in the system's use shall last no more than three hours'

- 'the source code for every component shall contain a change history of the following form ...'

- 'the system shall be constructed so that the language of screen messages can be changed without change to procedural code'.

In particular, when someone places an order for a software system, they can expect to describe the quality they expect of it as a collection of attributes, some functional (what they want it to do), some non-functional (how well they want it to do it, and how they want it to 'look'). Note how cost and timeliness requirements are quality attributes just like any other.

HEADLINE

Quality attributes are either functional (what a thing should do) or non-functional (what a thing should be like). Cost and timeliness are simply non-functional attributes.

When we deliver the system, these *user-driven* quality attributes will be checked for at some form of acceptance test to make sure we have delivered the quality we contracted to deliver. They are therefore our ultimate target. However, to achieve them we must make sure that every step we make from the start to the end of the development keeps high our chances of successful delivery. So we can expect to be defining *developer-driven* quality attributes for all of the intermediate products of the development process: high level designs, low level designs, test plans, project plans, build schema, and so on. Our expectation is that by building quality into the intermediate products we shall deliver quality in the final products, those items that go to the customer.

> ## HEADLINE
>
> Good food needs good ingredients. We achieve quality in the final product through quality in the intermediate products.

Let's take three examples.

We might require that *a particular component* is of certain quality in terms of attributes such as:

- its functional attributes must be such and such

- it must occupy less than 1 Kb of memory

- it must in the worst case execute in less than 3 ms

- it must have been successfully tested on data from all combinations of single samples from the following ranges …

- at least 50% of source code lines must be annotation

- its McCabe complexity must be less than 12.

When, in its component test specification, we define *the particular tests* to be carried out on a particular component, we will define the quality of those tests with (solely non-functional) attributes such as:

- given condition *C1* and input *I1* the component will produce output *O1*

- given condition *C2* and input *I2* the component will produce output *O2*.

Similarly, we might require that *every test specification* is of particular quality in the form of (solely non-functional) attributes such as

- it must conform to the standard document layout for versioned documents

- it must identify test cases separately

- for each test case it must specify the input values, the starting conditions, and the expected output values

- it must be approved as appropriate by the Technical Authority for the relevant subsystem before use.

Specifications and standards

There is an important difference between these three examples. In the first and second we are defining the quality attributes of a single object, in this case, say, the component *AS123 Build User Profile Transaction* and the tests for that component. Where we define the quality attributes of a single object we write a *specification*, so we will produce a specification of component *AS123* and a specification of the component test for *AS123*. In the third example we are defining the quality attributes of a *class* of objects, in this case *all* component test specifications. Where we define the quality attributes of a class of objects we write a *standard*, so we will produce a document called, say, *Standard for test component specifications*.

HEADLINE

A *standard* defines the quality attributes of a *class* of products.

A *specification* defines the quality attributes of a *single* product.

Typically we will write specifications during the project at an appropriate point in development. We cannot say what each subsystem or component must do or be like until we have reached that point in the specification/refinement process. Standards, on the other hand, may already be in place before the project starts, or we might write them specifically for the project.

We can get our standards from a number of sources:

- *International standards* – typically standards issued by ISO or by ISO/IEC, such as ISO/IEC 12119 on the quality requirements and testing for software packages.

- *National standards* – standards issued by a national standards body such as BSI (in the UK), ANSI (in the USA), DIN (in Germany) and AFNOR (in France), e.g. British Standard BS 7925 Part 2 on software component testing.

- *Industry standards* (national or international) – standards issued by trade associations or industry bodies for regulatory or advisory purposes, e.g. the IEEE in the USA, the IEE and BCS in the UK.

- *Corporate standards* – standards prepared by an organisation for its internal use, typically in a Quality Management System of some sort (see below for more on this topic).

- *Project standards* – standards prepared by a project for its specific use, e.g. covering the precise mechanisms to be used for the control of changes on that project.

In the software development world, it is relatively rare for standards in the first two groups to be mandatory. Industry standards are commonly used, however, especially where safety criticality is an issue, such as in transportation, energy and medical devices. Which standards we choose to 'impose' on our project might therefore be decided for us to a degree but they can also be self-inflicted and care must be taken in selecting only those standards which truly reflect the quality demands of our customer.

One of the leading bodies in the software engineering scene is the IEEE in the USA. It supports a number of projects involved in standards making and standards revision. IEEE standards are frequently adopted as US standards by ANSI. They include:

- IEEE 610.12-1990 Glossary of Software Engineering Terminology

- IEEE 829-1983 (R1991) Software Test Documentation

- IEEE 1008-1987 (R1993) Software Unit Testing

- IEEE 1012-1986 (R1992) Software Verification and Validation Plans

- IEEE 1058.1-1987 (R1993) Software Project Management Plans

- IEEE 1063-1987 (R1993) Software User Documentation

- IEEE 1228-1994 Software Safety Plans

- IEEE 730-1998 Software Quality Assurance Plans

- IEEE 828-1998 Software Configuration Management Plans

- IEEE 1028-1997 Software Reviews

- IEEE 1219-1998 Software Maintenance.

(These are clearly under constant review and an up-to-date list can be obtained from http://www.ieee.org/catalog.)

Because of the broadness of the area they try to cover, standards from international and national bodies are frequently general and hence somewhat weak. Many organisations take these standards and then adapt them for their own use, customising them to their own situation, and thereby giving them a sharper edge. A collection of such local standards typically forms the bulk of an organisation's *Quality Manual*, complementing descriptions of the overall statement of policy, quality management structures and responsibilities, and so on.

A typical Quality Manual would contain standards covering all the major products of concern to the organisation in question, such as

- System Specification

- System Design

- Component Specification

- C++ code (or whatever languages are used locally)

- Test Plans

- Acceptance Test Specifications

- and of course standards themselves!

Additionally, a Quality Manual could contain standards on related topics such as:

- Project Plans

- Project Progress Reports

- Reviews, Walkthroughs and Inspections

- Change Control records

- Project Debrief Reports.

The Quality Manual presents the standards in force in the organisation. It is like a top-level Quality Plan for that organisation, a plan that is then refined as necessary for each development project when it draws up its own Quality Plan.

Defining quality attributes

Make them testable

Quality attributes – both user-driven and developer-driven – would be meaningless if we could not test that they had been achieved, so it is important that, when we state what level of quality something should have, we should be able to express that level in a testable form. Attributes such as 'the design must be extensible', 'the code must be easily maintainable and well structured', 'the manual must be easy to use', 'the test plan must be thorough', and 'the performance must be acceptable' are all quite useless. We must be precise enough to be able to devise a test that the attribute has been achieved. In an example above, the word 'confidently' in 'a warehouse employee shall be able to use the system confidently after two hours' tuition' is clearly not precise enough (did you notice that?), and we would want to replace the vague notion of *confidence* with something such as 'without more than one fault in 100 predetermined transactions over three hours of use'.

All this should be easier with functional attributes: provided we can express those attributes in a precise and unambiguous fashion (not a trivial matter) we shall be able to check that the item in question possesses them and is therefore of the requisite quality, in that respect at least. Typically we set up the necessary conditions, provide some inputs and check we get the expected outputs. Some other quality attributes can be made precise with numerical values, such as 'the software must occupy less than 320 Kb when delivered'. In such cases, the necessary precision is there and we simply have to be certain we can actually make the measurement – something that is not always easy with, for instance, performance figures that might require the construction of quite elaborate environments to check them out.

HEADLINE
All quality attributes must be testable.

Gilb's 'System Attribute Specification'

Possibly one of the most pragmatic approaches to the definition, measurement and achievement of quality attributes for systems is that of Tom Gilb in the techniques he refers to as *System Attribute Specification* (Gilb 1987).

Gilb uses a technique whereby unquantified and untestable attributes (such as *the system shall be secure against unwanted intrusion*) are quantified and made testable by refinement. Thus, a system's security might be measured by the number of unauthorised intrusions achieved by an 'assault' test team in a certain period, *and* by the amount of effort that was required to make the first intrusion. An attribute such as *it shall be easily maintainable* might first be decomposed into the ease with which the system can be changed in the event of a fault's being found *and* the ease with which an enhancement can be made. The first of these might be further decomposed in terms of the time for the first ten faults found in operation to be corrected. The second might be decomposed in terms of the time taken to add a new transaction and screen to the system *and* the time taken to add a new field to a screen enquiry *and* the time taken to add a new data item to a report.

Once the decomposition has proceeded as far as quantifiable and testable attributes, Gilb recommends that for each one the following should be specified: a measuring concept (e.g. number of intrusions in one week), a measuring tool (e.g. the test log), a worst permissible value (e.g. five), a planned value (e.g. two), the best or state-of-the-art value (zero?), and today's value where there is one. Gilb provides a number of guidelines for steering this process. The planned value becomes a design goal, and as development proceeds so the designers ensure that their design is adequately addressing the goal.

Non-functional attributes and ISO/IEC ISO 9126

As a first step towards the standardisation of non-functional quality attributes, the ISO/IEC joint committee responsible for software engineering standards has issued an International Standard ISO 9126 entitled *Information technology – Software product evaluation – Quality characteristics and guidelines for their use*.

This standard is brief since it is intended to be only a starting point for further development, but it usefully divides software quality attributes into six broad areas which, it says, are designed to overlap as little as possible:

- *functionality* – those attributes that characterise what the software does (i.e. my *functional attributes*)

- *reliability* – those attributes to do with the software's ability to maintain its level of performance under stated conditions for stated periods of time

- *usability* – those attributes to do with the effort needed to use the software and the individual assessment of such use by a stated or implied set of users

- *efficiency* – those attributes concerned with the relationship between the level of performance of the software and the level of resources used under stated conditions

- *maintainability* – those attributes to do with the effort needed to make specified modifications

- *portability* – those attributes concerned with the ability of the software to be transferred from one environment to another.

The standard goes on to present guidelines for using these quality characteristics and, in particular, proposes an evaluation process model whereby quality characteristics are defined – probably as refinements or specialisations of the six above – metrics are chosen against which the software can be measured, rating levels are defined against which the resulting measurements can be compared, and finally an assessment is made against those ratings. The outcome is a decision as to whether the software is acceptable or unacceptable.

We can see how Gilb's approach fits the standard's process model with its measuring concept, measuring tool, and worst permissible, planned and best values.

Quality factoring

Consider the range of quality attributes that we might require of a C++ code component:

- the component yields certain specified outputs for certain specified inputs

- it always runs in less than a certain amount of time

- it occupies no more than a certain amount of memory

- its source is commented to a particular degree

- its source satisfies a certain set of style rules

- it contains no unreachable code

- it contains no variables that are read before being written, or that are written but never read.

And here are quality attributes that we might require of a design in the form of a finite state machine:

- for every event in every state an action and a new state are defined

- every state is reachable by some sequence of events from the initial state *s1*

- the state sequence *s5*, *s7*, *s3*, *s3* can never occur

- state *s12* can never be reached without state *s6* having been reached beforehand.

But where do such quality attributes come from? What made us choose these?

When we talk about the final system, it is clear where its quality attributes come from: the customer. And we define those quality attributes in the System Specification. That specification will tell us all about the functional and non-functional attributes required in the final system. But how do we decide what the quality attributes of the *intermediate* products are? For instance, what quality attributes should we define for our design, our code, our test plans, and so on? And what should they be derived from?

The answer to this last question is simple: *from the quality attributes of the system itself.* There is nothing else from which they might come.

It is here that we need to revisit the notion of *quality* and its equivalent description as 'fitness for purpose'.

Quality factoring down the specification chain

I always become worried when people start to use the term *quality* in isolation, especially as an adjective: 'this is a quality piece of software', 'this is high quality software', 'what are you doing about quality?', and so on. There is the suggestion that quality is something absolute, something out there, a sort of Platonic ideal that exists somewhere and that we all strive for. It is far from this. It is precisely what we define it to be. And, ultimately, *it is what the client wants to pay for.* If system *A* has more (or more stringent) quality attributes than system *B*, then we can expect it to cost more than system *B*. A car with the property that it is less likely to skid in the wet under braking will cost more than one without that property. To the client, therefore, quality is *not* free; there will be a level of quality (or more precisely a set of quality attributes) that they will be prepared to pay for and that in some way makes some economic sense to them. You don't spend £100 on a component that will last 20 years if your need is for a £10 component that will last 5 years.

To illustrate this, let me mention something that was raised on several occasions at seminars where I gave presentations on so-called *Zero Defect Development*. Attendees often assume that 'zero defect software ' must never fail. In answer to questions I often make the statement that a piece of software could crash and yet be defect free. If the program is for experimental use only or just a prototype that is to be experimented with, we could well specify that it should have an MTBF of two hours in continuous use. If we produce a program that only crashes about every four hours we will have satisfied the specification: the program will be defect free in that it possesses all the required quality attributes. If the program took us two weeks to develop we would perhaps have got value for money. To make it fault-free (i.e. totally correct) would require far, far longer – even if we could ever know we had achieved total correctness.

So the definition of the quality of a system lies with the client. What are they prepared to pay for? How much is economically useful to them? What does their business demand and what will it pay for it? Every client that tells you they don't want a gold-plated system understands that – from their perspective – quality is not free.

But as far as you the *developer* are concerned, quality *must* be free, in the sense that to build to a lower quality than that required will lose you money because you will have to rework to achieve the quality wanted ('right first time' is the catchphrase that captures the message here); and to build to a higher quality will cost you more but bring you nothing: spending an extra £100 000 putting in performance that was not asked for is unlikely to earn you an extra £100 000 in a fixed price contract – that's gold plating and your client will not pay for it.

The lesson is clear: all quality attributes of all products during development must be derived from the quality attributes of the system to be delivered. This immediately suggests the notion of what I shall call *quality factoring*. We take the quality attributes required of the final system and factor these into quality attributes in the design, in the code, in the user manuals, in the test specifications, in the project plans – in fact into everything we produce. Let's take an example: performance.

In the specification of some system, let's suppose there is a requirement (quality attribute) for a certain level of performance. Let's imagine that it is that the system should be able to process up to twelve transactions per second over a sustained period of ten minutes without any other loading, irrespective of transaction type, each transaction having a transit time of less than 0.5 s (with suitable definitions). We can straight away factor this attribute into one in our design. Our design must display this level of performance, and we shall want to check that it does. That check might be done with a mathematical model of the proposed design, or perhaps with some prototyping.

Let me give you a real example of this. Earlier in the book I described a sonar system I was involved with where our design involved a network of communicating processes that triggered each other depending on the mode in which the system was running (live data, recorded data or simulated data) and on failure conditions in the surrounding electronics (noisy data, missing clock signals etc.). The system was required by the client to support the tracking of a certain number of objects at any one time. Would our design handle this?

The tracking capability was a quality attribute of the final system, and could be factored into a quality attribute that had to be displayed by our design. How would we check whether our design satisfied it? The answer was to build the basic tasking primitives, to construct a number of dummy tasks of about the right size and duration, to build them into the triggering network we had designed, and to put the whole software mock-up into the target processor and watch what happened with some simple simulated data.

When we tried this we noticed that some processes were getting into memory too late – the design had to be changed so that they went into locked partitions in memory. Others were holding too much memory for too long unnecessarily – they had to be split. After some adjustments to the process network we achieved a structure that gave us confidence that the actual system of processes would achieve the required tracking performance. So far so good.

Now we came to the next level of design where we were designing in detail each individual process down to the component level. We could not forget the performance issue. Our mock-up had assumed a certain size and approximate running time for each process. If these estimates were significantly missed in reality then we could be in trouble. So the performance quality attributes on the design had to be factored further down into individual components. If we had been very stringent (and we weren't) we could have set size and execution time limits for each and every component, thereby continuing the factoring right down to the code. In fact we only did it for a selected few that were seen as critical – the others had only broad requirements.

Standing back from this we can see that we developed a chain of quality factoring and that this chain was carried through the specifications: some factor of performance was required in system, subsystem, and component specifications, and the quality factoring passed down the specification chain.

Now this business of performance is a simple one with which to demonstrate the principle of quality factoring, but let's take a slightly less obvious case: 'usability'. If we have done a good job on the specification of the system, we will have defined the usability of the system in terms that will allow us to check it out in the delivered software. Let's suppose that the definition we came up with is as follows (it's not perfect but it will do for illustrative purposes):

> The system shall be usable with confidence by a new operator without previous experience of computer-based systems within one day of full-time use after up to one day of training. 'With confidence' means 'without having more than one transaction attempt in ten rejected by the system because of operator error, without referring to the paper manual more than once per twenty transactions, and achieving thirty successful transactions per hour'.

How shall we factor this quality attribute over intermediate products? Clearly, we shall have to factor attributes into the specifications for the design, for the help facilities on the system, for the user interface, for the user manuals, and for the training courses and their materials. For example:

- we might require certain ease-of-use attributes to appear in the user interface, such as a maximum number of key strokes required, or a limit on the possibility of user error through the use of pull down menus and point-and-click working, or the use of visual cues to indicate the stage that has been reached in a transaction

- we might require a minimum level of direct hands-on working in the one-day training course, plus a specified emphasis on the most common transactions that the operator is likely to see

- we might require certain functions in the design of the screen handling software that permit good 'undo' facilities.

The factoring here is obviously more complex, and two questions arise:

- how do we decide how to factor an attribute in one product into a number of attributes defined on quite different products?

- how do we decide that the factored attributes in some sense 'sum' to the original one?

There is no answer to first question! The question is the same as 'how do you design software?'. It is a matter for experience, imagination, creativity. And it is the subject of other books.

As for the second, one of the few people to tackle this directly is Tom Gilb in his *Design by Objectives* (Gilb 1987). Briefly, his method requires you to decompose the various non-functional attributes until at some point you have testable sub-attributes at the lowest level. You then identify actions you will take, or attributes of your system design, or whatever, that (will) contribute in some fashion to those sub-attributes, ascribing a figure to the 'size' of that contribution, expressed as a crude percentage. If the total of the contributions to a given sub-attribute is large enough – for instance, over 150% – you judge that you have probably done enough. This might make a mathematician blanch but, as Gilb put it at a workshop when criticised for his cavalier approach to mathematics, 'if you can tell me a better way of doing this, I'll sell it!'.

Quality factoring into standards

So far we have identified the flow of quality attributes from the System Specification down through the specification chain. We saw earlier that quality attributes can also be specified in standards in which the quality attributes for an entire *class* of products are laid out, for components written in C++ for instance. So, we can ask the same question: 'where do the quality attributes defined in standards come from?'. To answer this we need to go back to the levels of standard that we might come across:

1　International standards

2　National standards

3　Industry standards (national or international)

4　Corporate standards

5　Project standards.

I have one reservation about them all (though I must make it clear that I support standardisation activities and serve on the UK national standards committee responsible for standards in software development!).

I have argued in some detail that (a) quality is fitness for purpose and hence will vary from system to system, and (b) primary quality attributes are factored into quality attributes for intermediate products. The implication of this is that one cannot write a standard for, say, component specifications that will apply to all systems. As an example suppose we were to write a standard that defined what checks were to be applied during code reviews. Such a standard would list items like:

- there shall be no unreachable code

- no variable shall be read before being written to

- the component shall contain a change history record detailing all changes made subsequent to the first successful completion of component testing

- pointer arrays shall not be used.

But we can easily imagine situations where these quality attributes would be too stringent: a prototype piece of software intended only to explore some facet of design and then to be discarded, for instance. And we can just as easily imagine a situation where they would not be stringent enough: for safety-critical software we might well wish to add a number of additional attributes (such as amenability to semantic analysis). To have one standard for all situations is clearly an impossibility and so it is vitally important when using standards (whether local to your organisation or international) to be sure that wherever necessary you adjust them to the requirements of the job in hand.

At Praxis, project Quality Plans were always reviewed by the Quality Manager. Their job was to ensure that the Plan concerned was fit for purpose, in particular that the quality levels being called for were appropriate to the system in hand. It was as common for the Quality Manager to propose that the levels be turned down as turned up; project managers would not uncommonly call up standards from the company's Quality Manual which were relevant but which were too stringent or too extensive for the system being built. In exactly the same way that we factor the required quality of the final system down into intermediate products through their specifications, so we factor quality down into intermediate products through the standards that apply to them. There is no point in calling up a standard appropriate for the writing of code in a safety-critical environment on a project that is preparing an experimental prototype for a customer. Our standards must be fit for purpose too, and that means 'relevant to the system we are building and the quality demands of our customer'.

Of course there are some situations where you might not have the luxury of questioning whether a standard is or is not applicable: your client might demand it, or you might be required to use it by legislation. Clearly these are special cases that require special handling. Nick Birrell and I once met the first of these cases and felt it proper to convince our client that our standard was best. We were developing a complex call billing system for telephone exchanges. The client wanted us to prepare the design in the form of flowcharts, but we felt that this was inappropriate to a multi-process, real-time system. Nick had decided to use the SARA design technique, as its fit with the problem was excellent (see Birrell (1988) for a summary). Flowcharts simply didn't come into the running, but the client's Quality Assurance staff expected them as part of their normal quality standards. It needed some careful argument of our case to get them to agree to a design expressed in the diagrams and text of SARA.

So let me finish this section by voicing a word of caution against the blind use of standards – whatever their source. Quality attributes will vary from project to project. It is important not to set them too high or too low by simply calling up a standard 'off the shelf'.

Quality achievement, control and preservation defined

Now that we have a clear idea of what quality is and how we can go about defining quality attributes, we can start to define the three quality-related processes that we shall want to plan for on our project.

DEFINITIONS

Quality achievement – how we build the quality in.

Quality control – how we check that quality has been built in.

Quality preservation – how we make sure that the quality stays in, despite any changes we make.

Quality always has to be built in at the point of production, and the software development methods that are at our disposal are largely designed to ensure that the right quality is achieved in the first place. Quality control comes along close behind to check that those methods have been successful and to discover where they have not, so that faults can be found and corrected. Quality preservation ensures that we do not destroy the quality of things when (as we surely shall) we have to change them.

Let's take the three processes in turn.

Quality achievement

A software system is as much an artefact as a chair. If we want to build a good chair, we will make the joints with a saw and glue, perhaps some pins. That way the joints are strong and the chair robust – a quality attribute we will look for in any chair designed for everyday use. A nail would make a joint but not a robust joint; the joint would not have the required quality and the chair would not have the required quality. Quality is clearly only going to be achieved in an artefact if we use the right tool for the right job.

HEADLINE

Hammers are best for nails, spanners for nuts, screwdrivers for screws. Quality is achieved by using the right tool for the right job. Software quality is achieved by using the right methods for specification, for design, for coding, for testing.

The real engineering in software engineering is what we do when we specify, when we design, when we code, when we devise tests. The engineering tools we use are the methods for specification, for design, for coding and for testing. Because engineering happens in the head, those methods are *intellectual* tools – tools that we use to think and reason about things. A method for design will help us to think and reason about designs.

I can think of two methods for making a chair. The first involves buying a large piece of wood, bigger than the intended chair and using a hammer and chisels to carve away at it until I have produced the chair with its seat, back and legs as a single piece of wood. The second – more conventional method – involves buying some planks, using a saw to prepare embryonic legs, back and seat, and then a variety of tools to cut them to their desired shapes and fit them together.

The two methods differ radically in the way we think about the construction of the chair: in the first case our approach is one where the chair is 'discovered' inside a block of wood; in the second case the approach is one about components that are individually made and then assembled. The same is true of software engineering methods: each has its own approach – I shall later call it a *computational model* – which we use to think about the problem in a certain way.

There is another dimension to this: the team dimension. When we work as a design team, we must think as a team, and to do this we must share a language for design that will allow us to share design proposals and to reason about them together – to explore them, experiment with them, alter them and test them. The language of joinery is one that has concepts of joints, runners, veneers. In software engineering methods we will also look for a language – perhaps the 'language' of the Data Flow Diagram in which we 'talk' about activities, the data flows between them, and the datastores in which our data is kept.

Finally, as we construct our chair, how can we check whether that rail is true, that joint square, that shine sufficient? Does the approach we have used give us ways of checking the quality of what we are doing? For instance, a jig will help us check as we proceed. We shall make the same demands on our software development methods and look for ways in which they can help us analyse what we have done and see whether it is good.

HEADLINE

In summary, a good method is one that offers

a language for talking about specification, design, whatever

a way of constructing the product

ways of checking whether the product is good.

If our method does these three things well we shall produce a good product – in short we shall build quality into it. This will be the subject of Chapter 6.

Quality control

We are doing quality control whenever we check that a given item has a certain attribute. Anything that could be considered to be 'testing' is a form of quality control, provided we do it against a definition of the attributes we are checking for. Checking that a design covers all the requirements in a system's specification, testing a component against its specification, running a spelling checker over a user manual, measuring the response time of a transaction processing system – these are all quality control activities.

Where we find that a quality attribute is missing we say that the product has a *fault*. Part of the larger quality control process is then to correct that fault and check again that the quality attribute is now there.

Varieties of quality control: checking for attributes

Let's look again at the attributes that we had as examples of the two types, and for each let's invent a quality control activity or two:

Quality attribute	Quality control activity
When the pressure sensor reading climbs through a pressure level of 3.2 bar, the relief valve control line shall be set to open	Analyse the software connecting the sensor reading to the valve control and verify this behaviour will be its effect Set up a situation where the pressure climbs through 3.2 bar and observe the relief valve control line setting
At the request of the user from a menu, the account status shall be printed with the following data displayed as shown in figure 4.6: ...	Request account status against a 'representative' set of customer accounts and check the printed reports
All relevant data shall be secured to disc before any transaction is cleared	Analyse the design, in particular checking the locations of data updates at the point where every transaction is cleared
If x<0 the component shall return the value zero	Analyse the path taken through the component's code for an input of x<0, checking that it returns zero Compile and run the component's code with inputs of -1, -10 and -1 000, and check it returns zero in each case
With no other load present the system shall complete any type *B* transaction within 1.5 s, the duration being that time from the operator's pressing the ENTER key to screen acknowledgement	Run a 'representative' set of type *B* transactions and time them in some way
The system shall be capable of operation on a computer with 64 Mb of memory	Install the system on a 64 Mb memory computer and run a 'representative' set of scenarios
The system shall give uninterrupted service despite any power outages of up to 2s in duration	Examine the specification of the UPS for the system and verify it provides such uninterrupted supply Run the system with a 'representative' set of scenarios and switch off the power during them for periods between 0 s and 2 s
Each component specification shall define the input variables, the valid range for each, ...	Read the component specification checking that the required information is supplied
The system will be ready for use by 23rd August next year	Examine the plan for the project and challenge the predicted date of 1st July next year Come 23rd August next year, see if the system is ready for use

The system shall have a failure rate not exceeding one in 10^4 demands under all conditions	Left as an exercise for the reader!
A warehouse employee shall be able to use the system without more than one fault in sixty predetermined transactions over three hours of use after two hours' tuition	Train a 'representative' set of employees and measure their performance
Every test report shall state the version of each component used in the test, ...	Read each test report and check that it states the component versions
The system shall be designed so that the addition of a new type A transaction does not require changes to existing software	Analyse the design and construction of the software to confirm this property
The system will cost less than £1.4m to develop	Examine the plan for the project and challenge the predicted total cost of £1.3m When development is complete, check the total costs
The training course in the system's use shall last no more than three hours	Examine the training course schedule and materials and verify that it is unlikely to last more than three hours Give the training course to a 'representative' set of trainees and time the course
The source code for every component shall contain a change history of the following form ...	Examine the source code for each component and verify that the change history is of the right form
The system shall be constructed so that the language of screen messages can be changed without change to procedural code	Analyse the screen handling design to verify it has this property Change the screen language to German and verify that no procedural code had to be changed

Where appropriate, I have given two quality control activities for each attribute: one that involves 'running' the product concerned, often with a 'representative' sample of scenarios, and one that uses *analysis* of the product, without 'running' it. I want to show that, in many cases, if we can demonstrate by analysis that something has an attribute then we shall have very strong evidence, but that if we check for the attribute by running the object – by 'testing' it – we shall only have sampled its behaviour, and this is much weaker. Look back at the table and see whether you agree. There is clearly a spectrum here: at one end we have activities that perhaps give complete confidence, and at the other activities that perhaps give only slight confidence.

Since we want to define a quality control activity for every product during development it makes sense to look at how the development methods we choose for each product can themselves contribute to quality control. Some methods are good in that they offer us built-in quality control opportunities. Others do not and we must then apply general quality control actions to make up for this deficiency. In Chapter 6 I shall take this a step further and look at the *verification & validation potential* of the methods that we use – the degree to which they help us verify the products – specifications, designs, code, etc. – that we produce; and in Chapter 7 we shall look briefly at some of the generic 'review' techniques that are available to us in the cases where our methods don't help much.

How much quality control?

The examples in the table above raise another question. I purposely used the weasel word 'representative' in several cases. I wanted to emphasise the problem that, when we do quality control and especially when we do traditional testing, we are often only *sampling* the attribute of the product concerned. We try a handful of cases from possible millions. We could take a big sample or a small sample – just how much is enough?

For some attributes there is no problem. For a C++ component, we might set a non-functional attribute for memory occupancy. Thus: 'the memory occupancy of the component must not exceed 2 Kb'. Such attributes are relatively easy to define, and we have a simple way of checking that the component satisfies them: compile and assemble it to measure its memory occupancy.

Conformance to the functional part of the specification is generally another matter. This problem – the major part of what is normally referred to as *verification*– is hard and in general we have no guaranteed methods of checking for perfection. We know, for instance, that we cannot in general *prove* by testing that a component conforms to its specification. Testing is only ever sampling. So, if we cannot achieve perfection, it is even more important that we define what level of checking – what level of sampling – we feel will be sufficient for our purposes.

The question to be asked by the software engineer here is 'how much testing should I do to ensure the required quality of this system (/subsystem/component/procedure)?'. But it has no simple answer. The responsibility remains with the engineer firstly to decide, at the time that the quality control operations are defined, what level of checking (i.e. testing) is deemed to be sufficient, and secondly to record that decision in the Quality Plan. Systems with a high quality requirement, in the sense that they must not fail to behave as specified, will demand more extensive and detailed testing than, perhaps, a test tool for a non-critical system. So, the questions we must ask are: How critical is the quality of this product to the overall quality of the final product? How critical is the quality of the overall product? Can the quality of this product be more cost effectively established in this way or that?

Thus, the quality required from the user interface of a test tool being developed for a project is likely to be less than that required of the final product. Central database functions in an administrative software system are likely to be more thoroughly tested than a little used and marginal report facility. Stringent user-driven quality requirements will generate stringent developer-driven quality requirements, as we saw above.

In summary, and perhaps disappointingly, there is no simple answer to the question 'how much quality control?' – it has to be answered specifically for each product on each project. Moreover, as an industry we know relatively little about the precise fault-finding power of different testing methods. In the general case it is impossible to determine it just by looking at the method itself. However, there is an increasing body of empirical evidence being collected around the industry that can be referred to for some indications. See for example (Jones 1996).

A central principle of quality control

I have had quite a lot to say about quality control and the forms it can take. In Chapter 7 we shall look in detail at the precise form that our planning for it will take. But I want to introduce a little more 'theory'. Firstly, let's stand back and look at the general notion of *quality management*. We can define one central principle for doing it.

> ## HEADLINE
> The central principle of quality management is
>> say what you'll do
>> do it
>> record that you have done it.

If we apply this to quality control we see the following.

HEADLINE

Quality control is a five step-process:

    1   define the attribute(s)

    2   define the attribute check procedure

    3   carry out the check procedure

    4   record the result

    5   take and record any corrective action.

Steps 1 and 2 are planning steps that we shall carry out before the product requires quality control operations on it – they say what we will do. In step 3 we carry out the planned actions and in step 4 we record what happened. Step 5 is vital: it closes the loop by ensuring that, if the product fails the check, the fault is traced, corrected and the corrective action is recorded as having been taken. It is all too easy to spot problems and then never quite get round to solving them and correcting the faults. Step 5 ensures that they are solved and that a trace is left to that effect.

Say what you will do, do it, record it, take any necessary actions.

1: Say what you'll do

When a project is started it will begin by doing a great deal of planning work to ensure that development takes place in an ordered fashion. Your Quality Plan will identify the products that the project will produce during development – specifications, designs, code, manuals, prototypes, etc. – and the activities that will produce them. It will then identify what quality attributes and levels are expected from all these products and what quality control actions will be taken to check that the required quality has been achieved for each.

2: Do it

For each activity in the development process, we have now defined a quality control action that we will carry out on the product of that activity to check it has the required quality attributes to the required level. When the product has been finished it is then submitted to those checks. For example:

- the System Specification is reviewed in a Structured Walkthrough using a checklist drawn from the organisation's Quality Manual, together with additional questions specific to this project

- the design is simulated to check that process interactions are correct and that overall timings meet the system requirements; it is then checked to ensure that all the system requirements have been translated into the design in some way

- the component design is checked to ensure that it satisfies the specification

- the component code is tested against the predetermined test cases, and statically analysed to check that there are no anomalous data usages

- a subsystem is constructed from components and its memory occupancy checked against the pre-set maximum

- the entire system is timed for the speed of transaction processing on a test database of predetermined size and with a predetermined set of transactions

- a novice user is given a pre-set amount of training and practice and their performance is measured to ensure the required usability of the system.

3: Record it

Once you have checked an item's quality – and taken any corrective action if it is lacking in some way – you might feel that the job is complete. It is not. It is important that you then record the results of the check and the fact that the corrective action has been taken.

The quality control record is made up of the definition of the check and the required results, the actual results in some form (paper or electronic record), and a record of any corrective action that was required. You will probably want to make sure that such records bear signatures (written or electronic) of those with the authority and responsibility. For instance, a moderator will sign off the report from a Fagan Inspection indicating that all the problems noted were satisfactorily resolved; or a team leader might sign off the record of a successful component test indicating that version 10 of component *AS123* satisfactorily passed the planned test cases and could proceed to integration.

Quality control records are important for two reasons.

Firstly, quality control actions – reviews, component tests, whatever – throw up faults. Each and every one has to be corrected. If we don't list a fault then there's considerable danger that we will forget it; as a result it never actually gets corrected and it creeps through into the next stage of development where it will be much more expensive to correct.

HEADLINE

Recording faults found and corrective actions taken is not bureaucracy – it is simply good and secure management.

Secondly, an important feature of any Quality Management System is that it is visibly being used and this in turn requires that it is auditable. That audit might be carried out by the local Quality Assurance group, who will be checking firstly whether the Quality Management System itself is working effectively, i.e. to the organisation's benefit, and secondly whether the organisation – and our project in particular – is carrying out the company's quality policy. An audit might also be done by an external assessment body with the task of checking that the conformance certificate of our Quality Management System is still justified (but more of this later in the chapter).

Quality preservation

I use the term *quality preservation* in the following sense.

DEFINITION

Quality preservation: the techniques and processes necessary to ensure that the quality of a product is not damaged by subsequent change.

We know that changing something is a good way of introducing a fault into it, as well as the change you intended to make. If I take the source of a component that I have already tested and got working correctly and I try to optimise it, I stand a very good chance of introducing faults into the code. The situation becomes worse – much worse – when we start making changes to *sets* of things at the same time. There we are, the project sailing along, the System Specification agreed, the design well under way, some early components in testing. And the client wants to change something. It means a change to the System Specification, with a knock-on into the design and some changes to components that have already been completed. We now have to make a set of changes across a number of products in a way that leaves them consistent, and we have to do this without stopping the project. The scope for introducing faults is, as we all know from experience, enormous.

Key to solving this problem is knowing what we have, knowing what state it is in, and having a process that ensures that all the consequences are followed through and the resulting new set of products still have the quality they started out with. I shall refer to this generally as *change management*, and in Chapter 8 we shall see that it has three parts – identification control, change control and configuration control – which together will allow us to preserve the quality we have so carefully established in our products.

On our project we shall therefore need to plan for the style of quality preservation appropriate to the job in hand. If the work is a small system being done by one person we can choose a change management process that provides a relatively light level of control. If we shall have 100 people working on a 2MLOC system replacing 25 legacy systems over a two-year period, we shall want something pretty robust and probably close to tyrannical to keep control.

The Quality Plan

We shall take each of the three project-level quality processes in a great deal more detail in the next three chapters. Our aim here is to understand what sorts of issues we must address when we think about the quality of our work and the final system. This is a good moment to pull the threads together to see how our Quality Plan for the project should look.

ISO 8402 defines a *Quality Plan* thus:

> **DEFINITION**
>
> *Quality Plan*: a document setting out the specific quality practices, resources and activities relevant to a particular product, process, service, contract or project.

We can be more precise.

> ## HEADLINE
>
> Our project's *Quality Plan* will describe the quality achievement, quality control and quality preservation approach that will be used in the project.

In Chapter 2 I introduced the contents list of a Risk & Quality Plan. Figure 5-1 shows the part relating to quality, and I hope that you can now see what sort of things we shall be putting in each section.

Quality assurance and Quality Management Systems

So far I have addressed quality really just from the point of view of the individual project, though we have seen that we can expect some of the standards that we shall call up on our project to come from the organisation that we belong to, and that those standards probably live in some sort of Quality Manual that itself is the description of the Quality Management System that the organisation operates. This is the right moment to pick these environmental matters a bit more closely, though I shall not return to them after this chapter.

ISO 8402 defines a Quality Management System (QMS) as follows:

> ## DEFINITIONS
>
> *Quality Management System*: the organisational structure, responsibilities, procedures, activities, capabilities and resources that together aim to ensure that products, processes or services will satisfy stated or implied needs.

A QMS is a statement by management of the strategy and tactics that will be used across the organisation to achieve the required quality in whatever is produced. It sets the framework within which our software development project will define its own approach to quality.

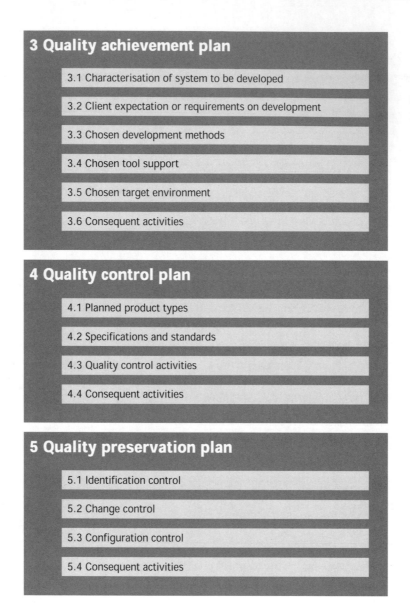

Figure 5-1. Contents list of a Quality Plan

A great deal of work has been done in industry in general and in the software engineering industry in particular to define what constitutes a QMS, and this has culminated in national and international standards for them. They are of increasing importance to software engineering organisations as many purchasers of software realise the benefits of requiring that some form of QMS has been used in the development of the software they are buying.

Perhaps the most important general standard for QMSs is the international standard ISO 9001. Because of its importance I want to look at it in some detail.

ISO 9001 covers any QMS in any industry, so its requirements need to be carefully 'interpreted' for the software engineering industry. Guidance on its use in software development is available from a further international standard ISO 9000-3, which you should have as your bible if you are planning to use ISO 9001 to steer your software development QMS.

ISO 9001 as amplified by ISO 9000-3 defines requirements for a QMS in twenty major areas:

- *Management responsibility* – the organisation must 'define and document management policy and objectives for and commitment to quality' and must 'ensure that this policy is understood, implemented and maintained at all levels in the organisation'. In particular the responsibilities of all staff who perform and verify work affecting quality have to be defined, and the senior management must systematically review the operation of the QMS to ensure it remains suitable and effective.

- *Quality system* – this is where the standard calls for a quality plan for a project. The requirements listed are covered largely by the Quality Plan I shall describe.

- *Contract review* – this is included to ensure that a contract (in our case to produce a software system) starts out with a mutually agreed set of requirements for the system and that the developer is capable of delivering it to the purchaser. Without these safeguards, all else is futile!

- *Design control* – the standard requires that the developer has and uses procedures to control and verify the quality of the design of the system to ensure it meets its requirements. These procedures should cover planning, identification of the inputs to the design process, identifying what form the design should take and what properties it should have, the verification of the design against the requirements, and how changes in the design will be handled. ISO 9000-3 lists a number of areas that should be addressed according to context, and you will find that our Quality Plan will again largely cover the requirements of the standard.

- *Document and data control* – this is an especially important area for software development where so much of what is produced takes the form of documents or data in some form: specifications, designs, code, test data, etc. ISO 9001 calls for procedures for document approval and issue, and for the handling of changes. Control of all these generally comes under the heading of 'configuration management', 'change management', 'configuration control' , 'change control' or some other rearrangement of thcsc words – I usc the term *change management* to cover the topic, and deal with it in more detail in Chapter 8, where we look at planning for quality preservation.

- *Purchasing* – this section of the standard requires procedures for the verification, storage and maintenance of bought-in items. It's increasingly common for third party software to be included in a delivered system, and for that third party to issue a stream of new versions, part updates, corrections and the like – we need to ensure that we have ways of handling these properly so that the right version is included in the system we release to our client. So, if you plan to incorporate someone else's software or work in your own system you need to consider the assessment of your subcontractors' and suppliers' ability to meet quality requirements, what records should be kept about purchased items, and the verification that bought-in items satisfy the requirements on them.

- *Control of customer-supplied product* – the standard says that, even if your customer has supplied you with some software that you will integrate into their final system, this does not absolve you from establishing the quality of that software for yourself.

- *Product identification and traceability* – this has always been an important issue for software developers who, like other engineers, build their systems from many small components. Again, I shall deal with this under *change management*.

- *Process control* – this is a general requirement that the production process itself be planned and monitored. ISO 9000-3 'interprets' this to cover the replication, delivery and installation of software.

- *Inspection and testing* – the standard requires that inspection and testing should take place during the development process, on the completed system before it is delivered for use, and on bought-in items before they are incorporated. It also requires here, as in most other areas, that records be kept of the results of tests. This will be entirely covered by the quality control part of our Quality Plan.

- *Control of inspection, measuring and test equipment* – 'equipment' here means software tools in particular. These must themselves be properly controlled with respect to quality, version, etc.

- *Inspection and test status* – so that the quality of all items at all stages of their development should be clearly known, the standard requires that their test status should be shown in some way at all times. As examples, the design specification of a system should say whether or not it has been reviewed or is only at draft status; a code component should say whether it has been successfully compiled, has passed its tests successfully, or has been frozen as 'definitive' for integration purposes, and so on.

- *Control of nonconforming product* – this is a requirement that items that do not meet their requirements cannot be used inadvertently. The state of products should be determinable from quality control records – our quality preservation plan will largely cover this.

- *Corrective and preventive action* – if a fault is found in an item when a quality control check is carried out on it there are two things that must be done: firstly the fault must be removed from the item, and secondly the processes involved in its production need to be checked to see if they should be changed to avoid such a fault appearing in future items of that type.

- *Handling, storage, packaging, preservation and delivery* – again, this is not obviously of concern to the software engineer but an organisation that makes and sells a software product will need to consider its procedures for replicating the software reliably, for ensuring that the correct versions are reaching the correct buyers, that media – especially those with the product on them – are correctly stored to prevent corruption, and so on. Virus checking is part of this.

- *Control of quality records* – here the standard requires the developer to ensure that sufficient records are maintained to demonstrate that the required quality has been achieved and that the QMS is itself operating effectively. The first requirement effectively says that – as far as the purchaser is concerned – unrecorded quality actions never took place; the second requirement ensures that a poor QMS is not followed, lest it become a potential cause of poor quality itself.

- *Internal quality audits* – this continues the theme that the QMS itself must be subjected to review to maintain its effectiveness, and requires a system of quality audits whose findings are followed up and reported to management.

- *Training* – if staff are not adequately trained to do their jobs it is unlikely that their work will be of the necessary quality. This requirement covers the identification of training needs and the training itself.

- *Servicing* – an area that must be subject to the same care as production itself. ISO 9000-3 points us at plans and records for the maintenance and support of our system.

- *Statistical techniques* – the developer is required to 'establish, where appropriate, procedures for identifying adequate statistical techniques required for verifying the acceptability of product characteristics'. Because, as we shall see further in Chapter 10, measurement is a very difficult area for software development, ISO 9000-3 is reticent about saying more than that statistical techniques 'may be used'.

It should be clear from this short coverage of the ISO 9001 standard for QMSs that, taken seriously, quality requires investment and commitment from the software developer and management. Perhaps more importantly, nothing that it addresses is likely to be irrelevant to an organisation that takes software development seriously. The challenge is simple: if you think that one of the above areas is irrelevant, what would be the consequences if you did nothing at all about it?

> **HEADLINE**
>
> ISO 9001 and ISO 9000-3 provide a thorough basis for an organisation to build a relevant and value-adding Quality Management System.

QMS certification

As in many areas of standardisation, the effectiveness of a standard for QMSs comes from the existence of independent bodies that can certify that a given supplier's QMS conforms to the standard: so-called *certification*. Each country has its own certification bodies accredited to assess QMSs and issue certificates of conformance. Certification generally requires that the QMS is examined against the standard by independent assessors, and that it is observed to be running effectively over a reasonable period – having a system is not enough: it must be in use and be shown to be effective.

Once a certificate of conformance has been issued, the certification body will make periodic checks to ensure that the QMS remains in force and remains effective. Such a check done by a certification body in the UK can result in the assessors making *observations*, or noting *minor discrepancies* or *major discrepancies*. Major discrepancies are raised if the QMS or its operation is in some way sufficiently nonconformant to require withdrawal of the certificate unless immediate action is taken to remedy the situation. A minor discrepancy requires the organisation to take corrective action before, say, the next visit of the assessor. An observation is precisely that – an observation.

This constant and independent assessment of an organisation's QMS and its operation gives the certificate of conformance a strength that is important to those buying from the organisation. It engenders greater confidence in the latter's commitment to quality. But it is worth sounding a cautionary note here. An ISO 9001-certified QMS does not itself guarantee quality, nor does the possession of an ISO 9001-certified QMS allow an organisation to claim any particular quality in its products. Buy the car with the best safety record on the market and you can still drive it like an idiot. A bad driver can pass a driving test.

The QMS is a means that still has to be used. Moreover, a QMS is typically a prescriptive thing, telling developers what steps they must take to satisfy the organisation's policy on quality. The standards forming the Quality Manual should, if they are to be effective and testable, be prescriptive, and this can be counterproductive if certain measures are not taken. The system must be used, and used constructively. Following it by rote without an understanding of what it is trying to achieve may not produce any improvement in quality. This is a problem of attitude and culture, rather than a technical problem. In my consultancy work I am used to finding organisations for whom their QMS is an irritating appendage. It is always a cause for wonder that they persevere with this self-inflicted inefficiency rather than making it an asset.

All this is obvious, but it tells us that if we aspire to an ISO 9001 certificate for our QMS *and we want to get some real benefit from the achievement it represents* then we must live the spirit of the standard as much as the wording. It must be used in the spirit in which ISO 9001 is intended. In particular, that means not treating it as something that is simply tacked onto daily life, or as a bureaucratic ordeal. The sort of QMS I am thinking about is a QMS that is effective in promoting the business's effectiveness.

I once visited a large organisation that was well into a major Total Quality Management (TQM) programme. I had been invited to spend a day addressing about thirty of their IT delivery managers on the topic of ISO 9001 QMSs. I took on the assignment with some trepidation since, at the time, I felt rather apologetic about our rather traditional QMS when in the company of people in the midst of exciting TQM programmes, even though I had real evidence that 'quality' had a real meaning in Praxis and with our staff. ISO 9001 has this reputation of being a recipe for bureaucracy and the stifling of innovation – allegedly quite the reverse of TQM with its emphasis on innovation. Nevertheless, I prepared my one-day seminar.

At the end of the day, I was interested by the comments from the people who came. The gist of their feedback was that a QMS was just the thing they needed in their TQM programme. So far they had only heard a great deal of exhortations to measure, to control, to improve; they had received training in team building, process analysis, cause–effect graphing and all the paraphernalia of TQM, but they did not know what to do next (or even first). Some people had indeed started measuring things and putting graphs up at their desks, but when it came down to it, they had no foundations on which to build. They recognised that the real point of a QMS was that it could act as the focus they lacked.

HEADLINE

A QMS is a repository for everything we as a group agree is essential to achieving quality in the software we deliver to our clients; it is something to bring cohesion and hence lasting benefit to our organisation.

This 'repository' aspect of a QMS is one I want to draw attention to. Our QMS at Praxis was the major repository of our process, at least in so far as we wanted to capture that process in terms of process descriptions, as opposed to, say, training courses or in-house or purchased tools. It was also 'our' repository: it was originally developed by our engineers and it was maintained by our engineers, with an internal quality assurance team having editorial responsibility for it. It evolved year on year as the business evolved and technology changed. It proved to be one of the most enduring and unifying features of the company.

Interestingly, when I look back at the order in which we developed our QMS I find it ran roughly as follows:

1   have a standard format for documents and a standard approach to version control

2   have a standard way of peer reviewing anything and of closing faults, and start applying it to everything

3   institute a project-oriented approach under which all work is managed

4   have a standard approach to the planning and reporting of projects

5   start to define common technical processes and put in place standards for the products of those processes

6   concentrate on managing requirements.

This will look very familiar to anyone who has investigated the SEI's *Capability Maturity Model* (CMM, Paulk *et al* (1993)). It bears a very close resemblance to the order in which one ought to be doing things to lift oneself from level 1 in the CMM to (round about) level 3. It is about getting projects under basic control before worrying about technical issues. I once had discussions with a client who wanted to introduce quality-oriented practices into his IS department, was aware of the requirements of ISO 9001, and had been reading a lot about measurement. His brain was spinning from all the ideas that had been presented to him. I led him through CMM levels 2 and 3 and showed him how we had gone through that same foundation-laying and then up through the building, floor by floor. In particular, I could demonstrate to him why his uncertainty about measurement in an organisation with an *ad hoc* development process was making his brain spin; it was totally premature to think about process measurement when he did not have any defined processes in place.

The CMM gives us a good plan of action for achieving ISO 9001 certification starting from an *ad hoc* process, and ISO 9001 provides us with the notion of a Quality Management System, which reinforces the notion of the 'process asset repository' and gives us a framework for building our process capability. The two notions neatly support each other (I rather wish we had had the progression defined by the CMM when we started our QMS development). Establishing good software engineering practice by building through levels 2 and 3 will generate a QMS (whether or not we choose to call it that) and should, I assert, lead to an ISO 9001 certificate for that QMS. There are some pluses and minuses in each scheme but my point here is that the CMM and ISO 9001 are not alternatives from which one must be chosen. This is not a book on the CMM and you should be sure to read the authoritative texts on it.

ISO 9001's requirement that there should be an auditable trail showing that the plan–do–check–act cycle has been carried out is often turned inside out and portrayed as a demand for unnecessary bureaucracy. Those who run an ISO 9001 QMS properly – in other words *in a way that is appropriate for their business* – know that the only records you keep are those you need anyway for good quality management. It is hard to convince people who have seen or experienced an ineffective, bureaucratic QMS that bureaucracy is not a must-have of ISO 9001. In the Praxis QMS, because we had a wide variety of work for different clients on different architectures for different sorts of systems, we devolved engineering decisions about the development process to individual development projects and this extended to the choice of quality controls and records for the project. This was not a carte blanche to say 'we are not bothering' since the Quality Plan for the project had to be produced and had to be approved by management as appropriate for the job in hand. The rule for project managers is then simple: 'if you are doing something that you think does not add value to the engineering of quality into this system then you have only yourself to blame'. ISO 9001 does not require us to do things that do not make sense for our business. It does not prescribe bureaucratic processes, only areas that an organisation must address in some way, and it leaves how they should be addressed to the organisation.

Chapter recap

Quality is the totality of features and characteristics of a product that bear on its ability to satisfy stated or implied needs. Quality attributes must be defined in a way that allows their presence to be checked.

Quality achievement is how we build the quality in.

Quality control is how we check that quality has been built in. We can view quality control in the general case as a five-step process:

- define the quality attribute(s) and level(s)

- define the attribute check procedure

- carry out the check procedure

- record the result

- take and record any corrective action taken.

Quality preservation is how we make sure that the quality stays in, despite any changes we make.

Our Quality Plan assembles our strategy for each of these areas. It sits in a corporate framework of the organisation's QMS, which itself may be certificated to ISO 9001 as amplified by ISO 9000-3. See Figure 5-2.

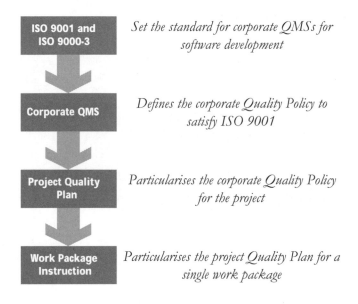

ISO 9001 and ISO 9000-3 — *Set the standard for corporate QMSs for software development*

Corporate QMS — *Defines the corporate Quality Policy to satisfy ISO 9001*

Project Quality Plan — *Particularises the corporate Quality Policy for the project*

Work Package Instruction — *Particularises the project Quality Plan for a single work package*

Figure 5-2. The quality hierarchy

Quality assurance is that aspect of the overall management function that determines and implements the overall quality intentions and objectives of the organisation as formally expressed by senior management. The corporate quality assurance policy sets the framework within which each software development team defines and carries out quality control activities. The policy is generally implemented in the form of a QMS and is normally described in a corporate Quality Manual. The accepted standard for QMSs is ISO 9001.

References

Flowers 1996

Software Failure: Management Failure. S Flowers. Wiley, Chichester, 1996

Gilb 1987

Design by Objectives. T Gilb. North-Holland, 1987

ISO 8402

ISO 8402: *Quality assurance – Vocabulary*

ISO 9001

ISO 9001: *Quality systems – Assurance model for design/development, production, installation, and servicing capability*

ISO 9126

ISO/IEC DIS 9126 : *Information technology – Software product evaluation – Quality characteristics and guidelines for their use.* 1990

Jones 1996

Software Quality – Analysis and Guidelines for Success. C Jones. International Thomson Computer Press, 1996

Paulk *et al* 1993

Capability Maturity Model for Software, Version 1.1. Mark Paulk *et al.* Software Engineering Institute, Carnegie Mellon University, report CMU/SEI-93-TR-24, 1993

6 Rivets or welding? Planning for quality achievement

Introduction

Quality achievement is about *methods*. It is about how we engineer quality into something, such as a design, during its production. Within any organisation there is a need for a common framework for software development within which different development approaches, methods and tools can be viewed. Approach, methods and tools must always be chosen to match the needs of the project in hand.

The purposes of this chapter are therefore

- to examine what makes a 'good' method

- to describe how to differentiate between different development methods in terms of their *computational models*

- to give you criteria for choosing the most appropriate methods for the problem in hand

- to illustrate how different methods and standards can be used to produce the different development layers.

What makes a 'good' method?

Not surprisingly, after the unrelenting emphasis in the preceding chapter on the notion of quality being synonymous with fitness for purpose, we shall expect to call a method 'good' if it too is fit for purpose, namely for producing a particular product such as a component test, or an Ada package, or a system specification, or whatever. But first, let's define what we mean by a 'method', a term I have bandied around without a clear definition so far. (I shall not distinguish in this book between a *method* and a *technique*. I prefer *method* in this context as it suggests 'contrivance' and the use of intelligence, while *technique* is what you have when you do something mechanically – you can have great piano technique but produce poor results. Equally, I shall not use the word *procedure*, which suggests something done by numbers: 1: do *A*, 2: do *B*, …)

DEFINITION

A method is a way of producing a product that

1   is defined

2   takes inputs

3   uses a notation and a syntax

4   offers heuristics for generating products in the notation

5   offers ways of analysing or verifying the resulting products.

So, a method – let's call it *M* – must first of all be *defined*. In other words, it had better be written down somewhere, not least so that I can pass it on to others, or train them in its use, or do it together with them.

Secondly, *M* will take certain *inputs*, perhaps the results of some other method. A coding method will take as input a component specification and perhaps a standard for the language concerned. A method for preparing a system specification will take as input the views of the intended users.

A method may be quite complex in that it consists of a network of steps that together yield the result and each step will then use its own method. Where I need to, I shall refer to the methods in the component steps as *sub-methods*.

I now want to look at topics 3, 4 and 5 in more detail and give some examples. (Please remember that this is not a book on software engineering methods, only on choosing them. However, to illustrate the ideas I shall outline how a number of methods work; you will need to go to the relevant literature for detail on using the methods concerned.)

Notation

My method M will give me a way of describing my output, a *notation* for my product. That notation might be one based on words, or mathematics, or certain sorts of pictures. And being a good notation it will have a syntax which allows me to ensure that the things I produce are (in the mathematical jargon) *well formed*. For instance, M might be 'data flow modelling' as a method for specifying the design of a system. In this case M is certainly defined – there are plenty of text books on the topic. Its notation is graphical and uses different blobs for activities, external entities and data stores, and arrows for data flows. Within the syntax there are 'rules' that say, for instance, that each data flow arrow must start at a blob and finish at another blob – you can't have data flows starting from nowhere or going nowhere.

The notation my method M uses is perhaps its most important feature. Its attributes determine many of the attributes of the method. Some methods use notations that are highly abstract – typically those that are mathematically based – while others have notations that are somewhat world-related or even strongly world-related. Each has its own degree of *worldliness*, something we need to consider as it will have a considerable effect on the usability of the method both by our staff and, where it's appropriate, by our customer.

EXAMPLES

Set theory as used in VDM is very abstract and not directly related to real-world things – some interpretation or translation is required.

The control and data flows of IDEF0 are somewhat abstract but model things in the real world to a degree.

The entity-attribute modelling of data modelling is closely related to real-world objects.

The *relevance* of a notation rests on how suited it is to capturing and representing the important issues. Some notations allow us to represent a restricted set of things; others allow us to say a great many things. How much we can say is often directly proportional to the worldliness of the notation. We can say many varied things in set theoretical terms if we are prepared to build a superstructure that connects the few abstractions of set theory to real-world ideas. Notations such as those within the UML (Unified Modeling Language) (Fowler 1997) allow us to represent certain things but they are the things that (in a certain context) are precisely what we want to talk about.

This question of relevance is central to our planning: it's the whole question of how we will get that screw to hold those two pieces of wood together: should we be using the spanner, the hammer or the screwdriver?

Notations also vary in the degree of *formality* with which their syntax and semantics are defined. When we step up to the white-board with the marker pen in our hand and start drawing blobs and boxes and lines and clouds for our design, we often start out doing a sort of graphical arm-waving, not applying any rules to how we draw the diagram (its syntax), or ascribing any clear meaning to the blobs, or arrows, or boxes of different shapes (its semantics). But if we draw a diagram with no defined syntax we will find it hard to verify that it says something meaningful. And if our diagram has no defined semantics we won't be able to verify that its meaning (assuming it is syntactically correct) is the one we wanted to express.

> ## HEADLINE
>
> A method's notation can be anything from arm-waving (with no defined syntax or semantics), through natural language (with very complex syntax and semantics), diagrams (with generally a small but defined syntax, and often no defined semantics), working models (with very varied syntax and semantics), and languages (with a generally small but well-defined syntax and semantics), to mathematics (with well-defined syntax and semantics of varying size).

It's immediately tempting to see that as the 'semantic content' or strength of a method's notation increases so does the 'V&V potential' of the method: the more you can read from something, the more you can check.

Heuristics

The fourth thing we shall look for in our method M is that it should offer some ways of producing the product – we have the language, how do we decide what to say? Now, we can't expect any method to work 'automatically' – we don't expect to just switch it on and have it generate a data flow diagram (DFD) automatically. This is where we as designers add the intellectual content and our experience. But any good text on DFDs will suggest ways of collecting data, structuring layers of DFDs, getting the right amount of detail at any one level, using a companion entity model as a basis for defining the data flows, and so on. These *method heuristics* are not guaranteed means of getting the untrained to produce high quality DFDs, but they do give us guidance and they embody collected experience.

> ## HEADLINE
>
> The heuristics for a method can range from strong ('for each box at level 2, define the ...'), through advisory ('in situation X it is often useful to ...'), to unstated ('you're on your own').

The strength of the heuristics affects the degree of creativity required from the person using the method: if a heuristic is strong, less thought and creativity are required from us to achieve a correct product (i.e. one that satisfies the quality criteria set for it); if a heuristic is weak then the method relies more on our creativity and skill to make the transformation from input to output. Was it one of the design aims of SSADM that it should be usable by less skilled staff than have traditionally been required? Certainly, SSADM breaks down the development process into many small steps, each of which can be prescribed in some detail. Also, as time goes by and experience with a method is gained, the heuristics for a method accumulate, as that experience shows that certain ways of going about the creative part prove to be more successful than others. These accumulated heuristics reduce the need for creativity on the part of the practitioner.

This is important. The more likely a method is to give 'correct' results if we follow it, the more valuable it will be to us.

> ## DEFINITION
>
> We can define the *correctness potential* of a method as the likelihood that its heuristics yield a correct product before verification and fault correction, and assuming the practitioner follows them correctly.

If I have to devise a sort routine, will I be more likely to get a program that works first time using Z or VDM? If I have to design a system to support an invoicing process, will I be better following a certain subset of SSADM or Gane and Sarson? If I have to code a statistical package, will I be better off using FORTRAN or Ada?

All things being equal, we would prefer methods with high correctness potential as they will reduce rework costs. But we might suspect that, in general, high correctness potential does not come free – there will be a price to pay, and we must always decide whether it is one we want to pay.

Analysis approaches

Finally and very importantly, will our method M give us ways of checking the quality of the things we produce? What questions can we ask of our DFDs? What checks can we make to ensure they are self-consistent?

Analysis approaches can range from strong ('construct the following proof obligations and carry out the proofs…'), through firm ('check that the diagrams are consistent according to the following criteria …'), to weak ('read the output through and see if it looks OK'). Strong approaches require less creativity from the practitioner (though they might require specialist skills, such as theorem proving). If an approach is to be amenable to mechanical checking, either by a machine or by practitioners following a cookbook, it needs to be stronger rather than weaker. To complement the correctness potential of a method we can therefore define its *verification and validation potential* or *V&V potential*.

DEFINITION

The *V&V potential* of a method is the degree to which its analysis approaches explicitly help us to find all the faults.

The power of the analysis approaches depends largely on how formally the syntax and semantics of the notation are defined. Let's take some examples.

If we write some Pascal, or Java, or C++ we can check – thanks to the formal syntax of the language – whether we have written a program, i.e. something with meaning; moreover, this can be done mechanically with a compiler. If we have formally defined semantics for the language we can decide what the meaning of the program is for given inputs, i.e. what it will do. But to check whether a given Pascal program is *correct* (i.e. it satisfies a specification) requires us to generate theorems whose truth would establish the program's correctness, and to do this we shall have to restrict ourselves to writing programs in a subset of Pascal and we shall have to add 'assertions' at various parts of the code to help things along; even then we would not be able to get those theorems proved mechanically, by a piece of software.

Suppose we decide to do data flow analysis as part of the design of our system and we draw DFDs. We can define a formal syntax for DFDs and use it to check (or more likely enforce with a tool) that only meaningful DFDs are drawn. Then we can define semantics for DFDs which will allow them to be animated by software to a degree so that validation ('does this look right?') can be done. Such an animation tool would show data flowing around some representation of the system, from activity to activity.

If we design our system in terms of a finite state machine (FSM) we can verify the design *totally* for defensiveness; in other words we can check that the design has a defined response for every possible event in every state. The verification of this attribute is total.

If we define the behaviour of our system in response to sequences of events using an FSM we can validate it partially – but, in a useful sense, exhaustively – against user expectations of its behaviour: we can mechanically derive a 'cover set' of finite event sequences and then eye-ball the behaviour of the system in response to those sequences.

If we write a program so that it is Dijkstra-structured (in particular without *goto*s) we will find it easier to reason about it than about one that is spaghetti. Moreover, we'll find it easier to derive test cases that achieve the various levels of test coverage.

In Chapter 7 we shall look at the concept of V&V potential in more detail.

HEADLINE

Formal methods such as VDM have strong V&V potential – the use of proof obligations in a VDM refinement guarantees the correctness of the refinement (assuming the correctness of the proof!).

Methods such as ER modelling have medium strength V&V potential – they give us some help in verifying what we produce by using them.

Methods such as 'making it up as you go along' have no V&V potential at all – they give us no help in checking the result.

In summary, when we use a method, the likelihood that the end-product is correct depends on four things, brought together in Figure 6-1:

- the *correctness of its inputs*: garbage in, garbage out; but a good method could help us ensure that faults are not propagated

- the *correctness potential* of the method: the likelihood that, by using its heuristics, we shall get a correct product before we do any verification and fault correction

- the *V&V potential* of the method: the degree to which the analysis approaches offered by the method help us find all faults

- our *competence* in carrying out the heuristics and analysis approaches of the method.

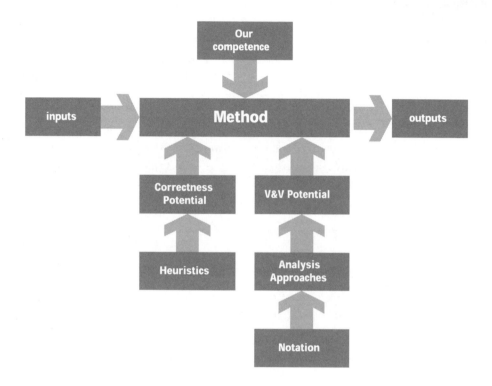

Figure 6-1. The parts of a method

Computational models

In an ideal world the three development layers that I introduced in Chapter 4 – User Layer, Architecture Layer and Implementation Layer – would be in a simple one-to-one relationship, making building systems a straightforward matter of refinement from start to end. Unfortunately, they rarely are, something due not least to the shortcomings of our target infrastructures: hardware, operating systems, databases, languages, compilers and so on. There is a *structure clash* (in Jackson's terms; Jackson 1975) between the structure of the real world and the structure of the target environment on which we build systems. The need for different development layers reflects this structure clash.

In the future I believe we should aim to use methods that reduce the number of different transformations we go through from problem statement to problem solution. This will mean using target environments onto which we can more easily map the structure of the real world and development methods that handle the structure clashes effectively when they are necessary. Also, it is frequently the case that an implementation that models the real world exactly (the ideal situation) or even closely would not have the necessary performance characteristics and it becomes necessary to transform the ideal structure into a structure that does.

We can be sure that all methods have at some time been inappropriately used, in other words used on systems where they simply 'weren't right'. When this happens the developers spend time trying to force square pegs into round holes: either they try to mangle the problem to make it fit the method, or mangle the method to make it 'work' on the problem. Neither of these is a very satisfactory approach to software development. Either results in a poor system and/or a bad reputation for the method – with one development team at least. I think that this mismatch can come about because the people choosing the method haven't looked at what I shall call the *computational model* of the method and compared it with the characteristics of the problem they are solving. (My thanks go to Clive Roberts for introducing me to this term.)

In simple terms we can think of a computational model of a method as being

- the *units of decomposition* that the model uses

- the sorts of *relationships* that the model defines between those units.

Let's take some examples.

The object-oriented computational model

If you are developing a system using object-oriented principles, in particular an object-oriented programming language (see, for instance, (Coad 1993)), then the computational model is the object-oriented model. In this model, at run-time, objects are created and have an existence of their own. And to make things happen they interact by passing messages to each other: 'redraw yourself in the current window', 'tell me how many items you contain', 'divide into three equal parts', or whatever.

In other words, the computational model is one in which independent objects, each containing its own private data, pass messages to each other, and in which there is no global data. This is quite different from the situation with a traditional procedural language where the computational model equivalent is one where functions (procedures, etc.) call one another, where global data (shared memory or files) is often used for inter-procedural communications, and where code and data are separate and there is a very loose connection between the two.

The computational model used by most object-oriented programming languages decomposes the world into class instances whose relationships are based on message passing, such as the UML's *interaction diagrams:* Figure 6-2 shows objects (dark boxes), their lifetimes falling vertically, and messages passing between them, sometimes iterated, sometimes conditional. Such a model concentrates on the data flow of the world, in particular which messages pass between object instances and thereby 'activate' each other. The model therefore also contributes to the understanding of the control structure of the world: which things activate which other things.

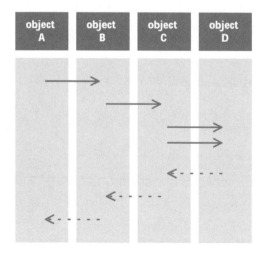

Figure 6-2. The UML's sequence diagrams

The computational model of object-oriented specification and design decomposes the world into classes and subclasses, with their methods and properties, related by specialisation and property classes (see the UML's *class diagrams* as an example). Such a model concentrates on the static structure, essentially of the data of the world. Figure 6-3 suggests the simplest form of class hierarchy where class *A* has three subclasses *A1*, *A2* and *A3*, the last having two subclasses of its own, *A3a* and *A3b*. Other notations in the UML capture further relationships between classes (see Fowler 1997, for instance).

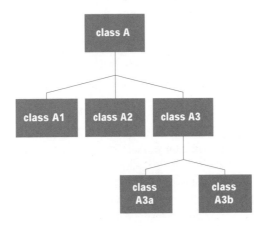

Figure 6-3. A simple class hierarchy

The computational model of JSP

The computational model that underlies JSP (Jackson Structured Programming (Jackson 1975)) is quite different. Here, our computational model shows the structure of a data item. Jackson uses this to posit that the structure of a program should be based on the structure of the data that it is processing. To over-simplify, the input data that is processed by a program can be defined in terms of a grammar that allows sequence, selection and iteration of data items.

For instance, data coming into a program that processes transactions at a cash dispenser might have the format

> opening transaction from the dispenser *then*
>
> {transaction from users of the dispenser} *then*
>
> closing transaction from the dispenser

where the curly brackets represent repetition (i.e. *iteration*). The *then*s (traditionally replaced by semicolons) represent *sequence*. A transaction from a user would itself have the structure

> carry out identification *then*
>
> [funds transfer *or* cash withdrawal *or* balance enquiry]

where the square brackets contain options (i.e. *selection*). (For simplicity, in this example we assume that only one of the three options can be exercised by the customer in any given transaction.) A funds transfer would itself have a structure:

> specify account to be debited *then*
> specify account to be credited *then*
> specify amount to be transferred

So we could describe the incoming data with a grammar thus:

> opening transaction from the dispenser
> *then*
> *repeat* until no more
>> transaction from users of the dispenser *i.e.*
>>> identification of user
>>> *then*
>>> funds transfer *i.e.*
>>>> number of account to be debited *then*
>>>> number of account to be credited *then*
>>>> amount to be transferred
>>> *or* cash withdrawal
>>>> …
>>> *or* balance enquiry
> *end repeat*
> *then*
> closing transaction from the dispenser

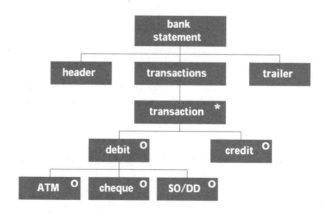

Figure 6-4. A simple JSP structure diagram

It only takes a little imagination to see how this can be turned directly into a program with the same logic. (Clearly, I have simplified away issues such as multiple input streams, error handling etc., but the principle remains the same.) The computational model of a JSP-designed program shows how the components of a data structure are related by sequence, selection and iteration. Figure 6-4 shows a JSP structure diagram as we might draw it showing the structure of a bank statement: the asterisk indicates an iterated data item and the circles denote optional data items.

The computational model of MASCOT

Let's take an example at the design level. If you are using the MASCOT method for the design of real-time systems (JIMCOM 1987) then you will design your system as a number of asynchronous communicating processes. Communication between processes is achieved through two sorts of data pipe: a *channel* which is a buffered queue, or a *pool* which is a simple global data area.

For each channel and pool you define *access mechanisms* that handle potentially asynchronous access by independent processes. To support your MASCOT design you can use a MASCOT kernel that supports a set of pre-defined primitive operations on which you build your communications and synchronisation as necessary.

In summary, we can see that the computational model of MASCOT has processes and datastores as the units of decomposition and their relationships are about data flow. So MASCOT concentrates on the flow of data around the world. Additionally, because of the access mechanisms defined for the datastores, MASCOT tells us about the dynamics of the control side of the world. This is quite a different scheme from the computational model used in Ada, where inter-process communication is synchronous and quite a different architecture results. The design ideas underlying MASCOT and Ada have different computational models. Attempting to build a MASCOT design on Ada requires a certain amount of contortion to make things fit – something that is very undesirable.

The computational model of entity life histories (ELHs)

When we draw an ELH for an entity we identify the 'grammar' of the states through which it can pass during its lifetime, just as JSP defined a data structure in terms of a grammar of smaller data items. Figure 6-5 shows the life history of the entity *bank account* in terms of the states through which it can pass (small circles and asterisks have the same meaning as for JSP structure diagrams).

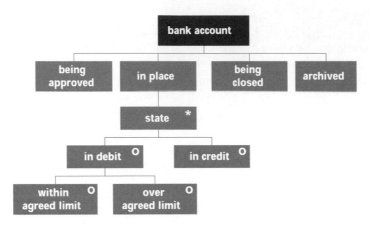

Figure 6-5. A simple entity life history

The ELH has nothing to say about *control* but it does tell us about the dynamics, over time, of our data. In real terms, we can expect events in the real world – certain actions by the holder of the bank account in the example of Figure 6-5, for example – to move the account from state to state.

The computational model of JSD

A related method is JSD (Jackson System Development; Jackson 1983, LBMS 1992). The principle is similar to that of the ELH. For each entity instance in the real world – take a particular bank account again – a process in the system tracks its history. A bank account is opened, undergoes a number of transactions, and is closed. A process in the system tracks each account's status as real-world events occur to it. Such processes are called *model processes* and they can communicate with one another in reflection of such communication between the real-world objects.

Into this real-world model we now insert new processes – *functional processes* – that generate outputs from the model. The overall computational model here is one of a network of cooperating processes, each of which has a status reflecting that of something in the real world or which uses that status information to produce outputs.

The computational model of Petri Nets

For something completely different let us look at the Petri Net (Peterson 1981), a model that captures concurrency in the world. See Figure 6-6 for an example of the basic form of Petri Net.

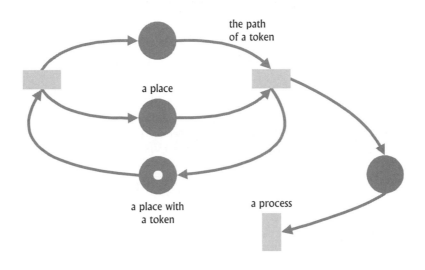

Figure 6-6. A simple Petri Net

Each rectangle represents a process, and each arrow represents the occurrence of an event detected by the process found at the beginning of the arrow. When a process completes, it places a 'token' in the 'place' (circle) on each of its outgoing arrows. As soon as the place on each incoming arrow to a process has a token in it, that process can be activated and all those incoming tokens are deleted (they are 'absorbed' by the process). Such a model can be 'run', and one can watch the tokens moving around and the processes firing as they do. (Strictly, in Petri Nets the processes appear as 'transitions' as they actually represent the transition of the net from one state (i.e. set of token positions) to another.)

Here, in abstract terms, the world is being decomposed into transitions that are related by their 'firing sets' of places. Closer to the real world, we can see that a Petri Net can capture the control dynamics of the world, showing us what causes what process to be activated. Note that the model has nothing to say about the data in the world, only on what conditions control is passed around between potentially concurrent processes.

The computational model of VDM

Finally, let's take an example from the specification area. If you specify a system using VDM (Jones 1986) you specify it in terms of a *state* – generally expressed in terms of sets of data elements and their values – and a set of *operations* that can act on the state and change it. Thus, a library system might be defined as a state consisting of the set of books (characterised by their titles and accession numbers, say), a set of borrowers (characterised by their names and addresses, and the number of books they are allowed on loan at any one time) and a set of borrowing relations between books and borrowers. Operations on the state such as *borrower X borrows book Y* cause changes on the state – in this case a change in the relationships between books and borrowers.

Before specifying a system with a method like this we would want to be sure that this computational model (operations on a state) was an appropriate one. I was once involved in a system in which we wanted to specify that an airborne system had carried out a certain set of manoeuvres on a given mission. This was tried in VDM but became unwieldy because VDM does not easily support the idea of 'journal' or a record of change over time – a notion that was crucial for what we wanted to describe when we defined this system.

Understanding the computational model implicit in the methods you are using is absolutely key if you are going to choose the best methods for your problem.

Views of a system

Let's stand back from this for a moment. When we define or describe or construct a software system we are building a model. A model concerns itself with some aspects of the thing it is modelling and not with others. A model of a building built to sell the plans to a buyer will concentrate on capturing the building's aesthetic qualities, showing how brilliantly it will fit in the existing cityscape, and suggesting a bold statement about the buyer's place in this world. A model of the same building constructed to analyse how well that design will stand up to an earthquake or to high winds will not be in the final colours that the buyer was so interested in.

When we specify or design a software system we will want to concentrate on those aspects that are the most important to us as modellers. If the performance of the system is critical, our design models had better allow us to represent and measure the performance properties of our design. If the safety properties are important then we had better have ways of expressing and establishing the presence (or otherwise) of those properties. If the integrity of data or its distribution is important then those aspects must be brought out by the methods we use. And so on.

Now, at a general level, a software system can be defined in terms of its data structures and its control structures. We can take static and dynamic views of each of these. Static views show the fixed aspects of the structure of the data or control. Dynamic views show how the data and control structures change in time or in place.

We thereby end up with six different viewpoints that we can take when looking at the different development layers. Each of these viewpoints is served by a number of different methods, as suggested in Figure 6-7.

In particular we can see that:

- JSP describes the static structure of data

- an entity–relationship model (ER model) shows the static relationships of one data entity to another

- an entity life history (ELH) shows how data (an entity) changes over time

- Z and VDM capture how the system state is affected by operations on it

- a data flow diagram (DFD) captures the movement of data around a group of processes but does not show the logic (i.e. when movement or processing happens) – extensions such as those devised by Ward and Mellor (Ward 1986) add this to simple DFDs

- an Activity–Channel–Pool diagram (ACP diagram) used in MASCOT shows the movement of data between different locations and the way that control flow is affected by the data flow

- a module calling hierarchy shows the static (i.e. coded) interrelationships between the modules in a program – what calls what, but not when

- a Petri Net shows how concurrent control moves around a network over time (i.e. the where) and the logic of that network, and captures the logic (i.e. the when)

- a Finite State Machine (or state transition diagram) shows how control changes on events (in particular the movement from state to state according to input)

- the formal methods CSP and CCS capture the flow of control between networks of connected, parallel processes

- the various modelling approaches in the UML – class diagrams, interaction diagrams etc. – address aspects across the matrix.

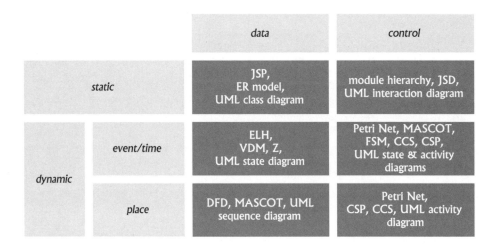

		data	control
static		JSP, ER model, UML class diagram	module hierarchy, JSD, UML interaction diagram
dynamic	event/time	ELH, VDM, Z, UML state diagram	Petri Net, MASCOT, FSM, CCS, CSP, UML state & activity diagrams
	place	DFD, MASCOT, UML sequence diagram	Petri Net, CSP, CCS, UML activity diagram

Figure 6-7. Some methods classified

In a given system one or more of these viewpoints will be more important and need emphasis. For a concurrent system, control aspects are crucial and we tend to concentrate on them. How are the processes organised? How do they synchronise? For an administrative system, we will concentrate more on the data aspects: what are the entities? How does data about them flow between agents? Where is the data located? Particular methods have particular strengths in particular areas so we can see that choosing a method (or methods) is a matter of matching strengths against critical aspects.

This analysis might lead us to choose several methods to cover a number of aspects within each development layer. The matrix can help us avoid the danger of relying on one method to do everything and is designed to assist in the choice of methods as part of the quality planning process as we shall see in more detail soon. Not for nothing, the 'wide-angle' approach SSADM uses

ELHs, DFDs and an ER model as its three principal modelling methods and can be seen quite clearly to concentrate on the data aspects of a system. Similarly, the UML and the method built on it, Objectory (Jacobson 1998), address aspects across both data and control.

Quality achievement in the Quality Plan

Now that we have a way of assessing which methods are potentially of most benefit to us for each of the development layers for our system, we can go on to look at how we use this analysis during quality achievement planning.

Choosing the appropriate method(s)

The process of choosing the most appropriate method is, put simply, one of finding the method that offers the most appropriate computational model for the development layer concerned. In other words, the computational model of the method must reflect some structural feature of what you are trying to capture. If, for instance, the real world (or the part you are auto-mating) is about data and how it moves around, then a method with data flow underpinning its computational model is the right method. If the real world is about serial files with a regular grammar then JSP has an appropriate computational model that helps you abstract the real world easily and fully. And so on.

The simple matrix in Figure 6-7 classifies computational models in a coarse way that should help you determine appropriateness at a coarse level. To take extreme cases by way of illustration, SSADM is unlikely to be suit-able for embedded systems because of its emphasis on the data aspects of a system, while MASCOT probably wouldn't make much sense for a database-based system using supplied forms and reports tools. However, what can be missed without an analysis such as this can be, for instance, the possibility of using VDM to give precise definitions of the effect of database updates, the use of a Finite State Machine (FSM) to give precise definition to the logic of a user interface, or the use of an ER model to provide input to an object-oriented design.

This discussion should make it clear that it is perfectly possible for one system to need a number of methods for a full attack. It is for this reason that some of the larger and all-encompassing methods pull together a selec-tion of methods that give good coverage of my classification matrix, and hence the possibility of covering all angles on any one system. They also run the danger, of course, of suggesting that the developer should throw all methods at every problem – an equally pointless and potentially dangerous act. The SSADM method favoured by the UK government for administrative system development combines DFDs, ER models and ELH models in the specification phase alone: the concentration is on data from three viewpoints which are then pulled together. Ward–Mellor and similar extensions of Yourdon add control logic in the form of FSMs to the data-oriented methods of 'traditional' Yourdon: DFDs and data dictionary.

In summary, the choice of methods goes thus:

1 Decide which are the most important aspects for the system or its subsystems: control or data, static or dynamic (temporal and local).

2 Choose the method(s) that promise the best fit.

3 Check that the computational model of the method matches the key characteristics of the development layer you are concerned with.

4 Determine the criticality of the system or its subsystems: low criticality means that methods with less formality can be used; high criticality means methods with greater formality should be used, thereby allowing greater V&V potential (see Chapter 7).

EXAMPLE

When it built the air traffic control information system at Heathrow, the Praxis team put together a portfolio of methods to address different aspects of the problem. At the specification level they treated the entire system (replicated servers, networks and PCs) as a black box and modelled its behaviour using the mathematical specification method VDM, adding finite state machines to model aspects of the user interface. At the architectural level a DFD decomposed the system into communicating subsystems and showed the data flows between them, with each subsystem individually specified in VDM. Some aspects of the concurrent behaviour of the overall system called for another mathematical approach, CCS.

Fitting the development layers into your process model

In Chapter 4 we examined a number of possible process models – possible unwindings of Boehm's Spiral Model – and we identified the major steps in terms of their products through the generic Work Breakdown Structure (WBS) of each. Those products were of course the different development layers that we have introduced in this chapter. When you sketch out your process model at the macro level (as in Figure 4-12 for instance), you will therefore be sketching out what sequence of what models you will produce (as well, of course, as all the minor and supporting intermediate products).

Now that you have chosen the methods you will use to produce those models you can make your WBS much more specific: instead of writing an activity such as *1220 Prepare System Specification* you will be able to make a more explicit expansion such as

1220   Prepare System Specification

      1210   Prepare layered DFD for entire system

      1220   Prepare Data Dictionary for all entities

      1230   Prepare VDM model of secure transactions

      1240   Prepare FSM model of secure transaction processing

etc.

We shall see in Chapter 7 how this will help us to decide what verification activities to incorporate in our development: having identified clearly what we will produce and how, we can make decisions about how to define and then verify the *quality* of those products and hence of the system overall. In Chapter 9 we shall also see how the more such detail we can provide the more likely our estimates are to be 'right', i.e. achievable and minimal. These are not just thought games!

Preparing the Quality Achievement Plan

In Chapter 2 we drew up the structure of our Risk & Quality Plan. We can now start to fill in the first of the quality-related sections. That structure is shown again in Figure 6-8.

Section 3.1: Characterisation of the system to be developed

This section lists the main characteristics of the system or perhaps different parts of the system that are pertinent to the choice of methods for those parts. This will come from an analysis of the system against the matrix in Figure 6-7 and a consideration of what would be an appropriate computational model. You can determine those characteristics by answering the following questions:

- Is the system principally a data-oriented system or a control-oriented system?

- Is the system a concurrent system?

- To what extent are we concerned with critical software?

- Is the target environment (on which the delivered system will run) also a suitable development environment?

(Remember that we must think about the User Layer and the Architecture Layer.) These questions are most relevant where a new development is being undertaken. Enhancement and porting of existing software are generally constrained by the way the existing software was originally constructed and the available documentation.

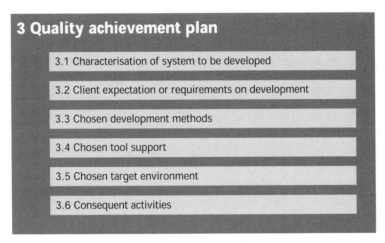

Figure 6-8. The quality achievement section of a Risk & Quality Plan

Is the system principally a data-oriented system or a control-oriented system?

We might decide that the relative or absolute timing of our system's actions is the most important architectural problem we shall face during design. Software controlling machinery or reacting to sensors in real time is typically like this. In this case we should consider our system to be principally a control-oriented system and we should look for design methods that fall in the *control* column of the methods matrix in Figure 6-7.

On the other hand, a system principally concerned with the processing of particular data structures can generally be considered a data-oriented system and is best approached using data-oriented methods. Software involving forms and reports using data in a database is typically data-oriented: transaction processing systems or batch data processing systems, for instance. We will look for design methods that fall in the *data* column of the methods matrix.

Many systems are a combination of these two extremes, of course, and we will need to take account of this. Often, data-oriented subsystems feature in a control-oriented system and a combination of methods is appropriate.

Is the system a concurrent system?

Suppose we have a system to build that requires some degree of concurrency: we need to deal with the relative priorities of the independent processes, the way they communicate, and how control passes between them. What is important here is whether the system must handle the problems of concurrent processing or each program can be treated as a free-standing serial process. We can ask such questions as 'does the designer want the system to retain control of the sequencing of processes?', and 'must the system have close control over the relative or absolute timing of processes and state changes?'.

A transaction processing system often requires the ability to handle a large number of simultaneous transactions. However, in some cases a transaction processing environment can be bought and integrated that handles the necessary simultaneity. In such a situation each transaction becomes a serial process and the designer need not worry about interactions between processes except the data aspects.

In situations where no off-the-shelf solution exists, handling concurrency becomes a problem for the developer and a different approach is required. In particular, the design of the system needs to address the dynamic control structure of the system, the control relationships between the separate processes, the concurrency model, and so on. In these cases we shall look particularly in the *control/dynamic* part of the methods matrix.

To what extent are we concerned with critical software?

The reliability we expect of our system will determine the approach we take to its development, the methods we use, and the tools we apply. Critical software with a high reliability requirement, such as software controlling a nuclear reactor or an aero-engine, demands the use of formal methods of specification, design, implementation and testing – methods with high correctness potential and high V&V potential. They will be costly to use, but we will decide that that is a cost worth paying, one that society will probably demand. So we shall choose methods from the methods matrix that satisfy those two criteria.

Section 3.2: Client expectations or requirements

We need to make sure we take note of the expectations or indeed requirements of our client in matters of how the system is to be engineered, whether or not we decide to take them on board.

It is increasingly common for the purchaser of a custom software system to demand that it be built using a particular method or with certain tools. The reasons for doing this are varied but very often the buyer intends to do subsequent maintenance and enhancement using their own staff. They may have house standards for development which we will have to fit in with so that their staff will be able to take over future work on the system without extra training or knowing about two development methods, two sets of tools and so on. It is this reason that underlay the US Department of Defense's push for Ada and the IDEF standards, and the UK Government's development of the SSADM development method for administrative systems.

In some cases we might find that our client wants to specify methods or tools that are really not appropriate, or that are even going to be counterproductive in some way. How we handle this will clearly be a matter for careful consideration. In some cases I have convinced a client of the benefits of doing it the way that I believe would be most cost-effective (not only for the development itself but also in the longer term). But this can look like arrogance. Step carefully.

Section 3.3: Chosen development methods

Here we will identify the methods or parts of methods that we have chosen for the parts of the system or entire system. If we choose a 'brand-name' method such as SSADM, or Booch, or Shlaer–Mellor we need to be explicit about whether we are doing it in its entirety or just those parts that make sense. If we are only using parts, we shall say which parts.

Section 3.4: Chosen tool support

List the tools that you want to use to support the methods you have chosen. The choice of tools is a non-trivial exercise in itself, and it is not one that I go into in this book, but we need to record our decisions in the plan because these choices will have implications for training, licence costs and so on that we must take into account. When we have prepared our Quality Control Plan (as described in Chapter 7) we might want to add further tools to this section to specifically support verification and validation activities.

Section 3.5: Chosen target environment

What system (hardware, operating system, DBMS, etc.) will our software run on when it is operational? This may well have been decided for us, or we might have a free hand. The reason for recording the decision here is that the choice will have implications not only for the delivery of that hardware and software (if it is our responsibility) but also for the development and maintenance environments, which in turn have further implications on procurement, which will have time and costs repercussions in our final plan. Easily forgotten, but frequently expensive.

From the target environment we can step backwards and ask similar questions about the development environment. What tools shall we need to develop the software? The following factors will influence our choice:

- the client's requirements or expectations

- the availability of tools to support the methods we have chosen

- the need for the development environment to be the same as or compatible with the target environment or the maintenance environment

- the availability of appropriate tools on our in-house development facilities

- the compatibility of the target environment with the systems available within our development facilities

- the cost of buying the tools against developing similar of our own.

Of crucial importance is the need to draw up a list of hardware and software to be purchased, a timescale for those purchases, and your requirements for any other development facilities.

And from the target environment and the development environment we can step forwards and ask more questions about the environment on which the system will be maintained after delivery.

If we are required to undertake maintenance and enhancement on behalf of our client, we will need to acquire and support the environment. It might need to be integrated into our own development facilities, and this in turn might have cost implications arising from the need to purchase extra hardware, tool licences and software licences, from rental or other charges for rented equipment, and from charges for the use of our facilities.

If our client is to take on the responsibility for maintenance, they might need to procure an environment of their own sufficient for maintenance and enhancement, and this environment would, assuming it is all of, or a subset of, the development environment, need to be shipped to them probably before delivery. If the development environment includes components of our facilities, the client would need to buy the necessary replacements. Licences originally purchased by us for development purposes would have to be transferred to the client or the client would need to purchase new licences.

All these costs must be recorded for the final costing of the project.

Section 3.6: Consequent activities

For each of the methods chosen in section 3.3, for each of the tools chosen in section 3.4 and for the environment components that appear in section 3.5, we will need to consider what training and familiarisation is going to be necessary for which staff. At project inception this should not be much of a problem, as we should have some idea of the staff we shall have. At bid time it can be a less exact science, but not knowing precisely who the team will be and their skills is not a reason for putting no provision in the plan for training. Murphy's Law says that if we include a provision for training we will get suitably skilled staff, and if we don't we won't. So we put it in!

We will also need to plan for the activities to procure, install, set up, maintain, and decommission the different environments.

Chapter recap

For successful software development you must pay attention to three aspects of quality: *quality achievement*, *quality control* and *quality assurance*. Quality achievement is about building quality in, i.e. having the right processes (methods) that ensure that you get things right first time.

The right choice of methods – i.e. the methods that lead efficiently to a correct system – requires you to match the strengths of your methods to the key characteristics of the problem you are trying to solve. This is the first step in quality planning.

Every method is about *modelling*. Most methods model in terms of data and/or control, and model their static and/or dynamic aspects. The dynamics of data and control relate either to how things change over time or as a result of events, or to how things move around. Every method assumes some form of *computational model* in terms of these aspects. Choosing the right method then becomes a question of matching the modelling 'language' and computational model of the method against the characteristics of the problem you are trying to solve. The method with the best fit is the method most likely to give you an efficient solution to your problem.

Your choice of methods will determine what sort of verification you will be able to do and will provide detailed input to your Resource Plan in terms of the products that you will produce and the activities that you will need to produce them.

OUTCOME

Analysis of the most appropriate methods leads to the quality achievement strategy for the project and in particular allows you to prepare the quality achievement section of your Risk & Quality Plan.

References

Coad 1993

Object-oriented programming. P Coad and J Nicola. Yourdon Press, New York, 1993

Fowler 1997

UML Distilled. M Fowler with K Scott. Addison-Wesley, Reading, MA, 1997

Jackson 1975

Principles of Program Design. M A Jackson. Academic Press, New York, 1975

Jackson 1983

System development. M Jackson. Prentice-Hall, Englewood Cliffs, 1983

Jacobson 1998

The Objectory software development process. I Jacobson, G Booch, J Rumbaugh. Addison-Wesley, Reading, 1998

JIMCOM 1987

The Official Handbook of MASCOT, version 3.1, issue 1. Issued by JIMCOM, available from RSRE, Malvern, 1987

Jones 1986

Systematic software development using VDM. C B Jones. Prentice-Hall, Englewood Cliffs, 1986

LBMS 1992

LBMS Jackson System Development: Method Manual, version 2.0. LBMS. Wiley, Chichester, 1992

Peterson 1981

Petri Net Theory and the Modelling of Systems. J L Peterson. Prentice-Hall, Englewood Cliffs, 1981

Ward 1986

Structured development for real-time systems. S J Mellor and P T Ward. Prentice-Hall, Englewood Cliffs, 1986

7 Is it watertight? Planning for quality control

Verification and validation

In Chapter 5 we analysed what constituted *quality* in software production and, hopefully, if we have chosen good methods with the understanding we gained in Chapter 6, we shall have produced a good specification, or design, or whatever. Our task now is to look at how we can check for that quality in the products coming out of the development process. Let's look more closely at the concepts involved.

In traditional manufacturing industries, quality control invariably includes the checking of the finished article to see if it has the quality required. Suppose you are in the business of making ball-bearings. You receive from your customer a specification of the ball-bearings required in terms of (non-functional) quality attributes such as weight, hardness and size, plus tolerances on all these at piece and batch level, say. You turn on the ball-bearing maker and out come ball-bearings. To be certain the customer will pay, you check that the ball-bearings meet the specification before you ship them: you carry out quality control on them. All well and good – your client will get the ball-bearings they want.

But you could have a large amount of below-spec ball-bearings that you will have to scrap. So you decide that rather than waiting to see what comes off the machine you will carry out quality control checks at various intermediate stages. So you will check the quality (i.e. composition) of the steel going into the top of the process; you will check that the dies in the forge remain correctly aligned over a production run; you will check the weight of the billets being cut off the steel wire you are using as input; and you will check that the temperature of the steel is correct at each stage.

For each of these intermediate quality control checks you will need to define quality attributes of some intermediate 'product' or process: the allowable range of composition and weight of the steel billets, the allowable temperature range of the steel, and the allowable distortions of the die. Each of these factors affects the quality of the final product. Indeed we can 'factor' the required quality level of the final product into these intermediate quality levels for intermediate products. If we get these intermediate quality levels right the quality level of the final product will be right. Problems are detected earlier in the process and hence can be cured before they get expensive in waste and rework costs.

Software production is no different. We cannot afford to go through the whole construction process before checking to see whether we have achieved what we set out to achieve, i.e. before seeing whether our software works. We need to carry out quality control checks at each stage of the development process, ideally on all the intermediate products: definitions, specifications, designs, code, user manuals, documentation – everything. And to do this we will need to define quality attributes that we will look for in each of these intermediate products.

HEADLINE

We can expect to factor our final requirements for the system into requirements on each and every intermediate product.

In software development we shy away from old-fashioned engineering terms like quality control, that smack of white-coated Quality Control staff walking around with micrometers and clipboards. We have borrowed two words – *verification* and *validation* – and we use them to mean *quality control*.

DEFINITIONS

Verification is checking that we have built the system right.

Validation is checking that we have built the right system.

This is a neat characterisation but let's go into the definitions in more detail.

When we verify something, say B, we do it by checking it against its specification, say A. We 'verify B against A'. B might itself be (or contain) a specification for C. Some obvious examples are verifying a coded component against its specification, verifying a component specification against the specification for the subsystem of which the component is part, verifying a completed system against the system specification. In each case we are asking 'have we built this thing right?', i.e. 'does it meet its specification?'.

Behind the notion of validation – 'have we built the right thing?' – lies the assumption that, despite all the specifications in this world, what the user or purchaser wants is ultimately only something in their head that can't be checked out in any other way than by showing them something. In other words, the only way we can validate something is by going to someone and saying 'is this what you wanted?'. There is no objective test in the way that there would be if we had a specification against which to check out the delivered item. Validation is almost a special case of verification in that it is the act of checking against the *requirements*. The difference is that those requirements might only be found in the mind of the user and might never have been expressed explicitly – even though a full specification of a particular system to *satisfy* those requirements might have been produced.

Now, it is the case that, finally, we have to ask people if what we've done is what they want. I might personally find this unsettling as a project manager because, while I can agree to a written specification, I find it hard to say that I'll satisfy whatever is in someone's head! Anyone who has done any amount of specification knows that if offered two options a user will want both, with an additional facility to choose between them!

What should be verified and validated?

Let's go back to the business of quality control throughout the process. Traditionally (and now I hope I'm referring to the distant past), V&V was limited to testing, and testing was limited to the testing of code, at component, subsystem or system level. But over the years the industry has realised that V&V could and should take place on *all* the items produced during development, and most importantly on the earlier items such as specifications.

In Figure 7-1 I have drawn a slightly different version of the simple V process model, showing only the main products that arise during development. On the left-hand side we see the chain of specifications from the 'expression' of the users' requirements, down to a specification of the system that will satisfy them, a design for such a system and finally specifications of components that feature in the design. Going up the right-hand side is the chain of increasingly large pieces of software, from the individual component at the bottom, up through part-systems ('threads', functions, layers, object sub-hierarchies, whatever), to the system ready for trial by its users to determine whether it is fit for use, finally reaching the system as it is in use. (You'll notice that the figure contains no arrows: this is because it is not a picture of a process – we are only concerned to list the main products that we could expect from any development project, no matter how they were produced within whatever process model.) Also, I have shown the right-hand software products in their state *before* V&V.

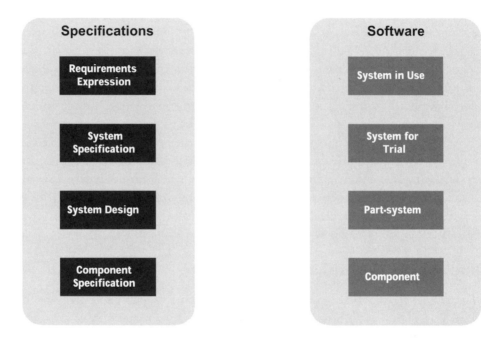

Figure 7-1. The main lifecycle products

Now let us start to look at the verification and validation opportunities that present themselves. The question we must of course ask is 'for each product, where are its quality attributes defined?', and we know from Chapter 5 that in each case the answer will be 'in a specification or a standard or both'.

Starting with the left-hand side of Figure 7-1, we can see that we can do several sorts of test on any specification:

- We can test it with respect to itself – here we are looking for *internal consistency* (Figure 7-2). In other words, does this specification contain any internal contradictions? Does this specification of a library loans system allow the possibility of a book being on loan to two people at the same time? Does this architecture specification in the design require the DBMS to lock all tables on reads but assume that this is not the case in some situations?

Figure 7-2. Self-consistency checking on a specification

- We can test it with respect to its preceding specification (except for the first of course, the Requirements Expression) – here we are particularly looking for *completeness* in the quality factoring that has gone on in the design process (Figure 7-3).

Figure 7-3. Verifying a specification against a previous specification

- We can test it (again except the first) with respect to its preceding specification for *behavioural equivalence* (Figure 7-3 again). In other words, does the thing described in our specification have the same behaviour as the thing called for in the superior specification? For instance, the superior specification calls for sixteen transaction types to be implemented in our component; have we covered them *and* carried down the precise operation of each of those sixteen types?

We can ask whether everything called for by the 'superior' specification finds its way into (perhaps a number of) subordinate specifications and if this specification that we are examining plays its, and all of its, part. For instance, the superior specification calls for a certain performance level to be achieved; does that get fully factored down into time budgets for individual components in their specifications?

- Finally we can test it against any standards that set the quality attributes for this class of object. So, if we have in our hands a System Specification, we can go to our *Standard for System Specifications*, read off the quality attributes required of all System Specifications and ensure that the one in our hands has them (Figure 7-4).

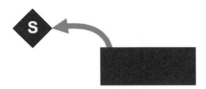

Figure 7-4. Verifying a specification against a standard

Going up the software side of Figure 7-1, we see that we can do the following sorts of test on any software item (component, subsystem, system):

- We can test it with respect to its corresponding specification – we are looking for *equivalence* (Figure 7-5). Does the code that we have produced to meet this specification for this component indeed meet that specification? Does it behave as required? Does it have all the functional and non-functional attributes required (speed, size, etc.)?

Figure 7-5. Verifying software against its specification

- As for a specification, we can test the code against any standards that set the quality attributes for that class of object (Figure 7-6). So, if we have in our hands a component in C++, does it meet the standard we have for C++ components, e.g. does it have the right headers, is it appropriately commented, is the layout as required, etc.?

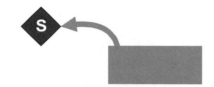

Figure 7-6. Verifying code against a standard

We can now draw Figure 7-7, on which every arrow represents a V&V opportunity. (Note that this covers more than the simple V process model in Figure 4-3 as we have now shown more than the straightforward specification-implementation testing.) In fact, I have also gone one step further. We know that we need, for instance, to verify a coded component against its specification, and when we do this we will of course (more of this later) write a component test specification which prescribes what tests we will do, with what inputs and what expected outputs. Immediately we have another intermediate product from our project … and we must think about what V&V we should apply to it – how do we know it is a good component test specification? This is clearly important: if our tests are poor we will let faults slip through and the quality of the final product will be jeopardised. So Figure 7-7 also shows the verification opportunity for all test specifications, an opportunity that will generally take the form of checking that the specification conforms to some standard that we have at corporate or project level.

The importance of this picture is that it points up *all* the different V&V opportunities, all the ways in which we can verify or validate the intermediate products of development to increase the chance of hitting the required quality level in the final delivered system. Of course, we shall have to look carefully at questions such as cost-effectiveness. Sure, we *could* do all this testing implied by the picture, but would it be worth it?

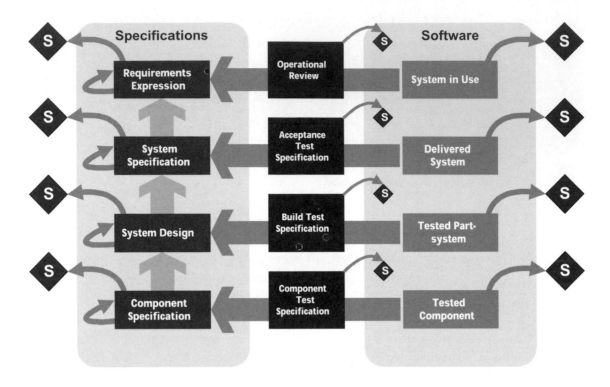

Figure 7-7. The complete set of verification opportunities

HEADLINE

Every product arising from the development process is a candidate for verification and/or validation.

What is good V&V?

We can expect to apply some level of V&V to practically everything we produce. But let's go one step further and ask: what is *good* V&V? We can summarise good V&V in two characteristics:

HEADLINE

Good V&V is *reliable* and *economical*.

When we say we want our V&V to be *reliable* we are simply saying that we want to be as sure as we can be that it will expose all the faults waiting to be found. When we say we want it to be *economical*, for instance in the case of component verification/testing, we mean that we want it to generate as few redundant test cases as possible, i.e. test cases that are unlikely to expose different faults.

Where exhaustive V&V of something simply isn't practical we have to make do with a manageable number of test cases. We would like those test cases to be as few as possible and yet still expose the faults in a product. In an ideal world we would also like our techniques for test case generation to detect the more 'important' faults with greater certainty – e.g. those that would cause loss of life before those that would cause an occasional need to repeat an input message. In general, as an industry we don't know how to do this yet.

Key to the reliability and economy of V&V is knowing how something was built, and in particular understanding the *V&V potential* of the methods used, the degree to which they support verification and validation of the products they are used to build. This is the topic we look at now.

The V&V potential of methods

In 1990, in the precursor of this book, I wrote 'Current testing practice can be caricatured as *over-the-wall* testing. Let's take the case of component testing. A software component is deemed ready for testing and then tossed over the wall to the testers. These poor folk have no knowledge of how the software was developed and hence cannot make use of any formality in the development method. They thereby throw away any chance of exploiting the potential the development methods might offer for helping in the verification and validation.'

As I write now, nearly a decade later, nothing seems to have changed and I can only repeat this today.

It's often said that the worst person to test a piece of code is the person who wrote it: they 'know' what it is supposed to do because they know what cases they wrote it to handle. So those are the cases that they test it on. An outside person doesn't know how it has been written and hence is less 'blinkered'. The easiest way of demonstrating this is to give someone else a program to use that you have written. No matter how much testing you have done, it seems that they will always break it within the first ten minutes of use. And this is generally because they will use the software in some way that you did not think of and hence did not test it on.

Now, I am not advocating that there is no need for independent V&V teams or for techniques of test data generation such as error guessing. Both of these techniques are of course needed. But we should not ignore the methods that were used to develop the software and thereby throw away opportunities to do really strong testing (i.e. testing that is both reliable and economical).

Traditional code testing techniques as described by most authors generally assume that an arbitrary piece of code has arrived for testing. The techniques apply irrespective of how the software was developed: error guessing, domain analysis, structural analysis etc. One's first reaction to this is pleasure that they are so generally applicable. But, as in so many situations, a generally applicable method can be so broad in its generality that it becomes all but useless in individual cases. It might cover all cases that one might want to consider when those cases are considered as a group, but when we try to apply it to a specific case we discover that its generality is actually its weakness: universally applicable – yet specifically inapplicable.

But we know that if, for instance, we prepare programs that are Dijkstra-structured (i.e. consist only of sequence, selection and iteration) then we have a much easier task when it comes to using structural analysis to determine the test cases we will apply. It becomes a great deal easier to traverse all 'long' path segments (e.g. LCSAJs of length one or two). In a sense this is because the meaning of a program that is Dijkstra-structured is easier to determine than one that is stiff with *goto*s. We also know that choosing test cases by analysing the input domain of the component (so-called *equivalence partitioning*, for instance) is much simplified if we have specified the component in terms of the different states that the component and its data can be in – the very basis of formal specification methods such as VDM and Z.

So far I have suggested that V&V potential relates only to the strength of the testing we can carry out on code, but, as I hinted in Chapter 6 when looking at what makes a good method, we can talk about the V&V potential of any method producing any product.

Methods that specifically support V&V are generally those that are more formal in nature, since that formality means that the semantics of the product are well defined and hence properties of the product can be more easily checked for.

EXAMPLES

Starting from a Z specification for a program, we can derive test data for that program systematically (Hayes 1986).

> Following McCabe and Schulmeyer (McCabe 1985) we can derive system test cases by analysis of the higher level Data Flow Diagrams for a system.
>
> If we use JSP (Jackson 1975) to design a program we start by defining a grammar for the incoming data streams that the program is to process. This allows us to generate representative sets of input test data directly from the grammar.

Many V&V checks can be automated if the meaning, i.e. semantics, of the representation we are using is well defined. At the very formal end of the spectrum there are formal methods that use mathematics and logic. Such methods offer mathematical proof as V&V steps on the products, for instance allowing the proof that a refinement of a piece of code preserves its functionality. Simpler cases include the use of static analysis tools (or some compilers) to check for anomalous code: sections of code that cannot be reached, variables that are never used, or that are read before they are written, and so on. Such analysers rely on the fact that the 'meaning' of a piece of code is formally defined.

In summary, a shortcoming of traditional V&V methods in general is that they do not use information about the way something was constructed to increase the reliability and efficiency of the testing of it. Moreover, we so rarely *build* for testing; i.e. we don't build for testability. The next section looks in more detail at the ways in which our current development methods can strengthen our V&V practices.

Method-specific V&V techniques

Verifying a specification

Let's suppose that we are writing program specifications using a formal (i.e. mathematical) specification method such as VDM (Jones 1986) or Z (Spivey 1989). The specifications we produce can be analysed mechanically or at least systematically. In particular, we can check for certain attributes such as consistency of operations and system invariants.

This is extremely powerful. A traditional component specification consisting of an informal description of the inputs and an informal description of how the outputs are to be derived from the inputs can rarely be checked for things like consistency – at least not with any degree of rigour worth speaking about. Let us take an example.

Suppose we want to specify a library system. We could define it informally in terms of the transactions that members of the library can carry out: registering as a member, borrowing a book and returning a book; and transactions that the librarian can make: registering a book, withdrawing a book temporarily for repair and deleting a worn-out book. We might add some rules such as a limit on the number of books that any member can have out at one time.

But we would probably not – in an informal specification – put down 'obvious' rules such as the fact that a member cannot borrow a book already on loan to someone else, that a book cannot be borrowed until it has been registered, or that books cannot 'disappear' from the system. But these are all properties we would want our library catalogue to have – and they are of course the sort of checks that programmers (might remember to) put into their code without being asked by the analyst via the specification.

But with a formal specification we can express those 'invariants' of the system (such as the fact that any book must either be available for loan, on loan or being repaired) in a mathematical and hence very precise way. By also describing the transactions as mathematical operations on the catalogue (itself described in an abstract way) we have all that we need to carry out rigorous, mathematical checks that each of the transactions *preserves* all the invariants of the system. (And, incidentally, those invariants can be used by the programmer to build defensive code into the software; this is no longer left to chance or their discretion.)

The crucial point is that *because* we have used a formal method like Z or VDM to write the specification, we have straight away given ourselves very powerful techniques for verifying the specification itself, or, to be more precise, to verify certain quality attributes in our specification. It would not be difficult to write an informal specification that defined transactions that in fact violated 'obvious' (and perhaps unrecorded) properties of the system. In this way, fewer specification faults are likely to be correctly coded up by the programmer. Quality is ensured at the earliest possible moment in development.

Validating a specification

We can go a step further. If our specification is indeed formally expressed and has formal semantics, we immediately open the possibility of using tools that can be used to 'animate' the specification. In effect we turn the specification 'automatically' into a prototype of the system it specifies. By executing the prototype we can validate whether the system we have specified is the one we want. Such tools are still rare and generally in the research environment, not surprisingly since the use of sufficiently formal specification methods is also a rare thing in our industry.

But there are simpler examples in use that do not require the use of algebra. If we can define sufficiently formally the database structure – the entities, their relationships and their attributes – that we plan to use for our customer service system and we can define the transactions we want to carry out on that database, we shall find off-the-shelf tool support, often from the database manufacturers, for automatically generating a database and the code for the transactions, at least to a first level of approximation as far as the form layouts are concerned. There is often very little distance in this case between a prototyping system and a system that automatically generates the final system. But either way, the formality with which we have prepared our specification has allowed us a direct, tool-supported, means for validating it.

Without such a facility the only way that we can validate our specification is by reading it and mentally animating it, perhaps with some visual aids.

Verifying a system design

Suppose we are designing a real-time system consisting of a number of independent but communicating processes that trigger each other. Such a system might be represented by the diagram shown in Figure 7-8 (which was explained in Chapter 6).

In a multi-process system of this sort it is not unusual for us to be able to define certain states of the system that we cannot permit. For instance we might want to ensure that there are no conditions under which two particular processes are running at the same time. To be able to do anything other than a very rigorous demonstration that our design does not let this happen would be very unsatisfactory. It would certainly not be enough just to try out a couple of sample firings of the net – we would want to have better proof than that. A Petri Net model allows just such a proof. It is easy to write an algorithm that generates *all* the possible states from a given starting state and checks whether any of them has the two processes concerned active at the same time.

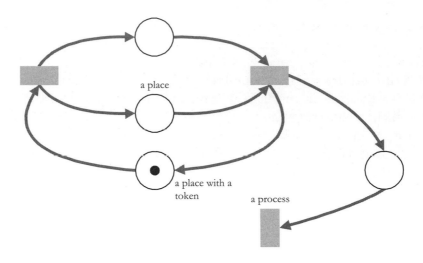

a place

a place with a
token

a process

Figure 7-8. A simple Petri Net

Because we have expressed our design in a formal way, very strong – indeed complete – verification of this important attribute becomes possible. We do not have to wait until the system has been integrated and all the processes put together for the first time to find out that there is indeed one strange situation in which the unthinkable happens and our system goes down. Similarly we could check that there is no undesirable loop in the running of the system, perhaps one from which the system cannot escape, such as some form of deadlock or livelock.

EXAMPLE

If we prepare a description of our system in terms of a hierarchy of Data Flow Diagrams, we get for free the possibility of checking that the diagrams up and down the hierarchy are consistent, in particular that the data flows shown into and out of activity A at level N correspond to the summaries for the subsystem at level N-1. Tools that support the preparation of DFDs will generally provide automatic checking of such attributes.

Verifying a program design

One of my favourite examples of how a well-chosen method can assist directly in the verification of a product is that of the use of Finite State Machines. Nick Birrell and I were building a system that was to capture television in digital form in real time so that it could be image-processed (for reasons we need not go into here) and then replayed in real time from the processed digital form. At the time (around 1981), sinking 18 megabytes of data a second in a form that could be addressed pixelwise for processing – which is what we had to do – was not an off-the-shelf facility.

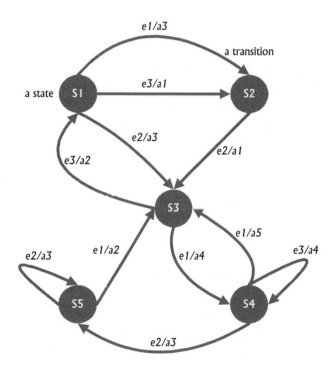

Figure 7-9. A simple Finite State Machine

As part of the solution the team built some digital framestores that could capture frames of TV and pass them to the controllers of a pair of very fast discs. These framestores were controlled by a microprocessor that was itself attached to a minicomputer. The software in the microprocessor had to run quickly as the gaps in TV signals when you can get things done (like moving disc heads) are quite small and you have to be quick to catch the various synchronisation signals. The user controlled the system from the minicomputer, which sent signals over a simple serial link to the microprocessor.

The problem was to design the program in the microprocessor so that it could handle any sequence of synchronisation signals, commands from the minicomputer, and other spontaneous events. A state transition diagram or Finite State Machine (FSM) solution sounded sensible (it had a 'computational model' that matched the problem). In an FSM, the system moves from one state to another depending on what events occur. Thus, in Figure 7-9, the system can be in one of five states, represented by circles, and can move from one state to another along the arcs between the circles. For instance, if the system is in state *s4* and event *e2* occurs, it moves to state *s5* and carries out action *a3*.

After doing some research, Nick Birrell came up with a paper by Chow (1978) describing a technique for generating sequences of events that would test an FSM design rigorously. We decided to use it.

Now, an FSM is a very simple design technique that has been used for decades in a host of different applications. Yet it offers a number of important V&V possibilities to the designer:

- If it is drawn up as a table, as in Figure 7-10, we can check that we have defined the effect of every event in every state. Thus in the diagrammatic form of Figure 7-9 we do not define the effect of event *e3* on state *s2*. But in the tabular form of Figure 7-10 we can readily see from a gap in the relevant cell in the matrix that our design was deficient. So we can verify *completeness* in our design.

- By using Chow's technique for deriving test sequences we can generate all sequences of states that the system can pass through and check that its action is what we want. In other words we have a rigorous validation procedure made directly possible by the design method. (This is touched on in Nick Birrell's paper, 1984.)

- A simple analysis of the FSM allows you to check what cycles there are in the design. Thus the system in Figure 7-9 has a number of cycles. In most software, cycles are of great interest. In particular, we are very often concerned with whether they are infinite or not, and whether they should be.

We used all these verification opportunities. The software in the microprocessor required a state table of some thirty or so inputs and nearly twenty states – not a trivial thing to define. But the method allowed us to verify the completeness of the definition and to validate the definition by using Chow's technique to generate test sequences of events. To do the validation, we wrote some software that took the definition of an FSM in textual format, generated the test event sequences, and then printed out the corresponding state changes and actions that the system would go through. By eyeballing the textual results we were able to check whether sequences looked right – we were after all looking to see that the design carried out our intuitively understood requirements.

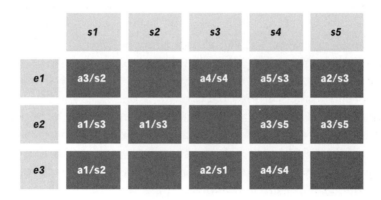

	s1	s2	s3	s4	s5
e1	a3/s2		a4/s4	a5/s3	a2/s3
e2	a1/s3	a1/s3		a3/s5	a3/s5
e3	a1/s2		a2/s1	a4/s4	

Figure 7-10. A tabular form of Figure 7-9

The success of the verification was considerable. During these simulations of the system driven from descriptions of the design (remember we had not yet written a word of the operational code), not only were we able to tidy up the design safely, but we discovered in an early version of the design that there was in fact one sequence of events where the system could lock up and get into an undesired cycle – 'hang' in other words. It only occurred when a certain sequence of commands coincided with a certain sequence of hardware events (synchronisation signals and so on) – a timing problem that we would never have stumbled on in any amount of testing, but that we could be certain would have happened at acceptance testing in front of the client!

When it came to testing the software in the microprocessor, the FSM definition again made things a great deal simpler – and indeed complete. We used the same Chow sequence generator to generate all the event sequences again, but this time used them to simulate the events occurring in the real world and to apply them to the actual software in real time to see whether it behaved according to the specification.

> ### EXAMPLE
>
> Suppose we are using a Finite State Machine (FSM) as a method for describing how our system will respond to events. An FSM model describes a system in terms of the different states it can be in and the transitions that occur between states in response to incoming events. With such a model we can easily check that the proposed system has desirable attributes such as not reaching certain states under certain input sequences, and not getting into a loop of states.

Verifying code

Let's now look at techniques of code production that allow us to verify the code in a much stronger way than the selection of a few test cases from the (generally) vast number of potential cases.

When we do dynamic testing, we apply a number of (hopefully) well-chosen test cases to the component and compare its action with that expected from the specification. The reason that we do this is that we have no other way of directly comparing the specification with its implementation, except in this trial and error fashion. Ideally, we would like to preserve the link between the specification and the code so that we could verify that we had achieved a correct implementation *in general* rather than on a small sample of the possible cases. This is where the techniques of *semantic analysis* and *compliance analysis* come in.

In outline, these techniques work as follows.

During the construction of the code, we use a formal approach. For instance, we specify the component in VDM. Our specification now takes the form of a set of *preconditions* for the component (assertions about the state of the system on entry to it), and a set of *postconditions* for it (assertions about the state of the system on exit). Typically, the preconditions limit the range of input variables, while the postconditions describe how the values of the output variables are related to the values of the input variables. These assertions are embedded at the start and end of the code, respectively, in a special extension to the language. As we develop the code, we derive new assertions about the state of variables at various points in the code, such as just before a conditional statement and at the start of a loop. Then we embed these assertions in the code in the same language extension that we used for the pre- and postconditions.

As development proceeds, the assertions which result from the reasoning about its correctness are embedded at various points. If the process is carried out properly there will then be a chain of assertions along each path through the program. A tool known as a *semantic analyser* can now be used to traverse the program. By taking the embedded assertions on a path and by interpreting the actual instructions on that path, the semantic analyser can construct a number of theorems which must be proved to be true if the code is to be proved to be consistent with the specification. The mechanisation of these proofs is still not an everyday possibility, and while proof checkers can assist, it is still the task of the programmer to develop the proof in the first instance.

The point of this is clear: if we use formal methods such as those described by Gries (1981), Jones (1986) or Dijkstra (1981) to construct our code from our specifications, we give ourselves V&V possibilities far stronger than the sampling techniques of traditional testing alone. If we have not had the benefit of such methods we are thrown back on sampling and must face the thorny question 'how much testing is enough?', or 'how many samples do we need before we are happy enough?'. To give testers a handle on this topic, researchers have devised a number of *coverage measures*. A coverage measure is a yardstick for the amount of testing you have done. Most text books on testing deal with the topic. You might also find useful British Standard BS 7925 Part 2, which defines fourteen ways of choosing test cases for a software component and then for each of those defines a coverage measure. For instance, we might choose test cases that together ensure that we have traversed every executable instruction in the component – we would say we have achieved '100% statement coverage'.

V&V potential comes from formalism

I have stressed how *formal* methods are the ones that have the strongest V&V potential – exactly what I observed when we were looking at methods for quality achievement. That strength derives from the fact that if something is formally expressed then its meaning is well defined, typically mathematically. And if something is well defined, we can apply logic to reason about it, and that reasoning will tend to be at a general level, rather than a form of sampling. General reasoning – 'in all cases …' – is clearly a powerful form of verification that meets our two criteria: that it should be reliable and economical.

Even traditional systematic methods can be improved simply by examining the underlying semantics and strengthening the method where necessary, as we saw in some examples above.

(I think it is worth noting here that I am *not* suggesting that by using formal methods and supporting tools you do away with the need for traditional testing. We have to recognise that any procedure that involves human beings is potentially error-prone and who would want to fly in an aircraft whose fly-by-wire software systems had only been proved correct and had never actually been tested with real data?)

So, reiterating the message of Chapter 6, when you look for the methods that you are going to use on your project you should be looking at each candidate for a number of properties:

- A *notation* of course and a syntax defining it, but a notation with well-defined semantics too. What does an arrow with a double head *mean*? What does it mean for an arrow to run from one sort of box to another? What are the implied dynamics of the system being drawn? And so on.

- *Heuristics* for developing descriptions in the notation. These might be expressed as a procedure or as checklists, though design (e.g. software development) is a creative and largely non-mechanisable act.

- *Good V&V potential*. We want techniques that help us to check out (test/verify) the descriptions produced, be they specifications, high level design, code, or whatever.

I believe that the V&V potential of a method is at least as important as, for instance, its simplicity in use. It is not enough that we should have an easy-to-understand diagram resulting from the use of a method. That diagram must also be amenable to strong verification. If it isn't then we have trouble ahead. Let me cite one case from outside the world of software development.

For some years now the world has used activity networks for project planning. An activity network consists of boxes representing activities, connected by arrows that represent the dependence of activities on each other. Annotation on the chart against an activity box shows the resources required for the activity and the cost of those resources, its planned duration, and perhaps an earliest start date. Figure 9-8 shows a simple activity network for a simple project.

The semantics of the chart are well understood, even if not expressed (though they could be) in mathematical form. Moreover, those semantics are sufficient for us (and, more importantly, a computer program) to deduce solely from the information on the chart the resource utilisation over time, the earliest and latest start and finish date of each activity, the total cost of the project, and so on. In particular we can – quite mechanically – determine whether in fact the project we have modelled with a particular chart is indeed feasible. We can in other words test the proposed design of the project against a number of attributes that we would wish it to have:

- *feasibility* – can that amount of work be done by those people in the time available with those resources?

- *economy* – is the total cost less than the amount we have to spend?

- *robustness* – is there enough slack in the resource and/or time usage to allow for a certain amount of overrun in key activities? And which are the critical activities, those whose slippage directly affects the end date?

- *flexibility* – is the degree of inter-dependence such that we could agree to take on additional work on the fly?

and so on.

With such a tool we can not only test our proposed 'design' for a project, but we can also explore different designs, something that it would be a pleasure to do for software specifications and designs. Computer support for activity network planning is now commonplace. There's clearly a lesson here.

Non-method-specific V&V techniques

Unfortunately, in many activities in software development, the way we produce a product does not offer us clear and reliable V&V opportunities. This might be either because the method of production we use is not formal (e.g. when writing a User Manual) or the resulting product is not amenable to such checks, for instance a design written in a natural language. In these situations we have to fall back on more general, less formal and hence less powerful V&V actions. They generally involve close human analysis – 'eyeballing' – of the product, relying on individuals to use their experience and perhaps ingenuity to find faults in it. A number of variations on this common theme have been proposed in the past, and I shall cover two of them here, referring to them generically as *reviews*. They are well established in the industry and I hesitate to repeat what has been said by so many before now, but they are not universally used and the messages bear repeating.

Structured Walkthroughs

In his book *Structured Walkthroughs* (Yourdon 1979), Ed Yourdon describes a general-purpose review technique which has been adopted by many organisations over the years in forms tailored to suit their purposes.

A Structured Walkthrough is an organised event at which a particular item – a specification, a code component, a chapter of a user guide, a test plan, or whatever – is scrutinised by a group of people looking at it from different perspectives and trying to find as many faults as they can in the item. The action centres on the producer of the item, who presents it to the other participants, who jointly look for faults. Any faults – or possible faults – found are recorded by a coordinator. The group concentrates on *fault detection* rather than fault correction, as it is the producer's responsibility after the walkthrough to take the record of faults found and make sure each is corrected in the item.

Yourdon identifies the following roles as appropriate:

- *the presenter* – the 'owner' of the item and probably the person who originally produced it

- *the coordinator* – someone to organise the walkthrough and chair it

- *the secretary* – who will ensure that the material is issued beforehand and that the records are taken and presented to the presenter

- *the maintenance oracle* – who represents the people who will one day be responsible for maintaining the item

- *the standards bearer* – who scrutinises the item for adherence to the local standards that apply to items of that sort

- *the user representative* – who checks that the item conforms to the views of its user (who might be the final user of the system or, in the case of a specification, say, the 'user' of that specification, namely the designer)

- any outsiders who can contribute to the scrutiny.

Crucial to the success of a walkthrough is the prior preparation done by the participants. It is the presenter's responsibility to choose the other participants who could most usefully contribute, to nominate a coordinator who will be able to run the walkthrough effectively, and to choose a time and place. Copies of the item to be reviewed are given to all participants sufficiently in advance for them each to do their own scrutiny of the item. The more individual work done by participants the more productive we will find the walkthrough will be. Participants take their comments and queries to the walkthrough and, with the guidance of the coordinator, present these and discuss them sufficiently to decide whether there is a fault or likelihood of a fault that demands further analysis by the producer of the item.

At the review, the item is scrutinised in whatever way makes most sense: a piece of text can be taken page by page, some source code procedure by procedure, a design diagram by diagram. These are the 'natural' and obvious ways of tackling the problem. However, a number of problems can arise.

Firstly, this serial approach to the walkthrough can lead people towards scrutinising what is there, and hence away from seeking what is not. In other words it makes it difficult to see deficiencies and gaps. This can in part be handled by the use of checklists. Many users of walkthroughs and related techniques maintain lists of specific questions that are always asked at such reviews (or, better, by participants during their preparation). Such checklists will generally be specific to particular products: system specifications, component code, test plans, etc. For instance, a checklist used to check the completeness of the coverage of a system specification might contain the following questions:

- have all inputs to the system been defined?

- have their sources been identified? (human agent, other machine, communications lines, peripheral types etc.)

- have their types been specified? (analogue, digital, electrical, acoustical, optical etc.)

- have the range, scaling, format, byte layout etc. been specified?

- have validity checks been specified?

- have the accuracy levels been defined?

- have all outputs from the system been defined?

- have all aspects of system performance been defined?

- what is the throughput of the system under different loads?

- what are the response times in different circumstances?

- what must be the system's response to failures of software, hardware, power etc.?

Such a checklist is designed to help check for completeness – an important quality of any item.

Now, an important aspect of a good Quality Management System is that it is constantly refined by looking to see how it has failed to find faults in past items. This process improvement feedback loop helps to reduce the likelihood that similar faults will creep through in the same way in the future. Thus, you might discover as development proceeds that an interface with another system does not operate as expected – this could happen as late as system integration when correction will be expensive. On investigation you find that the fault lay originally with the System Specification, which failed to specify the period for which data on an interface remained valid, and that this was not noticed when the System Specification was originally reviewed. This would lead you to add to your checklist a new check for completeness:

- for how long does the data on the input channel remain valid?

So the problem of checking for completeness in the product being reviewed can in part be dealt with by checklists.

A second problem that can arise from a serial approach to reviewing is that it makes it difficult for faults in the *overall* approach being taken to be spotted – 'high-level' faults, so to speak. This is a particular danger with text which, although it might be divided into chapters and sections is still a serial thing. Hierarchies of diagrams are less prone to such problems. This problem can in part be overcome again by the use of checklists that can, for instance, prompt reviewers into checking for the presence of a clear description of the overall strategy in a design, for a single diagram showing the interaction of processes, or for a summary timing diagram of the system's operation.

During the walkthrough it is the coordinator's responsibility to keep the discussion away from possible solutions since it is generally found to be a waste of time if six people argue over what should be one person's job, namely the producer's! It is also the coordinator's job to prevent the discussion from degenerating into arguments about style – all too easy, especially in the area of code and the use of the semicolon.

Once the participants have covered the item in full, it is customary to agree on whether it should be re-reviewed after the producer has corrected any faults detected, or whether the corrections are likely to be minor enough to allow the item to be accepted as having passed its V&V checks without a further walkthrough.

In addition to noting the importance of good preparation for walkthroughs if they are to be successful and cost-effective, we should note two other guidelines that have been adopted by most users of the technique.

Firstly, the item being reviewed should be small enough to be reviewed in no more than, say, two hours. Opinions vary according to people's stamina and concentration span, but this is probably around the limit of the period over which a group can operate effectively. It corresponds to perhaps ten pages of text, five to ten diagrams, or of the order of 200 lines of annotated code. That said, I once chaired a review of a substantial system specification that lasted two days – tiring but very effective.

Secondly, the item being reviewed should be considered complete by its producer. Finding faults is impossible if the item is incomplete. A participant might spot a problem, but is it just that such and such a section is missing at the moment?

Fagan Inspections

Fagan Inspections (Fagan 1976) are a general inspection technique that was developed within IBM. The overall principles are similar to those of a Yourdon walkthrough, but Fagan set his inspections in the wider context of planning, measurement and control. They serve two purposes: to find faults in a product, and to give greater control over fault detection through the collection of fault statistics. As with walkthroughs, the aim is detection and not correction, but faults are now classified in the record by type and severity so that profiles can be maintained to show up the commoner faults and to suggest how they can be avoided in the future. The emphasis as so often in this area is on feedback into the development process – learning from our mistakes.

A number of 'checkpoints' are defined during the development path. A checkpoint corresponds to the completion of some product or other: a design, some code, a test plan, and so on. For each checkpoint, 'exit criteria' are defined. These are quality levels that need to be reached by the product before it can pass the checkpoint. The inspection is the activity where the V&V check is made.

The original Fagan Inspections do not have the strong social emphasis of Yourdon's book (Yourdon 1979), but an important role is still there: a *moderator* is responsible for arranging, chairing and following up the inspection, much like Yourdon's *coordinator*. Around three further participants will be involved including the person responsible for the item being inspected. Fagan describes a four-phase process. Let us suppose that an inspection is to be carried out on a piece of design.

The procedure would then be as follows:

1   The designer presents the entire inspection team with an overview of the design and distributes the design documentation and any other relevant material.

2   The participants do their own preparation using the material supplied. Besides bringing their own knowledge to bear on their analysis of the design, they use the accumulated experience of past inspections of designs in their part of the organisation – in the form of *inspection guidelines* – in order to concentrate on looking in the areas

where faults have most frequently been found in the past. This is designed to optimise the effectiveness of the inspection by concentrating on 'high yield' problem areas.

3 The inspection itself now takes place. Someone nominated by the moderator walks through the product as for a Structured Walkthrough, and faults or potential faults are pointed out by the participants. Detection rather than correction being the order of the day, the moderator simply notes anything found, and, importantly, assigns it a severity and classifies it by type. As in walkthroughs, strong moderation is necessary if the inspection is not to waste effort and temper on the solution of problems, on issues of style, and so on.

4 After the inspection, the moderator produces the inspection report which then goes back to the item's producer for action. All the issues raised in the report must be resolved, and the moderator has the job of checking that their resolution is complete and satisfactory. Fagan recommends that if the level of reworking involves more than 5% of the item then the moderator should require another inspection of the item.

The notion of feedback is important. The records of faults found, together with their severity and type (see Figure 7-11), allow the organisation to refine the inspection guidelines used at step 2 above.

Like walkthroughs, inspections have a number of beneficial side effects that do not concern us directly here but that are worth noting as part of the justification for installing one of these techniques in your V&V:

- they spread understanding and knowledge around the team

- they allow easier transfer of ownership should staff leave or change responsibility

- they build team strength at the emotional level (if properly managed!)

- and they increase the level of shared ownership of the system by the team, without removing personal responsibility for the individual products.

Organisations often take the good points of Yourdon's and Fagan's techniques and combine the social aspects of the first with the feedback aspects of the second. As always this is an area where an organisation can set its own V&V standards.

Formal Review Report

Item under review	Code for component QT13T, issue 31.
Date	17th May 1999
Participants	Pode (author), MAO, TJH, GTAM
Re-review required by	21st May 1999
Project reference	P723.14.7

#	Location	Severity	Description of problem	Person responsible	Correction approved
1	line 63	major	loop bounds incorrectly calculated	Pode	MAO
2	line 71	minor	possibility of invalid data not handled	Pode	MAO
3	line 122	style	variable name in non-standard format	Pode	MAO
4	line 133	major	incorrect flag returned if SSAW>0	Pode	MAO
5	...				

Figure 7-11. A sample Formal Review Report

Building the Quality Control Plan

This chapter has been a rather philosophical one, and I think you, the reader, deserve an explanation of why this has been necessary. I believe the position and nature of V&V in software engineering has generally been poorly understood and poorly treated by the industry. We have simply not looked at the topic carefully enough, in particular at its position within the whole development framework and in the context of our development methods.

I hope the preceding philosophy has helped you to see more clearly just what V&V is all about and how it is completely bound up with an understanding of the development process model and with the methods that you use.

So, now that we have a better idea of the background to this V&V game, we are in a position to draw up sound procedures for developing the V&V strategy for our project. Back to the practicalities of planning software development!

In Chapter 4 we looked at how a consideration of the risks in our project led us to a choice of process model for the development. That process model was characterised by an overall WBS such as the one for incremental delivery, the first part of which went as follows:

1000   Plan overall development

2000   Develop kernel and increment 1 (jointly: INC1)

2100   Plan production of INC1

2200   Produce User Layer for INC1

    2210   Produce Requirements Expression for INC1

    2220   Produce System Specification for INC1

    2230   Produce Acceptance Test Specification for INC1

    2240   Produce Delivered INC1

2300   Produce Architecture Layer for INC1

    2310   Produce System Design for INC1

    2320   Produce Build Test Specifications for INC1

    2330   Produce Tested Part-systems for INC1

In Chapter 6 we looked at how the nature of the system to be built would determine what methods you should use to develop the development layers. This analysis allowed us to be more specific about production activities:

2300   Produce Architectural Layer for INC1

    2310   Produce System Design for INC1

    2311   Produce Logical Data Flow Diagrams

    2312   Produce Data Dictionary

    2313   Produce State Machine for AS Interface

etc.

In Chapter 7 we looked at the different forms that V&V activities could take.

We can now bring all this together and elaborate activities like *2313 Produce State Machine for AS Interface* with detail about the verification that will be used to check the product. In some cases, the V&V activity might be significantly large: component testing is such a case, where we need a whole test planning and test specification activity as well as the testing activity itself. In other cases, the V&V process might be quite small: checking the properties of the state machine, for instance, might be only a few hours' work and require no separately identified activity.

In the first case, we would want to add new work packages for those V&V activities – test planning, test specification and test execution – to the WBS. In the second case there would not be the need – we could assume that the V&V takes place at the end of the production activity, though in fact we will not rely on our memories: below we will look at how this sort of decision is recorded in the Quality Plan.

> ## HEADLINE
>
> In our detailed WBS we identify a V&V activity for every product, either explicitly or implicitly.

I proposed in Chapter 2 that the Quality Plan should contain a section on quality control as shown in Figure 7-12 and we can now examine its contents in more detail. It will:

- list all the types of product you will produce, final and intermediate

- define where their quality attributes will be defined (specification and/or standard)

- define how those attributes will be checked for (i.e. define how the V&V will be done).

The list of product types in section *4.1 Planned product types* will be steered significantly by our choice of methods in the Quality Achievement Plan – specific methods produce specific products. As we saw in Chapter 5, their attributes will be defined either in specifications or in standards or both, those standards being typically:

- for such products produced for use in this application domain

- for such products produced in this organisation

- for such products produced on this project.

We identify them for each product type in section *4.2 Specifications and standards* in the Quality Control Plan.

How the quality attributes will be checked for – the V&V activities – will have been deduced from our earlier analysis, particularly from the V&V potential of the methods we've chosen to use. We now list those activities for each product type in section *4.3 Quality control activities* in the Quality Control Plan. If our methods don't offer any way of checking the results or we aren't using any method to speak of then we will need to fall back on the non-method-specific V&V techniques, namely inspections, reviews and so on. But these should be our last resort as they are relatively weak and ill-focused.

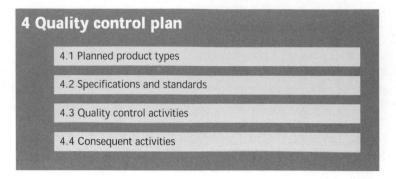

Figure 7-12. Contents list of a Quality Control Plan

In some cases we will be able to specify a tool that exists or that we can build to assist in the V&V. A static analysis tool can find unreachable code or anomalous data usage for us. We might choose to write a tool that allows us to look for desired or undesirable state sequences in a finite state machine; we might decide to write or buy a tool that allows us to carry out performance predictions for our chosen hardware configuration; and so on. The Quality Control Plan is the place to record these decisions. If a tool has to be built or bought and installed then we will need to plan activities to do this. We add those activities to section *4.4 Consequent activities*.

Finally, we need to remember those sources of quality attributes: specifications and standards. We must check that all the specifications we plan to write are covered by activities somewhere in the WBS, and also that any standards that are needed specifically for this project are covered by activities that will prepare them: add activities to do this to section *4.4 Consequent activities*.

Once you have finished you should, in particular, have definitions of all the arrows in Figure 7-7 relevant to your process model; and you should have elaborated your WBS with considerable detail about V&V activities.

Finally, it can be useful at this stage to identify levels of authorisation: who can approve specifications, component tests, source code, etc.?

Figure 7-12 lists the contents of the Quality Control Plan, but you might find it convenient to construct the plan as a table. as suggested in Figure 7-13.

Note how I have added at the end of the list some other products that arise during development and that we shall probably also want to submit to V&V: the very plans themselves, orders we place on suppliers for goods and

Item	Standard or spec	V&V method	V&V standard	V&V record	V&V approval
System Specification	QM3.1	review	QM2.2	Review Record	Client, Project Manager
Phase 2 system	System Specification	Acceptance Testing based on equivalence partitioning	QM6.5	annotated test output	Client
Acceptance Test Specification	QM6.5	review against System Specification	QM2.2	Review Record	Client, Project Manager
…	…	…	…	…	…
Project Plan	QM9.1	review	QM2.2	Review Record	Client, Managing Director
Risk Plan	QM9.1	review	QM2.2	Review Record	Client, Managing Director
Quality Plan	QM9.3	review	QM2.2	Review Record	Client, Managing Director
Project Progress Report	QM9.4	review	QM2.2	Review Record	Managing Director
Purchase Order	QM9.13	informal inspection	–	signature	Project Manager

Figure 7-13. A tabular Quality Control Plan

services, and our progress reports. This is of course a list that you must ensure is complete in your own environment. Again, a checklist in your QMS could be expected to cover this.

Chapter recap

While we would like to think that by choosing the right methods for software development we will attain all the necessary quality, human fallibility means that we have to provide the safety net of *quality control*. The earlier a fault is found the cheaper it is to remove it, and to be certain of delivering the desired quality attributes in the final system we need to check for the quality attributes in every intermediate product.

V&V is about checking for quality attributes. 'Good' V&V is V&V that is reliable and economical. Reliability can be achieved by using development methods with high *V&V potential*, i.e. methods that offer good possibilities for directed V&V. The problem of economy is less easily addressed. The more formal the method the stronger the V&V potential, so formal methods have greater attractions where there are more stringent quality requirements. A tool supporting a formal method is also more likely to be able to assist in V&V in a strong way than a tool supporting an informal method.

You should examine every V&V opportunity and assess how important it is for the successful delivery of your system. You must pitch the V&V at the right level for every product of the development process.

Given the methods you will use and the quality attributes to be checked you can draw up the V&V strategy in your Quality Plan. This will

- list all the types of product you will produce

- define where you will define their quality attributes

- define how you will check for those attributes.

OUTCOME

V&V planning yields the Quality Control Plan part of your overall Risk & Quality Plan.

References

Birrell 1984

Increasing productivity in embedded microprocessor software development. N D Birrell and D H S Blease. In *Australian Computer Conference —Programme and Papers*, pp66-81. Australian Computer Society, Sydney, 1984

Chow 1978

Testing software design modelled by finite-state machines. T S Chow. In *IEEE Transactions on Software Engineering*, **SE-4**, pp178-187. 1978

Dijkstra 1981

The Science of Programming. E W Dijkstra. Prentice-Hall, Englewood Cliffs, 1981

Fagan 1976

Design and code inspections to reduce errors in program development. M E Fagan. IBM Systems Journal, **15**, 3, pp182-211. 1976

Gries 1981

The Science of Programming. D Gries. Springer Verlag, Berlin, 1981

Hayes 1986

Specification directed module testing. I J Hayes. In *IEEE Transactions on Software Engineering*, **SE-12**, 1, pp124-133

Jackson 1975

Principles of Program Design. M A Jackson. Academic Press, New York, 1975

Jones 1986

Systematic software development using VDM. C B Jones. Prentice-Hall, Englewood Cliffs, 1986

McCabe 1985

System testing aided by structured analysis: a practical experience. T J McCabe & G G Schulmeyer. In *IEEE Transactions on Software Engineering*, **SE-11**, 9, pp917-921

Myers 1975

Reliable Software through Composite Design. G J Myers. Van Nostrand Rheinhold, New York, 1985

Spivey 1989

The Z Notation: A Reference Manual. M Spivey. Prentice-Hall, Englewood Cliffs, 1989

Yourdon 1979

Structured Walkthroughs. E Yourdon. Yourdon Press, New York, 1979

8 Stopping the rust: Planning for quality preservation

The dangers of entropy

About two decades ago, Alan J. Perlis said 'In the long run every program becomes rococo – then rubble.' Little changes. Except, I suspect, that today the piles of rubble are a great deal bigger than they were when Alan Perlis wrote those words.

When I was writing COBOL programs at the end of the 1960s, and merrily storing years as two digits (YEAR 'PICTURE' 99) I could not imagine that my software would still be running – and about to fail – three decades later. But much software has been surprisingly long-lived. Major systems that run railways, telephone switches and air traffic control systems are today well into their third decade. The cost of replacement increases year on year and the temptation to leave well alone becomes increasingly hard to resist. Over the lifetime of the software it will undergo many changes. In the early years the changes may be frequent, as the system and its environment settle down together. As time passes bits are added, until finally the whole thing becomes so fragile that no one dares touch its insides and the rubble that it has become is concreted up to prevent further decay. What started as a nice tidy structure has, over the years been bit by bit – or even wholesale – corrupted, distorted and even lost.

HEADLINE

Change increases the entropy of a system, in other words its disorder.

I was once called back to look at a real-time system that I had worked on several years previously. For some reason it had simply stopped working. After two weeks' work I had found over twenty faults that had been introduced into the software in the course of changes that had been made to it in the intervening period. It was, I thought, a credit to the design we had given it, that it had survived all that time with the faults that had been introduced – indeed, the internal resilience we had built in had worked wonderfully, in particular its robustness in the face of timing errors, which was where the faults had had most effect. But the last straw had just been added to the camel's back and it had dropped to its knees two weeks before – and I received that call.

But it is not just over the entire lifetime of a system that we need to worry about keeping entropy under control: we need to worry about the short run of the development of the system, as well as the long run of its entire working life. No software development proceeds cleanly through its development process. No one ever produces a specification, does the design, writes the code and puts the system together without finding reason to change things on the fly – perhaps because of faults detected – or without getting requests to make changes to the original specification, with all the consequent changes on design, code etc. If you have ever written and debugged a piece of software you will know that the best place to look for a fault is wherever you made the last change. Changed software is far more likely to contain errors that 'original' software. Life becomes geometrically worse when we have a *group* of people working on the same system, all making changes to different parts with consequent changes on yet more parts. Different parts of the system are at different stages of development – a component specification change here means twenty other components need to be altered, their test specifications revised and tests rerun, and so on.

Now entropy is inversely proportional to quality. As the disorder in a system (and a project!) increases so the quality of the products will fall. All that effort that we put into achieving quality in the first place and then making sure it was there with our verification and validation activities – all wasted … unless we plan to manage change during the project and thereby preserve that in-built quality.

Change management dissected

Imagine we are in the throes of our project. What have we produced? We'll check the project's working directories on the server. We find the System Specification, an Architecture Specification, a number of Subsystem Design

Specifications, many Component Specifications, a corresponding number of Component Test Specifications, component source code files, compiled versions etc. And we must not forget all the items being worked on that are in the private workspaces of the team members. Suppose Phil finds a fault in service component *SSX32*. He decides that the interface defined in its specification is wrong and must be changed, but this will in turn require a change to the code for all the components that use *SSX32*, some of which are completed and ready for integration, and others of which are still being worked on. How will we control the *set* of changes that flow out from this one fault? In this book I am not going to prescribe exactly what your change management strategy should be, any more than I can prescribe your methods strategy for you. But I shall say what sorts of things you should be thinking about when you write your Quality Plan for the project, which is after all what this book *is* about.

Identification control

The first and obvious requirement is that we must have the possibility of distinguishing one version of a component from another: does this version of the component precede or follow that one? Is this version one that I can rely on? what is its verification status? Who wrote it? When? So part one of the quality preservation strategy in your Quality Plan must be an *identification control* mechanism by which any and every product of the project must be *identified*, whether it be a technical document such as a coded component, a User Manual, or a training course slide-set, or a System Specification. In the general case we can expect that every product should carry the following identification data somewhere about its person:

- its name

- its version

- its status.

Any item falling under identification control we call a *configuration item*.

Naming conventions are popular points of dissension on any project, though perhaps less so now that most of our computer systems allow us to have filenames that are more than eight characters (how long has that taken?!) so we are no longer reduced to encoding component names, for instance, to BRT31A52 – which as everyone knows is version 3.1 (or is it 31?) of component A52 (whatever that is) in subsystem BRT (whatever that is). We simply need a unique and informative name.

Versioning schemes can be equally time-wasting in the invention. Two-level schemes are popular: 'version 8.12' indicating that this is the 12th minor update of the 8th major update, or some such interpretation. Again the detail is less important than having such a scheme. (I have a scary memory of a system built in the days of paper tape. We needed to recreate the system tape but the man who normally looked after that was on holiday. On his desk we found a box of unlabelled object tapes a subset of which, in the right order, would do the job. Fortunately one of the great but short-lived skills one possessed in those days was the ability to read binary headers on tapes to see what was on them. But in some cases we found two tapes for the same component, leaving us with the decision about which was the one to use. Fortunately things are no longer this way – or are they?)

The third item of information we need about a given version of a given product is its *status*. How far is this item reliable? Is it just a draft that someone has prepared? Has it been through its quality control? Has it been delivered for use? I don't think it is sufficient for something to be in a particular directory to attain a given status, or even to be given a certain filename – I believe a conscious action to change the source of a document or a code component to bear a new version number is what is required.

We might like to add to the identification the date that the version was created. Strictly perhaps, dates are irrelevant. We are only interested in knowing which version we are looking at. But a date can provide some useful redundancy and a cross-check. Similarly, with the author's name – a convenience.

In summary …

HEADLINE

Our quality preservation strategy will define exactly how we will identify each product we produce and its version and state.

Change control

Now that all product versions are uniquely identifiable we have a basis for change and its control.

Let's return to Phil and the fault he has found in component *SSX32*. We cannot allow him to just change it, with all the knock-on effects that will follow. We would be even more concerned if people started making changes to specifications, especially high-level ones like System Specifications and

Architecture Specifications, without some form of control being exercised. It's not just a question of the possibility of *technical* things going wrong as a result; we could very easily find ourselves in financial and contractual difficulties. Uncontrolled changes to specifications are a favourite way of ensuring failure, and 'scope creep' is a popular way of losing money and friends.

Again, my concern here is not to prescribe a particular change control mechanism but only to clarify what sort of thing we need to define in our quality preservation strategy. Most companies will have some form of change control in place and the usual constituents are:

- a process with steps for proposal, analysis, approval/rejection, implementation and closure of a change

- some form of process support, either in the form of paper forms or a computerised database containing the equivalent information, or even a specialised change management software package.

In the analysis step of the change control process we expect that all of the repercussions of making the change are worked out and costed, probably by the staff responsible for the items concerned. This will cover determining which versions of which development products are affected, right through to what the impact on the business and the user community might be. Some form of *Change Control Board* is often set up to consider changes and decide whether the costs justify the benefits, given the stage that the project is at. Costs can of course be not only money costs but also time costs, and it is often the latter that squash a proposed change, especially towards the end of development: postponing the change until the system is in the field might be preferable to delaying roll-out, despite the extra costs involved in changing a system that has gone into the world.

Assuming the change is approved, the necessary alterations will be made to new versions of the products affected, and retesting and new testing will be defined and carried out to ensure that no new faults have been introduced as a result of the change.

Whatever scheme you choose it should be very clearly defined, straightforward to follow, and unremittingly enforced!

It's not uncommon to use the same mechanisms for reporting faults in baselined products as for requesting changes – the process remains the same, only the information gathered might differ slightly. Also changes may be batched in order to reduce disruption.

> **HEADLINE**
>
> Our quality preservation strategy will define exactly how we will control changes to all configuration items.

Although it is a little tangential to our main thread of planning in this book, I believe it is worth sounding a note of caution here on the notion of the *conceptual integrity* of the system. My first real job in the industry was working on ICL's flagship operating system GEORGE. A team of 120 people – modest by today's standards – were working on up to three versions simultaneously – a major change control headache. The administrative side of things went well, with careful control that ensured that changes to the single multiversion source file were kept in step. But more important in many respects was the fact that there was a 'Design Team' who were responsible for ensuring that the system's philosophy and principles were maintained through all these changes being made by different hands. They were the guardians of GEORGE's conceptual integrity – if they didn't like the way a piece of design had been done then it didn't get through; they ensured that the system was built to a single set of architectural rules which were not broken by changes. The city of Bath was built very quickly over a short period of time to a single architectural vision, and its continuing beauty stands or falls by the degree to which planning regulations control changes in line with that vision. Software systems are much like cities: they can start with architectural integrity but unless planning regulations are enforced that control the changes that are made to individual buildings, the place very soon looks a mess.

Configuration control

We now have an orderly process which ensures that changes are properly considered – not least with respect to other changes that might be going on in the same or related areas of the system – and that they are followed through to a tidy conclusion. We are now in a position to bring in the notion of the *baseline*.

There are a number of reasons why we will want to 'baseline' our development now and then:

- you want to review a set of design documents together to ensure that they describe a consistent and feasible design that meets the specification

- you want to prepare a subset of the system for integration testing

- you want to release a version of the system to the user community with a certain set of facilities.

In each case we take a set of products and declare them to form a baseline. We are saying 'these versions of these products together form a coherent set of things that, for some reason, we want to treat as a unit.' Baselines can provide stepping stones of progress. Our design might move through a series of baselines until we reach one that, at the review, passes the quality criteria we have set for going on to the next level of design. During integration we might build successive baselines of larger and larger subsets of the entire system, each baseline being tested as a unit, and forming a secure basis on which to build the next. Once the system is out in the field we might plan periodic releases, each of which will contain new facilities, remove old ones and solve earlier faults – each release will be a baseline that is a coherent unit. A baseline might consist of a whole set of versions of products from across the development layers; taken together those versions of those products form a coherent set – System Specification, System Design, certain Component Specifications, certain Component Test Specifications, certain versions of certain coded components and so on.

The metaphor that is often used in the baselining context is that of 'freezing' things. At the point when we decide that the design is stable enough for component specification to start we 'freeze' the design. Typically this really means that from that moment on changes will only be allowed to take place within the formal change control process that we have put in place. So we put together a group of design documents that form a consistent set and declare them to form a baseline, with everything in the baseline now under change control. At the point when we believe we have a working system we baseline it, issue it to our user base and use that baseline as the basis for future changes; we record the versions of all the items – software components and documents alike – and ensure that we have everything we need to reconstruct that baseline if we need to.

Configuration control is about the control of baselines: their definition, creation and documentation. As the project proceeds we shall constantly be identifying the upcoming baselines and what will be in each of them. At the start of the project, while we are planning, we must set out the process and machinery to make this baselining activity as easy as possible. We will need to say how we will collect the appropriate versions of the products that form the baseline, to record the baseline's contents, and to store it in a standard place. We will want an approval mechanism that involves the right people (perhaps the Design Authority for a design, a User Panel for a new system release). We may also need mechanisms to control the distribution of a new baseline and the withdrawal of old ones.

HEADLINE

Our quality preservation strategy will define exactly how we will define, produce and control baselines.

The need for rigorous configuration control is high in certain process models, especially evolutionary delivery and incremental delivery where several versions of the system might be in the field at a time. A further version might be in the final stages of development and two more coming through specification and design.

ISO 9001 and change management

By putting in place the sort of change management strategy I have described we shall satisfy several of the demands of ISO 9001, as expanded by ISO 9000-3, in particular:

- document and data control
- product identification and traceability
- inspection and test status
- control of nonconforming products.

Check back to their definitions in Chapter 5 to see that this is so.

The Quality Preservation Plan

Our quality preservation strategy, written up in our Quality Preservation Plan, will therefore consist of the following three items:

- a defined *identification control mechanism* listing all the product types that will be covered (often called *configuration items*) and defining the rules that apply to each type for its identification

- a defined *change control mechanism* including the process that will be used to control any change to any configuration item and describing any tools that will be used to support that process

- a defined *configuration control mechanism* including the definition of baselines, their creation and storage,

and we will need to include appropriate activities in our plans to make sure these mechanisms are put in place and then carried out. If we cannot point to these mechanisms on the shelf and ready to use today, then we shall have to make sure that we put entries in section *5.4 Consequent activities* for preparing them at the right moment in the project, and certainly well before they are needed. It is common for these mechanisms to be described in a separate document called a *Change Management Plan* or some such. But logically it is part of the Quality Plan of the project and to emphasise this I have brought it under that umbrella in section 5.

HEADLINE

Our Quality Preservation Plan will describe the project's

identification control mechanism – how we identify every configuration item and its version

change control mechanism – how we control any change to any configuration item

configuration control mechanism – how we define, create and store baselines.

One side effect of our Quality Preservation Plan is that we shall invent yet more products from the development process, in particular the records of change control and configuration control. Naturally we shall want to include them in our Quality Control Plan, identifying where their quality attributes will be defined (invariably in standards) and how their quality will be verified (typically by inspection and approval).

Chapter recap

Change increases the entropy of a system, in other words its disorder. Once we have developed a product and checked its quality attributes we shall want to ensure that any changes we make preserve that quality. The need for a quality preservation strategy becomes even more important to handle changes to multiple products at a time.

A prerequisite for managing change is to be able to identify every product, along with its version and its status. Procedures can then be devised that ensure that changes are properly assessed and executed. In many situations we want to associate versions of a given set of products that form a coherent set, that 'go together'. That set of versions is known as a *baseline* and we shall need a strategy for managing baselines.

Our quality preservation strategy therefore has three parts:

- an identification control strategy

- a change management strategy

- a configuration control strategy.

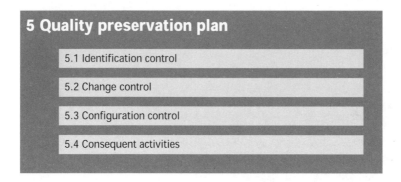

Figure 8-1. Contents list of a Quality Preservation Plan

OUTCOME

Quality preservation planning yields the Quality Preservation Plan section of your overall Risk & Quality Plan.

9 Pushing the boat out: crewing and provisioning

Time to launch

We have covered a lot of ground in the past chapters. The bulk of this has been about getting information about your project and the system it will build. It has been about making decisions about how the project will achieve its aim: namely to build the system to the right quality at a commercially acceptable level of risk. In this chapter we look at how you use the information you have gathered and the decisions you have made to prepare your *Resource Plan*, and at the factors that affect productivity on your project.

(Before we go further I must add that this not a book about estimating, a large topic that I leave to others – see for instance Capers Jones (1998). My aim is solely to show where estimating fits within the larger risk and quality planning approach I propose.)

In essence, what has come out of the risk and quality planning work has been a list of the activities, decisions and iterations that you need on your project in order to:

- carry through your risk management strategy to handle risks

- carry through the methods strategy you have chosen to achieve quality

- carry through the V&V strategy you have chosen to ensure quality has been achieved

- carry through the change management strategy you have chosen to preserve quality.

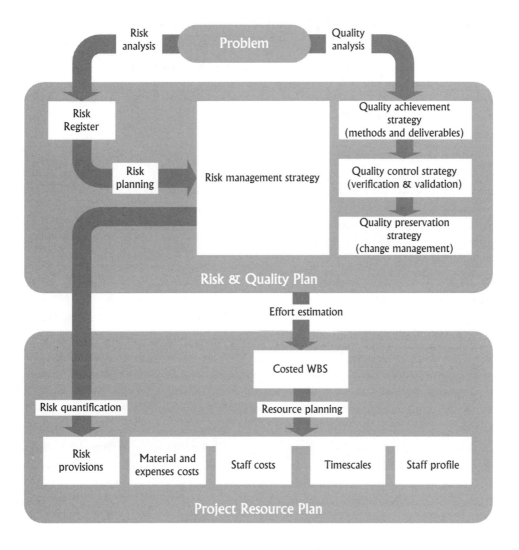

Figure 9-1. The big picture

This list of activities and iterations will form the major part of your Work Breakdown Structure (WBS). Figure 9-1 gives a detailed view of how we have arrived where we are. Notice how every decision you have made so far has led to the WBS, and remember my statement right at the outset that from technical considerations we would deduce managerial and commercial decisions. We have now reached that point.

Your next move is to complete some of the gaps in the WBS, to cost it, to deduce the timing and resourcing of the activities in it, and then to write all that up in your Resource Plan.

First, a note of reassurance

It would be easy to imagine that the process of risk and quality planning and all the analysis that is necessary to get to this point involve a massive undertaking, and an undertaking that is being called for at those moments when management time is in shortest supply, namely at bid time and at project inception.

Firstly, let me say that it is my experience that many of the decisions do not require significant prior analysis – they are obvious. Many choices might have been made for you, such as the methods you will use or the environments you will use. Others will be clear because you have done such a system before. In these cases, noting the decisions is a speedy affair. *But*, importantly, the process then asks you to check out the implications of these 'obvious' choices – it might still be the case that, although you are being asked to use a certain method, you have a team that is not fully trained, for instance. Miss this and you will have a project with a timescale that is inadequate and a budget that has no provision for training and familiarisation.

Secondly, when I have watched people (including myself) going through the bidding process, I have noticed how they do indeed deal with many of the issues that I have discussed above. But they address them in a relatively haphazard way and do not always follow through their thoughts by carrying the implications on into the Resource Plan for their bid. Where they don't, they end up with an unrealistic plan. The risk and quality planning process is designed to make sure you address all the issues and follow them through to their conclusion in a systematic way. The process should speed up your work and not slow it down. It should also make the figures in your bid or your Resource Plan more reliable, which is their most important attribute.

Above all, however many times you have done something, the risks and uncertainties are invariably different from one development to another. If there is one part of the planning process that I think is important above all others it is that analysis of what you don't know or don't have full control over. Handling the known is relatively easy and is what an inexperienced project manager will concentrate on. To be a better project manager you should concentrate more on what you don't know and what you are going to do about it. It's what is *not* known that kills projects.

As with your Risk & Quality Plan, you need to write all your resourcing decisions down for a number of reasons:

- because you will want to communicate them to others, in particular your project team who will use the plan as a work instruction

- because you will want to prove to others, typically line management and your client, that you have a feasible strategy for the project that stands an acceptable chance of success and that is well thought through

- because you have a bad memory.

It is important to remember that these are the only reasons you are writing a Resource Plan. All the thinking and decision making should now be complete, and recording things is just a straightforward matter of putting pen to paper. The 'only' remaining creative skills to be exercised will be to construct your project network and to estimate the duration of activities.

We start with the mechanics of project planning and project re-forecasting. Subsequent sections then deal with other factors affecting productivity (tools, training, and so forth) and with project metrics.

Preparing the Resource Plan

This section is the culmination of the processes I have presented in earlier chapters: it shows how all the decisions you have now made yield most of the input you require to draw up a full and realistic Resource Plan.

The Work Breakdown Structure

There is a strong tradition of hierarchical structures in our industry and so we take to a hierarchical decomposition of our projects into activities quite readily. If you have not come across a *Work Breakdown Structure* (WBS) before, read this section; otherwise skip to the next.

A WBS is best explained through an example. Imagine the following is a WBS for a project to build a house.

1000   Negotiation and planning
        1100   Agree target price with buyer
        1200   Negotiate materials prices with suppliers
        1300   Draw up ground plans
        1400   Get plans agreed by local planning department
        1500   ...
2000   Construction
        2100   Clear ground to correct levels
        2200   Prepare footings
        2300   Fabricate roof structures
        2400   ...
3000   Fitting out
        3100   Install electrical circuits
        3200   Install plumbing
        3300   Install air conditioning
        3400   Decorate interior
                3410   Plaster where necessary
                3420   Wallpaper as specified
                3430   Paint as specified
                3440   Carpet as specified
                ...
        3500   Carry out final inspection and cleaning

The main groupings of activities are *1000 Negotiation and planning, 2000 Construction* and *3000 Fitting out*. Anything needed to get from the initial agreement to handing over the keys to the new owner must appear within one of these three main groupings. Each grouping is then decomposed into a number of smaller activities. The sum of the subordinate activities is exactly equal to the main activity, no more and no less. This decomposition can be taken down any number of levels, though I have never worked on a project that could not be adequately handled with five levels. I have shown some of the decomposition of house building above. Every activity required to get the house built must appear at some level in the WBS.

I strongly recommend that you use imperative verbs at least for the lower level WBS activities: *Prepare System Specification* rather than just *System Specification*. You are after all defining activities! You should also suggest the required *outcome*, for instance *Get price agreed* rather than *Discuss price, Review design and close off faults* rather than just *Review design*.

Note that I have drawn up the WBS for the house building in more or less the order that things would happen in time. Clearly there is some parallelism around: roof structures can be prefabricated while foundations are going in, for instance. But overall there is a flow of time through the WBS. However, you might choose to structure your WBS around the structure of what you are building. For instance, your system might consist of three relatively independent subsystems: Account Transaction Processing, Mail Shot Processing and Credit Worthiness Assessment. You could structure your WBS thus:

1000	Prepare overall design
2000	Design subsystems
	2100	Design Account Transaction Processing
	2200	Design Mail Shot Processing
	2300	Design Credit Worthiness Assessment
3000	Implement subsystems
	3100	Implement Account Transaction Processing
	3200	Implement Mail Shot Processing
	3300	Implement Credit Worthiness Assessment
4000	Integrate subsystems

...

or thus

1000	Prepare overall design
2000	Construct Account Transaction Processing
	2100	Design Account Transaction Processing
	2200	Implement Account Transaction Processing
3000	Construct Mail Shot Processing
	3100	Design Mail Shot Processing
	3200	Implement Mail Shot Processing
4000	Construct Credit Worthiness Assessment
	4100	Design Credit Worthiness Assessment
	4200	Implement Credit Worthiness Assessment
5000	Integrate subsystems

...

I would generally favour the second approach because it is easier for the separate teams that you will probably have working on the different subsystems once the overall design has been done to see their own work separated, rather than mixed up with everyone else's. Also, the potential parallelism is expressed at the correct (i.e. high) level. But this is not a crucial issue – the work packages at the bottom level are the same.

Inputs to the WBS

Because you are going to use the WBS as a basis for your costed Resource Plan, there is a vital point to be remembered:

HEADLINE

If an activity is not in your WBS you will have to do it in zero time and for free.

Completeness is therefore the key attribute of a good WBS, and in this section we shall look at how the results of risk and quality planning provide the major part of your WBS.

I shall refer to an item at any level in the WBS as a *work package*.

Input from risk planning: the risk management strategy

First, let's look again at the form that these various inputs can take. As predicted in Chapter 2, our analysis of risk leads to the identification of

- an overall shape – a process model – for your project, e.g. *a three-phase project with two intervening review points*

- decision points at which one of a number of alternative paths is chosen, e.g. *if a relational database will suffice use one, otherwise develop a purpose-built file-handler*

- iterations, e.g. *refine the prototype until the user is satisfied*

- process fragments for minor risk reduction measures, e.g. *train new staff in VB before component specification begins*, or *validate system against simulator before integration with real hardware.*

The first question is: how do each of these find their way into our plan, into the WBS and the network?

- The process model obviously has a major effect on the structure of the project because that is exactly what it is about. When we draw up the structure and high level items of the WBS we will use the structure of the process model as we saw in Chapter 4. When we construct the network we shall reflect the overall logic of the chosen process model in the overall logic of the network.

- A decision point will generally involve an activity to make the decision, e.g. *4522 Evaluate the available relational databases*, followed by two or more alternative paths (sets of activities with their logic). The question here is: how should these alternatives be shown?

  Firstly we should note that we should at least have a good idea of the possible outcomes of the decision. If we don't then we shouldn't be planning the project beyond such a critical decision – we should have limited our (commercial) commitment to what we can reasonably predict. So the sort of decision in *4522 Evaluate the available relational databases* is fine: subsequent activities will either be independent of the outcome (do the design with database *A* or with database *B* as the target), or, at worst, might depend slightly on the outcome. For instance, if database *B* is chosen we might need to add further activities for training if we only have experience of database *A*.

  When it comes to constructing the WBS it should therefore be possible to put in *all* activities that might result from *all* the possible outcomes. And when we choose durations we can pick the longest from the alternatives.

  This might not sound entirely satisfactory, but our starting point should be to cover against the 'worst' case, i.e. the most expensive outcome of the decision. Later on we might assess the relative likelihoods of the different outcomes given whatever prior understanding we might have, and then adjust the durations on the basis of that. Resource planning is never an exact science!

- Iterations cannot be shown in a WBS or in a network, so you will need at this stage to put a bound on the iterations, perhaps budgeting and planning for three, decreasing tours. You can either sum the iterations and show them once, or keep them separate.

- Process fragments are dealt with in the obvious way: we have defined them in a way that positions them in the project to reduce risk at the appropriate moment, so we need only insert them into the WBS and activity network at the appropriate point.

Input from quality planning: the quality management strategy

In Chapter 6 we looked at how your choice of methods is determined by the sort of system you are building. In particular we looked at how generic activities such as *Prepare User Layer* are defined by the methods you use. So when you draw up the WBS at this stage of the planning process you can be quite specific about what activities you will have, given those methods. Thus, if you believe some of the notations of the UML are appropriate you will replace the generic activity *Prepare User Layer* by activities that prepare class diagrams and activity diagrams; if you are using SSADM, it can be replaced by a whole set of activities to do with the preparation of Entity Life Histories, Data Flow Diagrams, Technical Options and the like. Your WBS will name these activities and their products explicitly, e.g. *Prepare and agree Entity Life Histories*.

In Chapter 7 we looked at how verification and validation take place throughout development, and we defined validation and/or verification for every product of development as appropriate; so you could expect to see these V&V activities throughout your WBS. Moreover, because of the analysis you have done of the methods and of V&V that you can do, your WBS can be very specific about the precise verification activities. *2300 Verify design* would be a weak specification of an activity: you should be able to break this down into, for instance, *2310 Verify performance through simulation*, *2320 Verify database integrity preservation*, *2330 Validate functionality through prototype screens*, and so on in the WBS. All these activities will also appear in the network for the project.

In Chapter 8 we looked at how to plan to preserve quality through a change management strategy. Depending on the precise mechanisms you chose, you will have identified activities necessary to set up the mechanisms and support for your identification control, change control and configuration control. And you will also have defined activities that will occur during the project – perhaps to do with baseline production at key points during the build phases. All these activities can now be added to the WBS and inserted in the network.

Filling in the gaps

Risk and quality planning are designed to help you generate all the crucial activities of your project. But there may be other activities which will not have been thrown up directly by the analysis of risk and quality. Precisely what they are will depend on your particular environment, but the sort of things I am thinking about include:

- preparing documentation plans
- preparing maintenance documentation
- preparing support material

- handling any change-over from existing systems (data conversion, parallel running etc.)

- preparing user documentation

- training users (including preparing materials)

- project debriefing

- the collection and analysis of metrics.

I would advise that you construct your own checklist of such activities and make sure you scan it whenever you are drawing up your project plans. If you miss one out and it's non-trivial *you will have to do it for nothing*.

Costing the Work Breakdown Structure

Finally, we come to the one bit of black magic in this book. Under an innocuous sounding heading, we have to tackle the great unsolved problem of software engineering: estimating. How long will it take? How many staff will we need?

This is not a book about estimating models – you should refer to the specialised literature on this – but a glimpse of the processes is all that we need here to show how they fit into the overall resource planning business.

It's an advantage if you don't expect there to be some magic formula that will help you here. The only real guide is straight experience. In the software houses where I have worked, when the moment comes for the estimates to be made for a competitive bid, it's the old hands who are brought out in their wheelchairs to do the estimate. Experience, experience, and more experience. There are of course various 'estimating models' that you can use, but they are only as good as the experience that is crystallised in the parameters in their formulae. Any estimating model worthy of the name will give you a way to calibrate it against *your* experience in *your* organisation with *your* sort of staff on the sort of projects *you* normally tackle. In other words – against *your* experience.

It is therefore quite obvious that if you never record your own experiences you will never learn to estimate. On the down side, if your technical environment changes constantly you will find it that much harder to learn from the past. In Chapter 10 I shall recommend the simple statistics you should keep to help you develop at least a 'feel' for how long things take.

There are two ways to cost your WBS: the *holistic* approach and the *analytic* approach. Let's take them in turn.

The holistic estimating approach

In the holistic approach you start with an estimate of the 'size' of the problem you are going to solve, and you derive from it an estimate of the total amount of effort an enterprise like that would take. You then take that total figure and break it down over the various activities using further experience about what proportion of the total project effort each activity takes.

The holistic (top-down) approach is adopted by, for instance, the COCOMO estimating model (Boehm 1981). This model has many ramifications so I shall restrict myself to the general scheme and leave the detail to Boehm's classic text.

For the COCOMO model the estimate of the problem size is expressed as the number of lines of code that will be developed for the system. The unit generally used is the KLOC (thousand lines of code). (Suitable definitions of things like a line of code are of course necessary but they are peripheral to this discussion.) The model then requires an estimate of fifteen so-called *cost drivers*:

- required software reliability
- database size
- product complexity
- execution time constraint
- main storage constraint
- virtual machine volatility
- computer turnaround time
- analyst capability
- applications experience
- programmer capability
- virtual machine experience
- programming language experience
- use of modern programming practices
- use of software tools
- required development schedule.

Some of these are showing their age: 'computer turnaround time' harks back to the days when computer systems were few and accessed in batch jobs in a queue – how long would it be between the time when the clerk collected your job from your desk and returned the results from the computer operators? Scales are defined for these drivers and it should be clear that much of the risk and quality planning analysis described earlier in this book will help you to make estimates of these costs drivers against the scales. The model will then, if suitably calibrated, give you an estimate of the total amount of effort required for the development, plus estimates of how that should be divided over the various phases of development. This would be a starting point for putting figures against the individual activities in your WBS.

Another popular holistic estimating approach is *Function Point Analysis* (Symons 1991). The approach is very similar to COCOMO except that the initial 'size' estimate is made in terms of the 'amount of functionality' that is being delivered, rather than the number of lines of source code that will deliver it. For certain classes of systems, in particular forms-based transaction systems, 'function points' are much more readily estimated than lines of code, especially where code is automatically generated from some other specification of the software. The result is the same as with COCOMO: a total figure for the effort for the project, together with indications of how it should be broken down across the phases of the project.

Clearly, as you divide the effort down over smaller and smaller activities so you will need to exercise your judgement about what proportions to use. That judgement will come from experience – i.e. from records you have kept of past actual results. I have figures from a project carried out in the late 1970s. The proportion of effort consumed by each of the major phases is shown approximately in Figure 9-2, and subsequent figures show the proportions for sample projects up to the present day.

What is interesting about these figures, which I do not pretend are about entirely comparable systems or are statistically reliable, is that the proportion of effort that goes on 'management' activities has remained a constant: one in every five effort-days will be spent on some aspect of management, be it managing the client, managing the project team, managing the development environment, managing releases and baselines, etc. This is borne out by the observations of colleagues on other projects and seems a reliable starting point. Secondly, we can see in microcosm the trends in software development over the decades: the trend was clearly towards a greater concentration on the definition and design phases and the effort profile has changed. But most recently design, in the architectural sense, has dropped back again – the project captured in Figure 9-6 was one that used a rapid DSDM prototyping cycle with a tool kit that provided an architectural basis, leaving the 'designer' only to capture requirements at the screen interface.

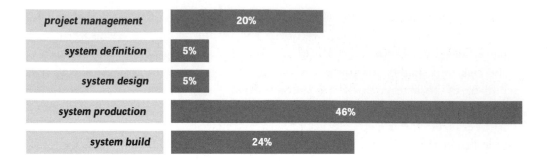

Figure 9-2. Effort profile of a late 1970s project

There are of course no magic numbers that apply universally – projects can vary enormously and the projects in the figures are a tiny sample, but you should establish a profile for projects in your organisation, both so that you can use them as a basis for costing your WBS when estimating holistically, and also so that you can take steps to change the proportions if you feel they are not right – for instance, continuing the emphasis on early activities.

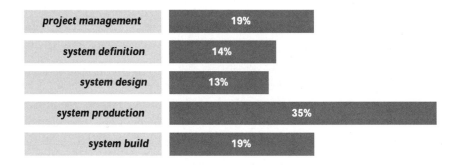

Figure 9-3. Effort profile of an early 1980s project

The result of a top-down holistic approach will be a costed WBS, with an estimate of the duration of each of the activities in some appropriate unit such as weeks.

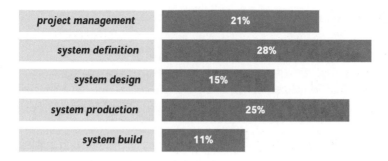

Figure 9-4. Effort profile of a late 1980s project

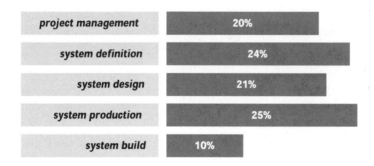

Figure 9-5. Effort profile of an early 1990s project

Figure 9-6. Effort profile of a late 1990s project

The analytic estimating approach

In the analytic approach you start from the detailed WBS and ascribe a duration to each activity. By totalling the estimates for the individual activities you get a figure for the total effort for the entire project. You still need in some sense to estimate the size of the system because, when you estimate how long the activity *2534 Code Transmission Algorithms* will take, you will need to have some idea of the 'size' of the Transmission Algorithms software.

There is little advice that anyone can give you here – you really are on your own! You will need to establish from your own experience and that of others just how long things take. Experience, experience, and more experience.

One tip worth following is to choose an appropriate unit for estimating durations. How do you decide what is 'appropriate'? Here are some points to remember when deciding.

If you choose a small unit such as days and have a small number of large activities you will tend to underestimate. If you choose a large unit such as months and have a large number of small activities (down in the one- and two-month area) then you will overestimate. Never estimate in anything smaller than a day. I once managed a project where estimates were required by senior management in hours. This could easily have led to hopeless underestimates, simply because you end up with very large numbers, and very large numbers always look *too* large, and so you tend to scale them down. The only way I could handle it was to do my estimates in days and weeks and then convert to hours for presentation purposes!

At bid time I would be surprised if anyone could estimate in anything finer than weeks. The acid test is whether I can discriminate between N units and $N+1$ units. For instance, will *2534 Code Transmission Algorithms* take 35 days or 36 days? If this is a meaningless, unanswerable question – I couldn't say which is more likely – then I am using too fine a scale. I move to weeks. Will *2534 Code Transmission Algorithms* take seven weeks or eight weeks? Yes, I can make a judgement on that. So I use weeks as my unit. If I couldn't I would move to months. Will *2534 Code Transmission Algorithms* take two months or three months? No, that feels too coarse. I had a manager once who reckoned 'it takes a week for a sh*t or a p*ss'. The smallest thing takes a week so there's no sense in estimating in any smaller units!

When doing a holistic estimate we made critical use of proportions for dividing estimates down over the activities in the WBS. These proportions have their place when you are using the analytic approach too. Once you have costed the entire WBS activity by activity you should add up the numbers so that you get totals for the major phases. Then check the proportions they have between them against the 'norms' that you have established from experience. This is a typical sort of sanity check that helps you spot anomalies. Where the proportions differ considerably, e.g. by more than a difference of 5%, I would suggest a careful look at the costings and either the production of a good reason for that difference or a change to the figures.

It is worth mentioning here a major difference between an estimate done for overall planning and an estimate done for actual project control. In the first case, it is only necessary to come up with an estimate of a feasible WBS – it does not have to be *the* WBS. This means that you might decompose your WBS to levels that give you a 'feeling' for the work rather than an accurate prediction of the activities that will be done. For instance, you might estimate the duration of the activities in a prototyping exercise at a much finer level than you could be totally confident about. It won't be until you get nearer the prototyping work that you will be in a position to do a breakdown and costing that you would be confident enough about to give a team member to act upon. This is fine. By all means estimate to a level of detail greater than that at which you are really confident *for costing purposes*, e.g. at bid time. But when you draw up the project plan you should leave your WBS at the higher level, and not refine it further until you have information on which to do it reliably – this will generally be closer to the time.

Making the estimate

Since you now don't expect there to be a magic formula, you will definitely want to use as many methods of estimating as you can in any given situation. In my opinion the analytic (bottom-up) method is the one to start with, though I would always expect it to generate an overestimate rather than an underestimate, especially if you have gone to considerable detail in your WBS. This is because you will tend to round up on each figure, and a lot of small roundings-up can become a very large rounding up when added together. On the plus side, the more detail you can go into in your WBS the more confidence you can have in being able to achieve your estimate – clearly a lot of WBS detail *should* mean a lot of understanding about how you are going to get the system developed.

Also, by costing the WBS directly, you will find it easier to inject your own experiences of how long things take in your situation – this is clearly not so easy with the holistic methods that require a good calibration to be effective *as well as* experience about the proportions for various activities.

However, if I can I then use holistic methods, no matter how coarse they are, to give a sanity check or two on the figures I get analytically. This is the whole point about estimating: you need as many ways of getting the estimate as you can find. When the results differ substantially you need to ask yourself why that is, and by answering the question – and it should not take long –

you will get more information about either the problem or your uncertainties. Either way, that's good value. It's for this reason that a number of independent estimates by different people will also help. Some people have a better feel about estimating some areas than others. So, by comparing their estimates and finding out why they are different you will know which ones are based on more reliable experience than others and you will start to get an overall feel for the 'real' answer.

This is a good moment to remind you that when you are starting a project an estimate is no longer a *prediction*. I have often heard people talking about estimates as if they were referring to the project as some sort of scientific phenomenon about which they were making a prediction and which they were then going to observe to see if their predictions were right. An estimate at project inception is a *management goal*, *a statement of intent*. It will only turn out 'right' if you as project manager manage the project to *make* it turn out right!

A popular sport for those coming across an estimating model like COCOMO for the first time (and I've done this) is to take an old project, 'run it through COCOMO', see what the model says the project should take, and then compare that with what it *did* take. The answers are invariably different. But we should not be surprised – the difference between a future project and an old project is that you can manage a future one, but the old one is history. On the future project you are going to use the estimate as a management *tool* to get things done in a certain time. No doubt on the old project that was run through COCOMO the project manager was using some other initial estimates as a management goal, and hence the comparison is not a valid one.

This is why the apparent poor 'accuracy' of estimating models like COCOMO is only apparent. When he calibrated COCOMO against his original 69 projects Barry Boehm found that, in rough terms, the calibration was within ±25% of the actual figure for two thirds of the projects. This sounds appalling. But he goes on to point out that a manager can handle a 25% 'error' either way, either by turning up the heat or turning it down (if allowed that luxury!). So an 'error' of that size is manageable. It's important therefore for you to have an idea of just how much ±% you think you could handle when you make your estimate.

Finally then, whichever approach you have used, once you have finished you will have a costed *Work Package Analysis* similar to the fragment in Figure 9-7. You will later update this on a monthly basis, as I describe below.

Planned days	Work package
	1000 Project Management
	1100 Initiate project
5	1110 Draft and agree Project Schedule
2	1120 Set up project file
15	1130 Prepare Risk Plan
10	1140 Prepare Quality Plan
15	1150 Prepare Resource Plan
	...
	1200 Monitor and report on project progress
	1210 ...
120	1300 Administer project
	1310 ...
	1400 Liaise with client
...	1410 ...
15	1500 Close and debrief project
	2000 Prepare User Layer
	2100 Specify requirements
55	2110 Analyse functional requirements
25	2120 Analyse performance requirements
30	2130 Produce outline design
20	2140 Define user interface through prototyping
	2200 Specify system
...	2210 ...
	2300 Specify acceptance criteria
...	2310 ...
	3000 Prepare Architectural Layer
...	3100 ...
	4000 Prepare Implementation Layer
...	4100 ...

Figure 9-7. A Work Package Analysis

Drawing the network

You now have a WBS with an effort estimate against each bottom-level activity. The next step is to draw all those activities onto an *activity network*, adding the inter-dependencies between them.

HEADLINE
Missing out a dependency reduces your plan to fiction.

There is no real way to spot all dependencies except to sit and stare at the network trying to decide, for each activity, what you will need to be able to start it. For instance, before you can start coding a component you must have completed its specification, of course. But you will probably also need to have the host machine and its development environment available to your programmers. You will need to have written a standard that defines the house style and programming rules. You might need to have the individual programmer trained in the facilities of the operating system they are to use. These are all dependencies to go on the network.

Among the activities and dependencies that you will put into your plan are of course the process fragments that arose from a consideration of the minor risks and uncertainties that you identified during risk planning. Check that they are all in the activity network and that their associated logic (*before* this and *after* that) is shown as dependencies.

Having got the logic right, you now allocate staff to the activities. You might be working with the names of real people, or simply 'programmer 1', 'programmer 2' etc. It makes little difference. What you should realise however is that as you allocate staff you are in effect adding new dependencies to the plan: unless the activities are only part-time activities, no team member can work on more than one at a time.

I have often been amazed – and alarmed – by seeing a project manager attempting to manage a significant project simply with a barchart. A barchart contains *no* indications of the dependencies from one activity to another; and in software development, as in any engineering activity, there are many dependencies. If you ignore them, you are working in the realms of fiction. There is no substitute for working with an activity network, and any tool that does not allow me to interact *directly* with my network gets a poor rating from me.

Having got the dependencies and the staff allocations onto your network, you now start to work with it. Your aim is clearly to devise a project that takes into account the estimates and the dependencies, *and* that brings the system in on time. This is where the trouble really starts. Almost without fail, the first network will show an end date that is too late – you have come up with 'the wrong answer'. There are other books on the tricks of project planning so I shall restrict myself to mentioning some of the basic ploys available to you. They all rest on the notion of the *critical path*.

> ## DEFINITION
> The critical path of a network (and there might be more than one) is the path formed by the longest sequence of dependent activities.

The crucial point is that if any activity on the critical path is shortened the end date comes in, and if any activity on the critical path is lengthened the end date goes out. So shortening the critical path is the key to bringing in the end date. Any project planning tool will give the necessary visibility to the critical path. Here are some ways of shortening the critical path:

- Long activities on the critical path can sometimes be split into two or more shorter and overlapping activities. There is a danger here if new dependencies are introduced between the sub-activities. The whole thing can become quite complex and hard to actually manage when the time comes. Moreover, by making the parts parallel – and hence done by different people – you might need to increase the total amount of effort in order to cope with the increased need for coordination between the staff.

  In other cases a long activity can be split into two parts, the first of which can be started earlier because it is not subject to the dependencies of the whole activity.

  Of course, some activities really cannot be split sensibly – a component design activity for instance. Putting two people on the job really makes no sense. (If it takes one woman nine months to have one baby, how long does it take nine?)

- Better staff can be put on critical path activities. In principle they will do the job more quickly.

- Sometimes activities appear on the critical path simply because of the way you have staffed them. Their dependencies with other activities have not made them critical, but the staff allocated to them have become fully or overloaded. For instance, it would be unusual if the activity *Train Users on System* were to prove critical, but it could be that it has become so because the staff you have allocated to it are also planned to do other *truly* critical work at the same time.

- In some instances, you can adjust the logic of the network and the activities to reduce the constraints and hence change the critical path's composition. Provided the new logic does not omit important dependencies this is fine.

One tenet that I believe in very strongly is the following:

> ## HEADLINE
>
> Start with the most highly constrained plan you can devise and – then and only then – be prepared to relax constraints. Not the other way round.

In other words, make sure that every possible dependency, however remote, goes into the first version of your network. Every dependency removed or ignored is a risk introduced, and it is only by explicitly removing them that you can know what risks you are introducing and then decide whether you want to take them. Taking risks is a commercial matter and not a technical matter.

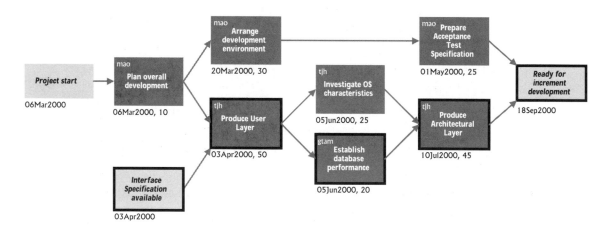

Figure 9-8. A simple activity network.

You should therefore start with a network that is 'correct' (i.e. adequate) on technical grounds and then use your commercial judgement to decide how much risk you are prepared to introduce in the cause of bringing the end date in.

Figure 9-8 shows an imaginary highest level activity breakdown for the first phase of a project to be run as an incremental delivery. Light grey boxes are *milestones* – stage points in the project; dark grey boxes are activities, showing, at their bottom left-hand corner, the calculated earliest start date and the number of days effort estimated for the work. Activities with black outlines are on the critical path.

You can see that the delivery of the interface specifications is currently a critical dependency too, and some experimentation with the database to determine its performance is also on the critical path. A moment's thought will suggest that there is no need for it to be so, if it were possible for it to start the moment that planning was complete, rather than waiting for the User Layer to have been finalised. There is clearly room for some manoeuvre here.

This is not a book on planning with activity networks so I shan't go into a lot of detail here about the use of slack, and hammocks, and lags, and the like, but I have some specific pieces of advice for anyone working with a network:

- Concentrate on where the critical path turns up.

- If a particularly risky activity turns up on the critical path, find a way to get it off: only have safe, predictable activities on the critical path.

- Keep yourself off the critical path: if the project goes critical you should be managing it, not doing the most critical work.

- If you plan to do more than manage the project, give yourself something unimportant to do, preferably something that can take the whole of the project without causing trouble. Don't be Technical Authority as well as Project Manager ('I like to keep a close eye on the technical side when I am managing') – that's pure selfishness as well as dangerous. There will be other people who will want to take on the role of Technical Authority – you should not expect to collect jobs like this.

- Don't let inexperienced staff work on critical activities if you can help it: they are already a risk in themselves.

- Don't let individuals work on two things at once unless it really makes sense. Take note of this yourself.

- Don't leave large gaps in people's timeline – time when they would be 'resting'. But there's no need at this stage to ensure that everyone is gainfully occupied every single day. You should leave a little slack in the plan for future use. (More subversion? Sure, but when the time comes to squeeze the project it's like any negotiation, it's nice to have a little you can give away without too much pain.)

Finally, spend as much time as you can just playing with your plan: see what the effect of likely delays would be (try slipping that hardware delivery by two weeks, or doubling the time that weak team member takes to get that component delivered), juggle the staff around the activities within their competence, and so on. Your aim should be to see where your plan is delicate, where the sensitivities are – in summary, what its *dynamics* are. Once you know those dynamics you will be able to respond more quickly and more appropriately when something *does* go wrong during the project. You'll know the likely effect almost without having to refer to your network.

Are plans programs?

This is a good moment to observe that our plans traditionally only capture sequence and sequential logic: 'this activity follows that activity', or 'this activity follows those activities'. When we looked at process models in detail in Chapters 3 and 4 and at the different ways we could manage risk in a project we discovered we wanted to be able to make decisions during our projects ('if this proves to be so, then do this, else do that'), and to have iterations ('do this until something is true'). In other words we would ideally like all the traditional *programming* constructs of sequence, selection and iteration.

But a 'normal' plan, of the sort that has always been drawn since PERT and related techniques were invented decades ago, shows only sequence, as if no decisions were going to be made downstream, and everything need only be done once to be right. What are we to do? It seems that a true plan must be closer to a program; it must be able to 'unroll' in a number of different ways, *each of which we have planned in advance*. Having alternative plans is nothing more than contingency planning – but how often do we show this in software development plans? And how often do we show explicitly the possibility of iteration?

Unfortunately we are not helped here by our project management tools. Until the time comes that I can express my project – as I would like to – as a program that can unwind in different ways (in the same way that the Spiral Model can unwind in different ways, for instance), I shall have to resort to half-truths in my networks, and in particular I shall have to compromise on the representation of iteration and decisions in my process model.

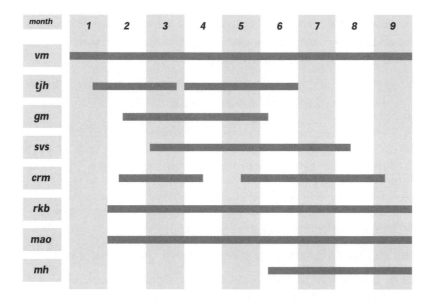

Figure 9-9. Effort profile by person

Deducing the effort profile

Once you have juggled staff, activities and dependencies until you get a project that looks feasible, you can read an effort profile from your network. (Note that you did not *start* with this picture!) An everyday project planning tool will generate one automatically for you. Ignore those few days mid-project when someone is between activities. You'll end up with a simple barchart such as that in Figure 9-9. Imagine how pointless it would have been to have started trying to draw up such a barchart right at the beginning.

Deducing costs and milestones

Now comes the moment of truth – the moment when you have all the information at hand to determine when you can deliver the system and what the total cost will be.

By using the appropriate day cost for each of your staff, you can determine from your effort profile what the total effort cost will be. Again, an everyday project planning tool will do this for you. To get the full project cost you will need to add a whole host of other costs – often referred to as *materials and expenses (M&E)* – some of which will have been thrown up by your risk and quality planning, and others of which you will need to remember, from checklists, company procedures, or whatever. Here is a selection of some of the things you will need to consider:

- fees for training courses (in methods, in the use of support tools or embedded packages, in languages, etc.)

- software licence fees for the development, target and maintenance environments (database management systems, specialist applications, component libraries, compilers, operating systems, communications packages, planning tools, CASE systems, etc.)

- travel and accommodation costs (during training, visiting suppliers, visiting your client, users, the site, etc.)

- hire of specialist or spare equipment for the duration of the project.

The sum of the planned effort costs and the M&E is what I shall call the *base cost* (*BASE*) of the project, the cost of the things you are planning to do. Note how it has been derived from technical considerations of the project.

To this *BASE* figure you must add the figure you arrived at on commercial grounds as the provision you would make for risks and opportunities. The result is your forecast cost to completion for the project, taking into account risks and opportunities.

HEADLINE

The forecast cost to completion of your project is the sum of the base cost and the provision for risks and opportunities.

If you are bidding for work in a competitive situation, there will be a whole host of other considerations to be taken into account when coming up with the final *price* – for a price is never the development cost alone. When deriving your price you will consider items such as:

- inflation over the life of the project

- financing of cash flow (depending on the payment schedule you can negotiate with your client)

- any currency fluctuations

- profit.

These are definitely matters that I shall leave to your commercial judgement – the essentials probably remain the same but the detail will differ from one organisation to another.

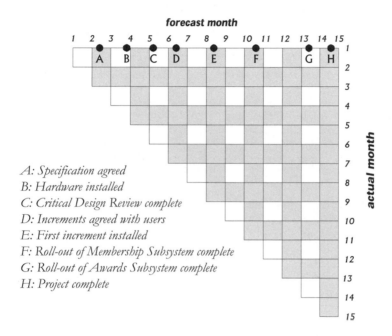

Figure 9-10. A milestone chart in its initial form

In the same way, you can provide a base forecast of the completion date of your project by reading off the end date of your network of planned activities, and then adding any timescale provision you have made for risks and opportunities.

Equally, you should read off perhaps between six and ten key points – *milestones* – from your project network that represent real achievement and use these to construct a *milestone chart*. Progress against the milestones can then be monitored as the project proceeds, and the milestone chart will provide a good summary of progress and forecasts to senior management and the client, who might not want all the gory detail. Figure 9-10 shows a simple milestone chart. There are (in this case) eight milestones labelled *A* to *H* plotted on the vertical axis ('actual month') against month 1, which is today. Each milestone is plotted on the horizontal ('forecast month') axis according to when our activity network says we expect that milestone to be achieved. As the months go by, we will reforecast the expected dates of the milestones and plot the new dates, moving down the chart month by month.

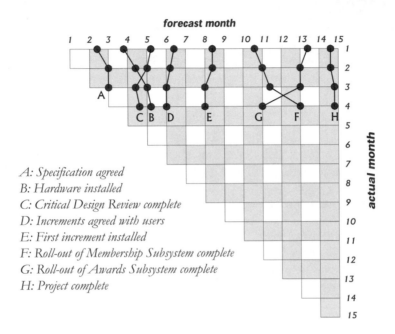

Figure 9-11. A milestone chart after three months

Figure 9-11 shows the chart as it might look three months later, at the start of month 4. We achieved the first milestone, *Specification agreed*, about two weeks late. The hardware installation is slipping badly, but we have made good progress on the work getting up to the Critical Design Review. The forecast for the first increment has changed a little and is not affected by the hardware slippage (we must have planned for this and ordered early). There have been some big changes in the roll-out, however, and we have swapped the order of the roll-out of the Membership and Awards subsystems, perhaps in response to the way that things were looking in the previous month.

Such a milestone chart gives a good quick indication of the way things are going, in particular the *trends*. It can also signal hopeless optimism. Figure 9-12 shows things slipping left, right and centre, with later milestones getting increasingly compressed. We are now in month 7, and only milestones *A* and

C have been achieved, whereas we should have achieved *A*, *B*, *C* and *D*. But, strangely, the end date will still be held!

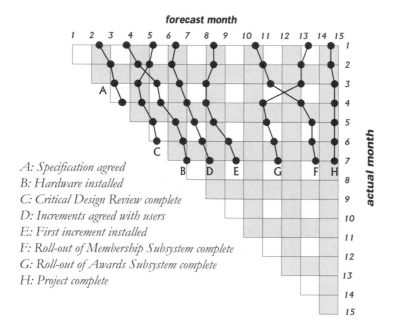

A: Specification agreed
B: Hardware installed
C: Critical Design Review complete
D: Increments agreed with users
E: First increment installed
F: Roll-out of Membership Subsystem complete
G: Roll-out of Awards Subsystem complete
H: Project complete

Figure 9-12. Hopeless optimism

Iterating to the 'right' answer

It seems to be a law of nature that when you have done your network, deduced your effort profile and deduced the delivery date and the cost of the project, they always seem out of line with the date and money you have been given. I personally take what is sometimes regarded by colleagues as a rather subversive view of this. It is that when the project manager is drawing up the plan for the first time they should do so without regard to the *external* constraints such as required delivery date or budget. This is the one exception to my earlier advice to start with a network with every conceivable constraint in it. They should aim to produce the ideal plan for the job in hand. This doesn't mean they are at liberty to produce a plan that takes as long as they like in delivering the system. They should simply use their best analysis to decide how long it should ideally take and how many staff should ideally be on the project team. And the plan should not assume that overtime will be worked from day one.

Once a feasible and workable plan has been produced, *then* is the time to start squeezing budget and timescale to meet the commercial requirements. The reason for doing it this way is simple: when you squeeze a project you introduce risk, by definition. And you, as project manager, have a responsibility to know precisely what risks you are taking. Indeed, nearly half of this book has been largely about identifying risks and planning to manage your way through them. Just chucking risk back into the plan now, without knowing you're doing it, would be madness!

The need to squeeze a project arises for commercial reasons, and for perfectly good commercial reasons very often. But commercial decisions are very much about risk analysis: how much risk to take and at what potential cost and at what potential pay-off. So new risk should only be put in a project *knowingly*. And that means squeezing the ideal project to fit the commercial necessities, and *not* starting off with a compressed project with no knowledge of the risks that have been introduced.

I think that this is a lot to do with people wanting to give the right answer – being keen to say they can do things – while keeping quiet about the risks that are causing them to curl their toes under the table and to bite their lips in horror.

> **HEADLINE**
>
> When finalising the Resource Plan the aim should be to separate technical decisions about feasibility from commercial decisions about risk taking.

A template for the Resource Plan

Exactly what shape your Resource Plan will take is very much a matter for local tradition (if you have any), but Figure 9-13 gives at least its likely contents.

Chapter recap

Your risk and quality planning work has yielded data in three areas: a process model and process fragments to handle risks and uncertainties, methods and their products, and a set of V&V activities. You now combine these in a single, hierarchical *Work Breakdown Structure* (WBS) together with other supporting activities. The completeness of this WBS is crucial to the realism of your plan.

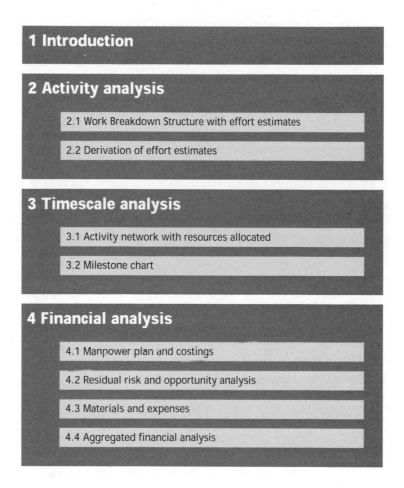

1 Introduction

2 Activity analysis

2.1 Work Breakdown Structure with effort estimates

2.2 Derivation of effort estimates

3 Timescale analysis

3.1 Activity network with resources allocated

3.2 Milestone chart

4 Financial analysis

4.1 Manpower plan and costings

4.2 Residual risk and opportunity analysis

4.3 Materials and expenses

4.4 Aggregated financial analysis

Figure 9-13: Contents list of a Resource Plan

You then cost your WBS by ascribing an amount of effort to each activity. You can derive your effort estimates in a variety of ways. If possible, you should use top-down (holistic) *and* bottom-up (analytic) methods, together with any sanity checks that you have.

Once you have a costed WBS, you can construct an activity network that contains all the activities and their interdependencies – the logic of your plan.

By ascribing individual staff or types of staff to the activities, you can derive a basic forecast end date and a base cost. If (when) these prove not to be acceptable you can apply various 'tricks' to shorten timescales. However, all such tricks generally introduce some new risk and so such compromises need to be taken knowingly – they might be acceptable on commercial grounds, and it is important to separate technical idealism from commercial realism.

By adding cost and timescale provisions to the base cost and basic end date you obtain your forecast cost to completion and forecast end date.

Your network will also provide forecast dates for project milestones which can be used in monitoring progress.

> ## OUTCOME
> Your Resource Plan provides you with the cost and timescale consequences of the technical analysis you have carried out in risk and quality planning, and it captures the commercial decisions you have taken about the appropriate level of provision for residual risks and opportunities.

We have achieved the aim we set ourselves: *either* a realistic and reliable plan on which to base our pricing and our bid for this project, *or* a realistic and reliable definition of the work we will now carry out.

In the first case, let the bidding begin.

In the second, let the project begin.

References

Boehm 1981

Software Engineering Economics. B W Boehm. Prentice-Hall, Englewood Cliffs, 1981

Jones 1998

Estimating Software Costs. C Jones. McGraw Hill, 1998

Symons 1991

Software Sizing and Estimating. C R Symons, John Wiley & Sons, Chichester, 1991

10 The hand on the tiller and the Captain's log

Introduction

The Good Ship Project is launched and at sea, but hopefully not all at sea.

With an ocean to cross, your job as project manager is to keep the vessel heading in the right direction and, if I may continue the metaphor just a little further, you will need some navigation aids to tell you where you are at any one moment and some maps to help you skirt the rocks. And as you go, you will want to record the story for your own and your colleagues' benefit on future voyages.

Monitoring the project

In this chapter I present a simple but reliable way of regularly checking progress and reforecasting outcome. It's a way that has been successfully used in the software houses that I have worked in, i.e. in environments where reliable forecasts of future costs are vital to profitability. There is nothing special about it, but it falls out naturally from the planning method I have given in the previous chapters. If you have a project of small to medium size (say up to 50 person-years of effort) you will find it will work quite adequately without major effort on your part. As the project increases in size, particularly in terms of the number of people working on it, so the job becomes bigger and you might look for additional administrative support and some tool support to ease the burden.

Recording history is of course interesting but the real point of preparing your monthly report is to forecast the future, not to report on the past. So your first step must be to find out where your project stands against the plan in as much detail as you can. Knowing where your project is, you can forecast where it is going – or, rather, where you intend to *manage* it to go!

Since this is principally a book on *planning* I shall not get into detail, just enough to show how your plan can be a basis for rigorous monitoring.

Recording the past

Your first move must to be to find out exactly where you are on your plan. I assume that you have been doing this, at least informally, day in and day out anyway, and that you don't wait for the end of every month to find out what's going on. But at month-end you do it in detail.

For each work package that has been worked on during the last month find out the number of days that have been used on it. There are many ways you could collect this. A common one is to use some form of contract between the manager or team leader and the staff member. Such a work package contract would:

- identify the work package to be done (e.g. *3462 Prepare Acceptance Test Plan*)

- identify the inputs to be used (e.g. issue 2.1 of *System Specification* and issue 1.4 of *Project Overall Test Plan*)

- identify the outputs to be generated (e.g. a definitive issue of a document to be entitled *System Acceptance Test Plan* agreed with the client)

- define the quality level to be achieved, probably by reference to the project's Quality Control Plan (the term *exit criteria* is sometimes used here)

- define the amount of effort allowed (e.g. three weeks) and the required date.

This contract would be agreed with the staff member who would then start on the work. Each month each engineer updates the work package record with the time actually spent and their new estimate of how much work is still to go. When the work package is finished it is checked by the person who handed out the contract and the final amount of effort used is recorded on the contract. This should be a basic metric recorded for all work packages.

Forecasting the future

Now that you have collected your input data, you can take last month's report/forecast (or the original plan if you are at the end of your first month) and forecast again.

The process is simple:

1 For each work package that has been worked on during the last month but not finished, find out the number of days of effort that the staff member concerned reckons are required to finish it. It is not enough for them to subtract the number they have spent from the number you gave them at the start of the work package! You need a realistic estimate of what there is to go.

There is of course a great deal of psychology about getting these to-go figures. How you go about it is up to you – you might want to put the pressure on, or you might believe the person is so over-optimistic that you need to advise them otherwise! This is not a book on psychology, so I leave such matters up to you.

2 Update your Work Package Analysis (Figure 9-7) with the to-go figures you have collected. You'll get something like Figure 10-1, which also shows the effort used figure updated ('leaf' activities are in roman type). A little arithmetic will tell you what the forecast total of effort is now, as of today. You will use this as a cross-check in a minute.

3 Review the risk and opportunity profile of the project. There is a separate section on this below, but suffice it to note here that you should be checking whether the risk and opportunity management activities you currently have in place are still relevant, whether some need to be changed or moved or deleted, and whether new ones need to be added. As a result you can amend your WBS and activity network.

4 And now for the most important step: updating your network. (Precise details for doing this clearly depend on the tool you are using.) Delete or mark as 'completed' each completed activity. If an activity has started but not finished, update its duration to the estimated effort to go, or mark it appropriately for the tool you are using. If an activity has not yet started you should nevertheless give a moment's thought to whether the original estimate is still sensible. Your experience to date on the project might lead you to revise some of the original estimates.

For instance, you might have got some way into coding work and discovered that your original estimates seem to be consistently about 15% under what is actually being achieved. You can turn the heat up under your programmers of course, or (better) find some ways of increasing their productivity. But you might also take a pragmatic view and adjust your forecasts on the network for the remaining coding activities.

5   Read off new dates from your updated network, both for intermediate milestones and for the final delivery and plot them as a new row on your milestone chart.

6   Finally, determine the new total cost to date and the new total to go, and add them to give the new value of *BASE*.

Used days	To-go days	Plan days	WP	Work package title
			1000	*Project Management*
			1100	*Initiate project*
6	0	5	1110	Draft and agree Project Schedule
1	0	2	1120	Set up project file
18	0	15	1130	Prepare Risk Plan
8	0	10	1140	Prepare Quality Plan
13	0	10	1150	Prepare Resource Plan
…	…	…	…	…
			1200	*Monitor and report on project progress*
16	85	105	1210	…
			1300	*Administer project*
26	85	120	1310	…
			1400	*Liaise with client*
			1410	…
0	15	15	1500	Close and debrief project
			2100	*Specify requirements*
62	0	55	2110	Analyse functional requirements
21	0	25	2120	Analyse performance requirements
24	0	30	2130	Produce outline design
32	0	20	2140	Define user interface through prototyping
			2200	*Specify system*
…	…	…	2210	…
…	…	…	…	…
255	1023	1450	totals	

Figure 10-1. A Work Package Analysis updated with to-go and forecast effort figures

As with the original planning work that you did, you will no doubt occasionally find that the cost and date you come up with at the month end is not the 'right' answer. If you are forecasting an overrun or overspend, your options are same as ever: reduce the scope of the work, turn up the heat under your staff, find new ways of doing things, or get an extension or more money.

I have known many project managers feel very reluctant to update their network every month. They feel it is an unnecessary burden. But it's clear to me that, if you don't, you are once again ignoring dependencies and the effect they will have on the end date. I cannot understand how anyone can predict a new end date *without* redoing the network. Ignore dependencies and you are in the realms of fiction.

If the above process sounds a lot, I can assure you it isn't. Before the days of spreadsheets I used to do the whole thing on pencil and paper. I would reckon on spending about two days at the end of the month preparing a full report including technical, timescale and financial status for my line management and the client at the expense of a set of calculator batteries. With spreadsheets and planning tools the effort is reduced to just that required to rework the network – and this is time well spent as you are getting to know the new dynamics of your project, exploring the effect of future events and the sensitivity of your project to different risks.

With the figures now all to hand, other analytical techniques such as *earned value analysis* can be used to give you further insight into the trends on your project.

HEADLINE

At the monthly review of the project, the spend to date and forecast to go figures are updated to give a new forecast base cost.

Reviewing the risk and opportunity profile

In Chapters 3 and 4 we went into a lot of detail to analyse the risks and the opportunities on our project, and I promised that we would use that analysis not just in the costing of the project (where we simply added a total provision to the base cost of the project) but also as a monitoring tool as the project progressed. That moment has come.

Part of our Risk and Opportunity Register might look like the following table (in which we have assessed impacts in terms of their effect on the costs rather than on the timescale):

#	Residual risk/opportunity	Best case (£K)	Chosen case (£K)	Worst case (£K)
...	...	...	...	...
17	New staff are slow to adopt new programming practices	0	5	20
18	Geoff may be borrowed for the SCOP maintenance work	0	0	10
19	The L27 driver from the SCOP project can be reused	-10	-15	-30
20	The new configuration control tool needs upgrading before the project end	0	5	20
21	We have miscalculated the licence requirements on the development environment	0	2	6
22	We fail to agree the L28 interface by the agreed date	0	5	20
...	...	...	...	...
	totals	30	65	75

In total, it is saying that the minimum provision we should make for residual risks is £30K and the maximum £75K. For the desired level of comfort we are choosing £65K. This figure takes into account the risks and the provisions. Let's now make a separate list for the risks and one for the opportunities and do the same arithmetic. We now get the following figures:

	Best case (£K)	Chosen case (£K)	Worst case (£K)
total provision for risks	50	95	125
total provision for opportunities	-20	-30	-50

If we now estimate that our base cost (*BASE*) will be £720K we could say that, at our chosen level of comfort, a total of £815K (£720K+£95K) would see us through all our risks without realising any opportunities and that a total of £690K (£720K-£30K) would require us to realise all our opportunities without any risks materialising. We could characterise the project's situation with those three figures: £690K, £720K, £815K, i.e. the base cost less the opportunity provision, the base cost, and the base cost plus the risk provision. Let's call them *BASE–*, *BASE* and *BASE+*.

Each month we revisit the Risk Register (step 3 above). Some risks will have materialised, some will have dissipated and others will still be lurking. We rework the list, deciding whether we are happy that the risk reduction measures that we have in place (if any) are still appropriate and adjusting the plan accordingly – this might mean adding some new activities to the plan or removing ones we now no longer feel necessary. Of course, new risks might break on the scene – perhaps some early experiences with the new object library have made us think that it will not give the performance we had taken for granted and there is now a chance we shall have to revisit the way we are using it in the design.

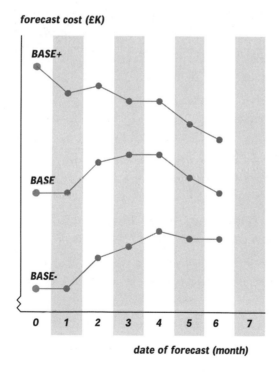

Figure 10-2. The provisions funnel

We do the same thing for opportunities, assessing the ones we knew about and checking for new ones.

If a risk materialises, its financial impact of course adds to the base cost *BASE* as money that has been spent (the impact), and we can remove any provision we made. That provision might or might not have been enough. If we realise an opportunity, the financial saving will reduce the base cost *BASE* as money that has or will be saved, and we can remove any provision we made.

By the time we have finished this analysis we shall have a new total line for risks and a new total line for opportunities. Our base cost forecast will probably also have changed and the new characterisation of the project's financial state might be £700K, £710K, £790K. Clearly we have lost some opportunities but also some risks. This is something that we can now track, month on month, in addition to all the other indicators that our planning and monitoring tool will give us. Figure 10-2 suggests how this can be done.

Each month the risks and opportunities are reassessed and the three figures calculated and plotted on a graph. To illustrate how it works, I have arranged that in this project only one thing has changed each month:

month 1 A risk has evaporated and the provision for it can be removed from *BASE+*.

month 2 A risk has materialised and its impact was greater than the provision. As a result, *BASE* rises (taking *BASE-* with it) but *BASE+* does not rise as much.

month 3 A risk has materialised and its impact was significantly less than the provision. As a result, *BASE* rises (taking *BASE-* with it) but *BASE+* falls more.

month 4 An opportunity has evaporated and its provision can be removed. As a result, *BASE-* rises.

month 5 An opportunity was realised and the gain was greater than the provision. As a result, *BASE* falls (taking *BASE+* with it) but *BASE-* falls less.

month 6 An opportunity was realised to the same level as the provision. As a result, *BASE-* stays where it is, but *BASE* falls, taking *BASE+* with it.

The resulting graph can give us some strong signals. If the three lines are converging the project is stabilising. If they are converging upwards it is stabilising towards a higher cost than anticipated; if they are converging downwards it is stabilising towards a lower cost than anticipated. If *BASE-* and *BASE* are not converging then opportunities remain and/or are arising and/or are not being realised – this could give us a warm feeling. If *BASE+*

and *BASE* are not converging then risks remain and/or are arising and/or are not being managed out – this should definitely give us cause for concern.

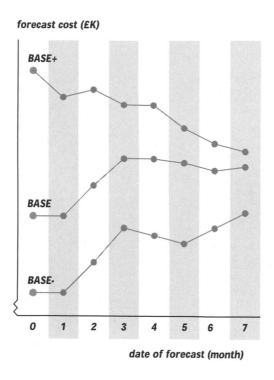

Figure 10-3. Cause for some comfort

Suppose our graph was looking like Figure 10-3. If we simply looked at the *BASE* figure – the sum of money spent and forecast cost still to come – we would get very concerned by the increase. But we would be somewhat comforted to see that the risks are being managed out of the project and there are some good opportunities still to be realised – perhaps it is time to concentrate on managing those to fruition.

   If our graph looked like Figure 10-4 but we only looked at the *BASE* figure we could start congratulating ourselves on how our forecast of the total cost of the project had been falling. But the moment we saw the lines for *BASE+* and *BASE-* our celebrations would look premature: the risk content on the project has also been climbing and we are running out of compensating opportunities.

The point I want to make from these pictures is that any forecasts that do not factor in the current risks and opportunities facing the project are not safe predictors of the project's future.

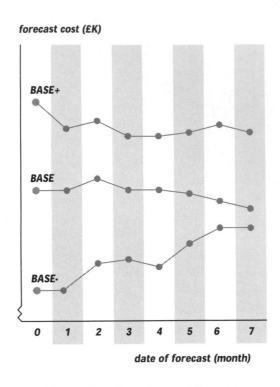

Figure 10-4. Cause for some discomfort

HEADLINE

The trend of risk and opportunity provision shows whether or not the project is being held under control.

The curse of measurement

Whenever the topic of measurement in software is brought up, Lord Kelvin, the nineteenth-century physicist, is bound to be quoted out of context from his *Popular Lectures*: 'When you can measure what you are speaking about and express it in numbers, you know something about it; but when you cannot measure, when you cannot express it in numbers, your knowledge is of a meagre and unsatisfactory kind: but you have scarcely, in your thoughts advanced to the stage of a science.' There then invariably follows the 'deduction' that software development is unscientific if nothing is being measured. We might just as well accuse scientists of being unscientific if they do not measure their own processes: counting the hypotheses they make daily, the number that successfully make it through one, two, and more predictions, and so on. What scientists do measure – and this is what Kelvin meant – is the *subject matter* of their science, measurements of flows, volumes, temperatures and so on; they don't measure science itself – that's the business of sociologists and academic funding committees. The analogy collapses since software engineering is not an observational science; it is a design process that applies technology. A proper parallel is with the designers and builders of bridges and buildings who apply mathematics in the development of their designs: we as software engineers apply logic and reasoning of a form appropriate to our subject matter – any look at a text on (mathematically) formal methods, on the theoretical underpinnings of object-oriented methods, on the mathematics of security or cryptography, or the 'calculus' of relational theory will show us behaving in a 'scientific' way.

Unfortunately there is a further analogy that is often used to goad us into more and more measurement: the manufacturing analogy. Software development, the argument goes, is just like any other manufacturing activity: people make things, in this case pieces of software, so why don't we apply the measurement techniques used in manufacturing industries and apply them directly to our software development projects and organisations?

I am certain that this is a very dangerous argument and I want to demolish it and then put something else in its place. But first let's see where the manufacturing analogy comes from. I want to look at both ISO 9001, which very definitely has its origins in the world of production lines, and the *Capability Maturity Model* (CMM), which was devised especially for the software world but has tried to base itself on the manufacturing paradigm.

Measurement in ISO 9001 and ISO 9000-3

In Chapter 5 we looked at the requirements of a QMS as called for by ISO 9001, at the general level, and ISO 9000-3 at the specific level of software. I want here to take a second look at a corner that I glossed over in the earlier treatment.

For the software developer ISO 9001 leaves openings in two areas. First, it calls for 'preventive action' which will include ways of 'detecting, analysing and eliminating potential causes of non-conformities'. ISO 9000-3 does not address this topic, based as it was on the earlier version of ISO 9001 which did not deal with it specifically. So we are left rather in the air currently. Second, ISO 9001 requires the supplier to 'identify the need for statistical techniques required for establishing, controlling and verifying process capability and product characteristics' and then to have 'procedures to implement and control the application' of those techniques. 'Process capability' is used here as a technical term defined (Ishikawa 1990) as 'the performance of a process over a certain period of time while in the statistically controlled state'; one way of putting it might be 'the degree of variation in the output of the process that is due to the process itself.'

ISO 9000-3 elaborates this by requiring the choice and use of quantitative measures of quality as a trigger for 'remedial action' should performance not meet targets defined for those measures, and as a way of defining 'specific improvement goals'. This is an open-ended definition because, as it admits, 'there are currently no universally accepted measures of software quality'. This (properly) lets ISO off the hook when it comes to trying to define any 'universal' measures, but it leaves the more practical question to be answered by the individual organisation: 'what will our measures be and how will we use them to assess statistical control or lack of it?'.

Measurement in the CMM's levels 4 and 5

For its part, the CMM also takes us into unknown waters in levels 4 and 5. I say 'unknown' because it seems clear that they are, at present, largely speculative. In his first book Humphrey's (Humphreys 1989) coverage of levels 4 and 5 was comparatively weak, reflecting the fact that the role of measurement for process improvement was still poorly understood. However it, and the subsequent authoritative text from the SEI (SEI 1995), proposed the translation of the techniques of statistical process control (SPC) (e.g. from Deming (1986) and Ishikawa (1990) sections 2.8 and 4.7.7), and the use of fault analysis for process improvement. I believe the ice becomes very thin at these two levels.

Humphrey says that 'Levels 4 and 5 are relatively unknown territory for the software industry. There are only a few examples of Level 4 and 5 software projects and organisations. There are too few to draw general conclusions about the characteristics of Level 4 and 5 organisations. The characteristics of these levels have been defined by analogy with other industries and the few examples in the software industry exhibiting this level of process capability'. Little appears to have changed since 1989 to provide any more examples to validate the definitions of levels 4 and 5. I know one organisation in the UK that could reasonably have laid claim to having a level 5 operation as far as measurement and process improvement are concerned. It was a maintenance group dedicated to handling change requests to a single system some decades old. Not quite the average situation of an IT development department moving new and legacy systems into client/server with RAD, or of a group developing new systems in avionics, or air traffic control, or medical instrumentation.

There is the danger that, while we might find a few organisations that meet the current level 4 and 5 requirements, they only validate the model *for organisations like them*. We will only get a useful validation if we perceive that those organisations *are representative* of the types of situations prevalent in our industry and that we can, by induction, demonstrate that levels 4 and 5 offer an effective route for the generality of organisations. I see no evidence that this has happened or will happen.

The CMM explicitly imports the work of Shewhart, Deming and Juran on statistical process control and calls for its use during the software development process. It requires that projects actively bring process variation within acceptable quantitative boundaries, using notions such as *mean* and *variance*. It talks about 'identifying *special causes of variation* within a *measurably stable* process and correcting … the circumstances that drove the transient variation to occur' (my italics). It follows traditional SPC principles: 'without controlling the process within *statistically narrow boundaries* (small variations in process measures), there is too much noise in the data to determine objectively whether a specific process improvement has an effect' (my italics), and it deduces that level 4's aim of bringing the process under statistical control must be achieved before level 5's aim of process improvement can be attempted. The SEI's book *The Capability Maturity Model: Guidelines for Improving the Software Process* (SEI 1995) is expressly clear about this use of SPC (pp. 19–20).

We need to look closely at the appropriateness of SPC to software development, since both ISO 9001 and levels 4 and 5 of the CMM rely on it. In particular, we need to ask 'can we give meaning to the notions of SPC and process capability when applied to the software development process?'.

SPC and software development

First we need to understand a little more about the style of SPC called for in the CMM and ISO 9001.

A glance at Ishikawa's book (1990, section 2.1) shows us that, of the Seven Tools of Quality Control (which include Pareto charts and histograms), the main one is the *control chart*, which involves 'statistically calculated control limit lines'. These control limits bound the statistical variation inherent in the process; the wider they are apart the less the capability of the process (Humphrey 1989, Chapter 15). Note that they are statistically calculated, on the assumption that the feature we are measuring about our process conforms to a normal distribution. It is the control chart style of SPC that makes possible what the CMM calls for in levels 4 and 5. (My investigations suggest, however, that most people in software development interpret SPC as Simply People Counting.)

Control charts are important to SPC because they allow the separation of what are called *special causes* and *common causes*. 'Special causes' are those that are due to a specific situation: things that are the responsibility of the individual worker, or due to faulty inputs to the process, or to machinery going out of alignment. 'Common causes' are those that are a property of the process itself: things whose prevention is in the hands of management as process owners. The control chart allows us to discriminate between these; given a set of measurements, statistical formulae give us upper and lower *control limits* which bound the inherent variability of the process. A value falling outside those limits is thus due to a special cause. A process which is 'under statistical control' is one that is free from variations other than those inherent in the process itself – the measurements consistently fall between the upper and lower control limits. Only such a process, the argument goes, can sensibly be the subject of process improvement, for, if the process is not under statistical control (i.e. free from special causes), we might find ourselves changing the process in response to effects generated by a special cause, with the result that we actually make the process worse. Hence the assumption underlying the two-stage approach of levels 4 and 5: first get the process under control by removing special causes (level 4), and then improve the process by removing common, i.e. systemic, causes.

But software development is not a manufacturing process.

In everyday software engineering situations we cannot expect to be able to apply manufacturing-style SPC; the software process – or any small part of it – is not a manufacturing process which we can adjust the knobs on. It is a *design* activity. As such it is largely an *intellectual* and a *sociological* activity, prone to many influences, including changes in the type of work being done, subtle differences in the complexity of solutions, changes in the technologies which the development group might be forced to use, changes in staff or recruitment policy, changes in general morale due to external factors, a new project manager on the client's side, and, perhaps above all, the learning that goes on inside the heads of the individuals – let alone any planned process improvements being put in place. On a manufacturing line, if I give the green knob half a turn I know – because there is a physical or chemical causal model available to me – that the widgets will be 0.01 mm thinner. In software engineering we simply do not have that strong causal model. If we have causal models at all they will be very complex, and, as a result, our ability to use measurement in the manufacturing sense will be correspondingly weakened. Why otherwise does COCOMO have 15 cost drivers and Mark II Function Point Analysis even more?

Moreover, we have no *a priori* reason to suppose that our software engineering processes behave in a normally distributed way. If we are to use statistics we will need other forms that do not make this assumption.

The use of measurement

Is this a counsel of despair? No, but it is a counsel of caution, especially to the definers of international standards. Am I against measurement? No, but I believe we have to be clear about what is a *valid* role for measurement in a sociological design activity carried out in an environment of learning. In particular we need statistical techniques that only make assumptions that are true of the software engineering environment and that use more complex causal models than SPC.

The great Lord Kelvin cannot be summoned to give evidence for the case for measurement on software projects. And I do not think that Dr Deming can appear either. Far more useful is the tag that 'you cannot manage what you cannot measure'.

I know that in everyday rough-and-ready terms I can use measurement in order to spot a potential problem: the module that seems to be taking more time to code than one would expect for its size; the module that has undergone more than its quota of changes given its size; the area of the specification that has generated the largest number of change requests from the users (what we might call Spotting Potential Chaos). However, this is not the same as using SPC with its assumption of an underlying statistical distribution model. By all means let us make simple measurements of fault densities and let us spot potential trouble-makers, but this is not an issue for statistical means, or subgroup ranges, or standard deviations, or upper and lower control limits, or control charts, or statistical analysis.

This is not a book on measurement (but I recommend *Software Metrics* Fenton 1991) so I shall restrict myself to an early experience of my own of the value of *indicators*.

On a project that Nick Birrell and I once worked on, we made frequent re-estimates of the size of the system. We estimated blind each time, that is, without looking at the last figures for a component. As the estimates came in we expectantly plotted them to see what was happening.

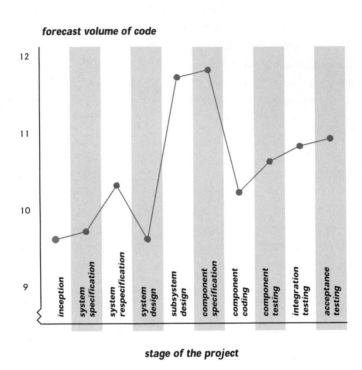

Figure 10-5. A history of size estimates

Figure 10-5 shows our estimates at various stages in development:

- at the start of the project
- twice during system specification
- on completion of overall system design
- on completion of subsystem design
- on completion of component specification
- at the end of component coding

- at the completion of component testing, about a year after subsystem design

- at the end of integration testing (i.e. ready for acceptance testing)

- after acceptance testing (i.e. at the entry to operational use).

Much of what happened was predictable. Until we really got into subsystem design our estimates were fairly constant – then they went bang! This was I suspect due to a combination of finally understanding in detail all the ramifications of what we were constructing, and of the fact that we were starting to estimate smaller chunks with the consequent increase in rounding up. As we actually got into writing the code, the volume dropped back a bit.

Overall we were 20% too low in our original estimates. The relative constancy of the estimates suggested to me that estimating KLOC, even from a system specification, is practical and sufficiently accurate for estimating purposes. At the point that we saw a large rise in volume of code we decided to take action to contain the problem. Having that early indication meant we could take early action. There really are very few other indicators that can give you as project manager early warning of possible overrun – too many measurements only tell you that things have already gone wrong: you've spent too much, or you've overrun.

I also know that I can keep my measurements over an extended period of time and perhaps, only perhaps, spot a trend. How do I respond to that trend? Suppose the trend represents an improvement. Can I congratulate myself on the process improvements I have recently put in place, or is it more likely that any improvement due to them is swamped by the fact that this is the second such system that this team has built?' Suppose the trend represents a degradation. What can I tell from it except that, for some reason, things have become worse?

So, all that my measurements are telling me is that things are better or worse, but I get no more help. (I can probably tell that things are going wrong, albeit a bit later, through my measurements of planned and actual effort use and schedule.) To get that help I must look to *fault analysis*: how did that fault get inserted and why did it escape detection until now? This tells us clearly what could be done to improve our production process and our verification process. Again we will look for trends so that we can tackle the big and/or expensive ones first, but this is still not a statistical question, simply one of recognising patterns and thinking through what we do. This for me is the constructive aspect of levels 4 and 5 – the institutionalised use of fault analysis to seek common causes and remove them – and it is an aspect that is consonant with ISO 9001.

Deming would not, I suspect, have liked my rough-and-ready approach, but I believe that we are in danger of being seduced by the lure of SPC. We are dealing with a sociological system, not a physical one; a soft system, not a hard one. If we demanded equivalent use of SPC by physicists we would be demanding from them the measurement and statistical analysis of their processes for developing hypotheses, designing experiments, carrying out experiments, and updating hypotheses. They do not do any of that; should we then accuse them of being unscientific?

So, for the everyday software development group's environment, I do not believe we can achieve a process which would in Deming's terms be recognisably under statistical control: the local influencing factors are too many and too strong, and too unavoidable. SPC in its traditional manufacturing sense is inappropriate for the software engineering *design* process. However, all is not lost. I believe we can find a formulation of levels 4 and 5 that still retains the notion of fault prevention and process improvement but that characterises them in ways that are meaningful for the software development process and the generality of software engineering groups.

For fault prevention, our use of measurement must be restricted to its power as an indicator in a very crude sense, that of pointing to *potential* trouble spots (Spotting Potential Chaos). We might use simple and robust data exploration (for instance, *box plots* described by Hoaglin *et al* (Hoaglin 1983)) to help us decide what is an 'outlier', i.e. what we wish to regard as anomalous and worthy of investigation, and we must then use our engineering judgement to decide if there was a genuine reason for the outlier or if it was an outlier only in terms of our crude discriminator. No algorithms or statistical formulae will replace that engineering judgement. In other words, we do not need to use a statistical algorithm to tell us which are the potential anomalies. We will look at *anything* that looks anomalous and make a decision. I believe this is both practical and methodologically sound (enough).

For process improvement we must still rely on fault analysis, but our use of fault analysis should be restricted to the search for patterns, not for statistical significance. We must use engineering judgement to spot those patterns. No pattern matching algorithm or spurious classification scheme will replace that engineering judgement.

We have now disconnected anomaly detection based on measurement from process improvement based on fault analysis, and thereby have effectively removed the ordering of levels 4 and 5. We are now using measurement in a realistic way, but it is not the way that either ISO 9001 or the CMM wants us to use it.

A level 5 organisation in my definition would therefore be one that was *routinely exploiting the measurement of quality in the refinement of its processes.* This would mean dropping the requirement for SPC and distribution-based statistical control and replacing it with the use of the 'simpler' approaches of histograms, box plots, Pareto charts, etc., as *indicators*. As a result, for example:

- an individual project would measure fault densities for some or all of its products

- the project would use coarse criteria based on those densities to identify potential trouble spots

- the organisation would consolidate fault density data at the organisation level for comparison by projects and for identification by management of processes needing attention

- the project would carry out causal analysis of faults in order to make local process improvements

- the organisation would consolidate project-level improvements at the organisational level as improvements to the 'corporate process'.

HEADLINE

The best measurements are those that can be used as predictive *indicators*, especially where they help you to spot potential chaos.

Adding indicators to the Resource Plan

Once your planning has advanced to the stage where you have a thorough strategy and a detailed work package analysis, the time is right to choose the indicators you believe will give you visibility of the inner workings and sensitivities of your project. Indicators that concentrate on fault detection and densities should come at the top of your list.

Knowing which indicators you want to use, you can finally add to the WBS activities for defining them in detail, for acquiring and installing any tool support for collecting and analysing them, and (if you think the task is worth identifying separately) for doing the regular analysis that will point up those areas of potential chaos.

Chapter recap

At regular intervals you find out what progress there has been on work packages that have started and reassess the effort required for future work packages. You also reassess the activities required for risk and opportunity management and across the project in general. You check that the dependencies you are showing on your activity network are all still valid and whether there are any new ones.

By updating your Work Package Analysis and activity network you obtain new forecasts of the base cost of the project and dates of future milestones.

You reassess the risk and opportunity profile of your project and revise the provisions you have made for the level of comfort you require.

By tracking the provisions funnel you can see whether your project is under control.

By measuring key indicators on your project you can spot potential trouble spots before they blossom into major trouble areas.

OUTCOME

As a result of the monthly review, you can prepare an up-to-date forecast of the future through an understanding of the past.

References

Deming 1986

Out of the Crisis. W E Deming. Cambridge University Press, Cambridge, 1986

Fenton 1991

Software Metrics – a rigorous approach. N E Fenton. Chapman & Hall, London, 1991

Hoaglin 1983

Understanding Robust and Exploratory Data Analysis. Edited by D C Hoaglin, F Mosteller, and J W Tukey. Wiley, Chichester, 1983

Humphreys 1989

Managing the software process. W S Humphreys. Addison-Wesley, Reading, 1989

Ishikawa 1990

Introduction to quality control. K Ishikawa, translated by J Loftus. 3A Corporation, 1990

SEI 1995

The Capability Maturity Model: Guidelines for Improving the Software Process. Software Engineering Institute. Addison-Wesley, Reading, 1995

11 *Blocks on the slipway*

Changing is hard

Over the years I have done a lot of work introducing and encouraging new software engineering methods into organisations. The response – as one would expect – has been mixed. Some of the blocks that people have to taking on new methods and tools start to sound familiar after a year or two. They have a similar pattern. Here are some variations on what we will quickly see is a common dilemma.

- We can't use a new and unfamiliar method on a fixed price contract because we increase the risk of exceeding our budget and/or timescales. We can't use a new method on a time and materials contract because the client won't stand for the bill for training and learning time, or for the increased timescales necessary to cover our training and familiarisation, or for the risk it represents.

- We can't use a new method on a real job because there is a risk that we will fail on it as a result. There's no point in trying out a new method on an artificial job created for the purpose because there aren't the pressures of a real job.

- The first project on which we use a new method must be one on which the method will succeed or the method will lose credibility right from the start. If we use a new method on a difficult project where it could fail then the outcome will not prove anything about the method. If we use a new method on an easy project and it succeeds then we shall have proved nothing.

- It's not possible to decide on methods at the start of a project because we don't know much about the system and hence what methods would be appropriate. It's not worth deciding on methods after a project has started because it's too late to do anything about training, tooling, planning and so on.

- It's no good sending our people willy-nilly on training courses on new methods because unless there is the immediacy of using it on a real project they won't be motivated to understand it. We can't send people on courses once a project has started because we probably haven't got the budget or the time for such luxuries, even if the client would buy the idea, i.e. it's too late.

- We can't introduce a new method on a small project because it will probably be too short and there will not be the time or budget for training. We can't introduce a new method on a large project because the increased risk and cost of failure would be too great.

- We can't use a new method on a project until we have seen it work on other projects.

- Training must take place on the project on which a new method is to be used. The cost of training cannot be borne on a single project because it is quite likely to be too large a proportion of up-front money.

- We cannot safely use a new method on a project unless we have a person on the team familiar with the use of that method. We don't have such a person because we haven't used the method before.

- What we are looking for on projects is reducing risk and increasing predictability. Traditional methods, being informal, increase risk and reduce predictability (because it is difficult to tell whether something is complete, consistent or correct if it is informally expressed or informally developed). However, we continue to use them and take the risks. Formal methods reduce risk and increase predictability because we can make positive statements about what we produce. However we do not use formal methods because we suspect they are more risky and we cannot predict how successful our use of them will be.

- We can't use a new method unless we have the tools to support it. But we don't mind using a traditional method even though there is no tool support.

- We could justify the use of a new method on a project if we could quantify the costs of using it. But we use traditional methods on projects even though we can't quantify the costs of using them (e.g. we are still unable to make reliable estimates).

- Tools that are generally applicable are generally weak. Strong tools are very specific and hence generally inapplicable.

- An important feature of new methods is that they tend to be powerful in particular areas. This makes them generally inapplicable. The traditional methods are weak in all areas. This makes them generally inapplicable.

Well, software engineers might seem a conservative lot, but of course they do have very real problems to face – generally today's problems – and managers will only make changes to the status quo if there is a pretty clear sign that there will be a pay-off not too far over their event horizon.

But breaking these dilemmas is clearly something that is necessary if new improved practices are to be taken on. The answer varies considerably and I have adopted a number of different approaches in different situations.

Breaking the blocks

Let me start by dividing the dilemmas into a number of basic problems faced by those wanting to introduce new methods. I then want to show how risk planning in particular can give you a framework in which to attack them. Here they are:

- Changing how we do things *before* a new project is started is wasted effort; changing how we doing things *after* a new project is started is effort that is too late.

- All new things must have proved their value before we try them.

- Trying new things on fake projects is unrealistic; trying new things on real projects is foolhardy.

Given that there are so many excellent reasons for not changing, it's a wonder that things do change. Here are some of the reasons that things change despite everything. It's useful to know what they are as you can use them as levers to break the blocks.

Have a champion. Having someone on the team – ideally the technical authority – who really wants the new method or tool to work can be 50% of the battle. It means you have someone who is committed to finding ways of making it successful, someone who won't give up at the first hurdle and go back to the old *ad hoc* methods. When Nick Birrell and I were involved in a telephone call billing system the choice of design method really was a difficult one: a network of microprocessors operating independently had to be coordinated in the real-time environment of a telephone exchange. Nick had read about Estrin's SARA method and felt it had a good match – the computational models were a good fit.

Although neither he nor the team had experience using it, Nick was sure it was the right answer and started by training the team in the methods at the beginning of the project. He drove the use of that method, adding project-specific detail and removing things that didn't work. Without his championship of the method it might not have been successful.

Get your customer to demand new practices. (But please let those practices be good ones and appropriate ones.) Government departments or major computer users often require particular methods or tools to be used in developments done for them. If you want the contract, you use the method required. This concentrates minds wonderfully in the supply side of the industry and the suppliers start to get their staff trained and to buy the tools. This clearly isn't the ideal way of going about things, since blanket rules such as this can be counterproductive unless sensitively handled – as most agencies know. But I suspect that – in the UK at least – the interest in methods has been beneficially increased by such pressures.

Find new things that really do let people do things better. Most software engineers are really very keen to do a good job. After all, getting software that works is most of the fun. A poor engineer must surely be an unhappy one. Methods can be of interest particularly to staff new to the industry. Old hands, who never learnt a method (perhaps because there weren't any when they started in the industry) are generally more reluctant to learn a method – simply because they have devised their own over years of experience. Throwing that experience away in favour of some 'alien' method is not an idea likely to attract anyone, particularly skilled staff. But young minds do not have this barrier to overcome; they accept methods because they are there.

Provided that the methods really do work, and are applied in the right places, and do not conflict with previously held views developed over years of experience, then such methods can be taken on quite smoothly.

The situation with tools is little different. Tools are not a million miles from toys and they can have an attraction for that reason. But from my observations I deduce that the same blocks occur as occur with methods. One of the major reasons that I have found people unwilling to use a new tool is not that it doesn't do X or Y, but that it doesn't automate *precisely* what they currently do by hand. A tool can have as many extra benefits and features, but if it doesn't work the way people work *now* then people won't want to use it: CASE tools that draw different shaped boxes from those used now, or that capture data in a slightly different fashion, languages that don't permit certain control or data structures, and so on. This must make life very difficult for the tool developer.

Handling the risks of innovation

If a new method is truly seen as a risk and yet you feel it is the correct choice, then you should simply apply the risk planning process recursively: treat the use of, say, the new method as a risk and decide what process model (or changes to the process model) and what process fragments you could use to reduce that risk downstream. Then work this back into your plan.

Possible process model changes might include a pilot phase on part of the system before the main development begins, and a parallel development with conventional methods on any area considered particularly dangerous. Additional plan fragments might be included for increased training, increased familiarisation activities, the use of external consultants in the method at critical points, and reviews of success at critical points (giving you the option of cutting your losses if the worst comes to the worst).

These additional activities will of course initially increase costs and possibly extend timescales. You must decide if those increases are acceptable and this will depend on the perspective you are taking. If your horizon does not extend beyond the current development project, it might be very hard to justify. This can be the case where one department is responsible for initial development and another for subsequent enhancement. It is not in the interests of the first department to invest more than it needs in doing its job.

If your decision horizon extends over the whole life of the project – i.e. beyond development, through enhancement, to final replacement – then the advantages of the new approach may outweigh increases in the development. This can be the case with a system that is likely to be subject to a lot of change – a little extra spent now to get a firm basis for the future can pay considerable dividends in the longer term. Calculating whole life costs is hard but can reveal the advantages of early investment.

If your horizon takes in all the projects in a department or company, it becomes easier to take on training, familiarisation, and tooling costs for the benefits that it can bring to you as a software engineering group. An investment (i.e. increased costs) on one project can lead to savings in subsequent projects, and such savings can be invested in part in further developments, thereby snowballing the benefits.

Getting the basic experience

Ultimately there is no substitute for using new methods on real projects with real pressures. But you might want to get the basic experience in a less risky way. Here are some simple suggestions.

- Use the new methods or tools in parallel with your traditional methods and tools. This could be done on just a part of the system if necessary. It has the advantage of giving you something real to work on without being totally reliant on the results.

  For instance, you might be interested in getting familiar with formal methods of specification, let's say Z. Find a part of the system that is amenable to specification in this way and specify that part of the system in your normal way and with Z. Have an activity to compare the results and the costs at the end. Squeeze as many lessons as you can out of the experience. Try Z on a bigger slice on the next system, or do just a part of the specification in Z alone, and the rest with your normal method.

- Less effective is to rework all or part of a completed development using the new method or tool. This is less satisfactory for all the obvious reasons, but it can be effective for simply getting to grips with the method and acquiring a deep understanding of its strengths and weaknesses. The engineers have time to explore and find out how it should be used, rather than unwittingly misusing it but getting by under pressure of time. It is rather like an extended real-life exercise at the end of the training course, with the opportunity to take a harder look at what is going on.

- The lowest risk approach is of course to watch someone else using the method, preferably a team that is expert in its use. This might be possible somewhere in your own organisation or even in another. Watching an expert use a method can reveal many insights that might take you years to discover by chance.

- Finally, in all cases it is well known that having an expert at hand – ideally on full-time secondment to the project – is essential. It is all too easy for a team starting with a new method to misunderstand basic principles or to use it in an inappropriate and ineffective way, without knowing. As a result they can quickly become disenchanted with the method and write it off as of no use. An expert can guide the team to an understanding of the principles and effective use at the point where they go wrong.

12 Diary of a voyage

Introduction

In this chapter I have put together a worked example, developed as an amalgam of many projects I have seen or taken part in, and which we used in our own training courses in Praxis. It starts with an *Invitation to Tender* (ITT) (or *Request for Quotation*, RFQ) from a company called Snoozo which is in the satellite TV advertising business and which wants a system to handle the scheduling of advert transmission. As you would expect, their ITT is full of problems awaiting the developer. (It's their right to set these problems – that's what they're paying us to solve.) The ITT appears below. Quite a bit of detail has been omitted where it is irrelevant to the subject matter of this book.

You'll then find the Risk Plan prepared at the time of bidding for the work. It illustrates the maxim 'write down what you don't know, as well as what you do know'. Then, there's a draft Quality Plan. The way that I have drawn it up, in quite a lot of detail, might be a bit too much to expect in some areas at bid time but it would be quite standard at project inception. Finally, there's the starting point of a Resource Plan for the project to do the work. The main point to note from the WBS of the Resource Plan is how its overall structure and many of the key details derive firstly from the Risk Plan and secondly from the Quality Plan. The precise form in which these three plans will appear will of course depend on your organisation's conventions – I have simply shown the main contents.

You might need to suspend your disbelief over some points, not least that some detail is absent. Remember though that the aim is to illustrate the major lessons of the preceding chapters.

The Invitation to Tender

This section describes the requirements of a system to support the Snoozo Satellite Advertising System. It is to be used by bidders to prepare a proposal to carry out the work identified below.

Snoozo plc have acquired the rights to transmission channels 326 and 327 of the Boresat European television satellite outside day-time broadcasting from mid-2001 to mid-2006. It is Snoozo's current intention to sell time to advertisers during the so-called 'night-time' period. Advertisements will consist of pre-recorded video features of varying length that will be transmitted at the appropriate time to Boresat for broadcasting. In the longer term all-day advertising channels may be leased and this should be borne in mind by bidders.

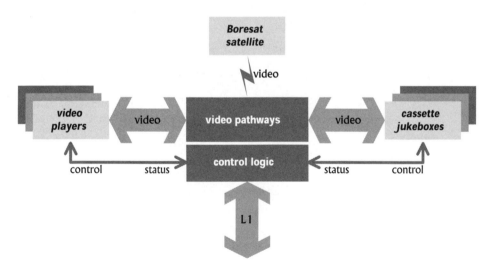

Figure 12-1. Simple block diagram of SULCS

Snoozo have already contracted with Horsefall Ltd of Auchtermuchty for the development of the video storage equipment, satellite up-link, and associated control system (SULCS).

The SULCS system

SULCS stores, transmits and deletes video adverts on a videotape jukebox under commands arriving on a serial link, *L1*. The structure of SULCS is currently expected to take the form shown in the block diagram in Figure 12-1. Briefly, videotapes from advertisers are mounted on videoplayers. On receipt of a command over the link *L1*, the advert is transferred from the videotape to a designated one of the 128 video cassettes in the jukebox. SULCS can also, on command via *L1*, ready up to three jukebox cassettes prior to transmission, and, on a further command, transmit the advert on one of those cassettes to the satellite via the up-link transmitter. SULCS can also carry out some housekeeping activities such as the erasure of cassettes and the ejection of defective cassettes, again on command from *L1*.

The contract to be placed

Snoozo now wish to place a contract for the development of the Advert Storage, Programming and Information Computer (ASPIC), which will:

- maintain records on stored adverts

- maintain transmission schedules

- control the Horsefall equipment during transmission of adverts at the predetermined times

- prepare invoices for advertisers on the basis of transmission time used.

The ASPIC system will need to be connected to SULCS for these functions.

Functional specification

ASPIC is required to carry out the following functions:

1   *maintenance of a database of stored adverts*

When a new advert is to be stored on the SULCS jukebox, this will be invoked by an operator on the ASPIC system. ASPIC will keep a database of what adverts are recorded on which jukebox. ASPIC will send commands to SULCS (on interface *L1*) to transfer the advert waiting on a given videoplayer onto a specified cassette. ASPIC will also instruct SULCS to delete adverts when they are no longer required for future transmission and are not marked for future but unspecified use.

1   *maintenance of a database of advertisers, and billing of advertisers*
    ASPIC will maintain a database of advertisers who place contracts
    with Snoozo. This database will also be used to accumulate details of
    the successful transmission of their adverts so that monthly invoices
    can be prepared.

2   *storage of newly received adverts*
    New advertising videos will be received on a regular basis (typically
    on a Friday) and they must be stored on SULCS ready for transmis-
    sion within six hours. This storage must be controlled by the video
    engineer from ASPIC. ASPIC must instruct the operator in the
    mounting of the videotape and then send commands to SULCS to
    transfer the advert(s) to a free jukebox cassette. ASPIC must get
    from the operator details on the advert(s) including requirements for
    its transmission, and must update the advert database accordingly.

3   *transmission of adverts*
    Although SULCS carries out the transfer of video from cassette to
    up-link equipment, it must do this under command from ASPIC.
    ASPIC must therefore take timely action to instruct SULCS to ready
    the appropriate cassettes and to begin transmissions at the specified
    times. SULCS timing information will be available from Horsefall.
    ASPIC must take appropriate action in the event of failure of
    SULCS. Successful transmission must be noted in the database for
    subsequent billing. It is a requirement that a blank screen should
    never be transmitted. In some cases one cassette might contain more
    than one advert, but no more than 100.

4   *connection with accounting system*
    Snoozo is currently updating its company accounting system and
    there could be a requirement to connect ASPIC to a remote Beeswax
    1901A PC in order to transfer invoice information periodically.

5   *transmission planning*
    In some situations it may be necessary for ASPIC to be able to assign
    transmission slots for adverts according to a number of criteria (yet
    to be determined) rather than using specific times. ASPIC must in
    such situations advise the operator of acceptable and available trans-
    mission times.

6   *future expansion*

Snoozo expect to require future enhancements in two areas. Firstly, in some installations videoplayers will be replaced or augmented by videodisc as the input medium. Secondly, the existing jukebox will, in some installations, be increased in capacity to 512 cassettes. Ideally these should be available for the start of broadcasting.

Figure 12-2 shows our understanding of the structure of the combined SULCS–ASPIC system.

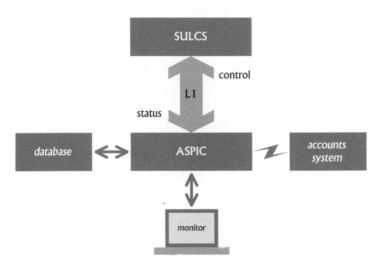

Figure 12-2. Simple block diagram of combined system

The supply

Bidders are required to present a proposal and plan of work to:

- prepare a specification of the entire ASPIC system to Snoozo's satisfaction

- propose for Snoozo's approval a hardware and software configuration for ASPIC

- design and implement the ASPIC system to the agreed specifications

- demonstrate the correct working of ASPIC in conjunction with a single 256-cassette SULCS.

Bidders can propose either to use an existing Beeswax 1904 available from Snoozo or to use new equipment. In the latter case the cost-effectiveness of the use of new equipment must be proved.

As from 3rd March 2001 one channel on Boresat will be available to the contractor for testing. Two channels are expected to be available from 12th April 2001. The system must go live on both channels on 15th May 2001.

The Risk & Quality Plan

1 Introduction

This section presents the Risk & Quality Plan for a project to develop the system whose requirements are defined above.

Snoozo plc have acquired the rights to transmission channels 326 and 327 of the Boresat European television satellite outside day-time broadcasting from mid-2001 to mid-2006. It is Snoozo's current intention to sell time to advertisers during the so-called 'night-time' period. Advertisements will consist of pre-recorded video features of varying length that will be transmitted at the appropriate time to Boresat for broadcasting.

Snoozo have already contracted with Horsefall Ltd of Auchtermuchty for the development of the video storage equipment, satellite up-link, and associated control system (SULCS).

The system to be developed is the Advert Storage, Programming and Information Computer (ASPIC), which will:

- maintain records on advertisers and stored adverts

- control the transfer of adverts onto SULCS

- control the Horsefall equipment (SULCS) during transmission of adverts at the predetermined times

- prepare invoice data for advertisers on the basis of transmission time used.

2 Risk management plan

2.1 Risks identified

The following risks have been identified:

1   We are not certain in detail what is required. The specification as it stands is too vague to give a reliable fixed price for the whole development.

2   It may be that we have problems with the interface to the SULCS system. An external contractor is already working on the equipment that will have to be controlled by ours, and they are geographically distant. The interface that they are presumably working on at this very minute is crucial. Getting it sorted out is an early priority.

3   It may be that we have problems get access to the SULCS system. It doesn't look as though it will be available until later than ideal. This could delay our verification work.

4   We are uncertain how the SULCS would work when operating with videodisc inputs rather than videotape. Presumably the interface between SULCS and ASPIC will change, but we do not know how.

5   We are uncertain how ASPIC will handle more than one SULCS and what implications there will be for performance etc. if the SULCS system is replicated at some point in the future.

6   We are uncertain whether the existing Beeswax machine will handle the load. We are uncertain about what other work it is doing at the same time.

7   We are uncertain who will use this system and what sort of interface they would accept at the single workstation. By all accounts the users will principally be video engineers, and their work patterns are not known.

8   Given that the real-time activity – the transmission of adverts – in principle causes update of the database, we are uncertain whether we can afford to leave these updates until during the day-time. What happens if the system fails between transmission and database update? Could the lost revenue be guessed at or what? These are issues for the design and do not lead to process model considerations.

9   We are uncertain about the arrival and loading of videos onto the jukebox. What sort of volumes are likely to arrive? Could they all be loaded into the jukebox in time for transmission start-up? Indeed, should the system be able to load new adverts during transmission time? If it can't there could be problems if the option to go to all-day advertising is taken up.

10 We are uncertain about the timing information on video transmission, which is going to be critical and will affect the design of the ASPIC real-time software. It is coming from Horsefall.

11 [etc., etc.]

2.2 Chosen risk reduction measures

Analysis of the risks and uncertainties suggests that the following features will be required in the project. (Numbering corresponds to risks numbering.) Two risks are sufficiently large to warrant significant process model structuring:

1 Because of the overall vagueness of the specification of ASPIC and the system it is to be connected to, we will split the project into a fixed price definition phase (phase 1) followed by an implementation phase (phase 2). For now the client will accept a budgetary estimate for the implementation phase. By the end of the definition phase we must have determined a fixed price for phase 2 and – if necessary – reduced functionality to bring it to within the budgetary estimate. This means we also do not want to be too optimistic with the budgetary estimate.

In summary, the first phase will deliver a system specification agreed with Snoozo, a SULCS–ASPIC interface specification agreed with Horsefall, and a firm price for the second phase.

4, 5 The two subsequent enhancements that are required are even less clear currently. The first two phases should concentrate on the basic system required for the first transmissions, using a 256-cassette jukebox. Activities in phase 2 (see below) should determine the enhancement requirements in sufficient detail for us to ensure that the architecture prepared in phase 2 will support them. Further phases can then be agreed to provide those enhancements once the initial system has been installed and has been proved in operation. If the scoping of the second phase requires it, we could also delay some of the less vital functionality to these later phases.

The overall process model is therefore as shown in Figure 12-3.

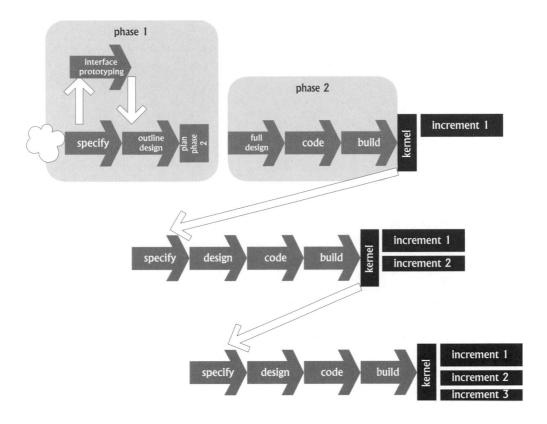

Figure 12-3. A skeleton for the Snoozo project

During phase 1 there must be the following process fragments (activities and dependencies):

1   *Prepare and agree* a system specification. This is a standard part of the basic process model so nothing extra is called for.

    Prepare phase 2 Risk, Quality and Resource Plans at the end of the phase once the system specification has been agreed. We would have to do these at the start of phase 2, but we will move them into phase 1 to allow us to do the fixed price estimate for phase 2.

2   *Agree* formal SULCS–ASPIC interface specification in the form of a state transition diagram/matrix, including timings, during the system specification activity and before phase 2 planning starts.

9   *Determine* worst case video loading timings and resultant loads, and check feasibility during the system specification activity and before phase 2 planning starts. We need to do some calculations about peak loading times and, if necessary, agree some constraints on the overall capacity of the system in the system specification.

5   *Establish* performance characteristics of the system with one and more than one SULCS, during an outline design activity.

6   We need an early activity to find out what spare capacity (of all sorts) there is on the existing machine and another activity to establish approximate loading profiles for the proposed system.

Establish the level of spare capacity of the existing Beeswax target machine and check its sufficiency before phase 2 planning starts and after the outline design is complete. If necessary, budget and design for a new machine.

During phase 2 there must be the following plan fragments:

1   Integration in the second phase should proceed in an order that makes the time-critical parts of the system available first for testing.

3   Since we don't expect to get early enough access to the SULCS system we will have to build some form of simulator to mimic the interface so that we can integrate well before we attach to the Horsefall kit.

Define, design and build a SULCS simulator, so that it is ready before the start of integration. (Is there some way this can be generated without writing too much code? In particular, can we generalise it for different protocols?)

Integrate with the SULCS simulator at earliest moment that this makes sense.

4   *Investigate* the effect of using videodiscs during the design so that the architecture can cope with this.

5   Since in future the SULCS system might be replicated our architecture must make ASPIC able to handle more than one SULCS at a time – a consideration for phase 2 design. Performance will also be an issue and we should do some coarse calculations early in the architectural design phase to check that, while the kit might be up to handling one system, it is also up to handling more than one (and perhaps finding out how many). We should also do an actual loading

measurement with the simulator when everything has been put together to see just what spare there might be.

Carry out performance calculations during architectural design phase.

Carry out performance measurements using simulator towards end of integration.

4,5 *Prepare and agree* details of the subsequent phases for the enhancements once the system has entered trials.

7 *Prototype* forms interface for users at start of phase 2.

10 *Review* SULCS timing characteristics with Horsefall before starting design. We need as a minimum a review activity with them on those timings, as well as some dependencies on them in the plan.

Phases 1 and 2 now look like the skeleton in Figure 12-4.

2.3 Residual risk assessment

[Not covered here.]

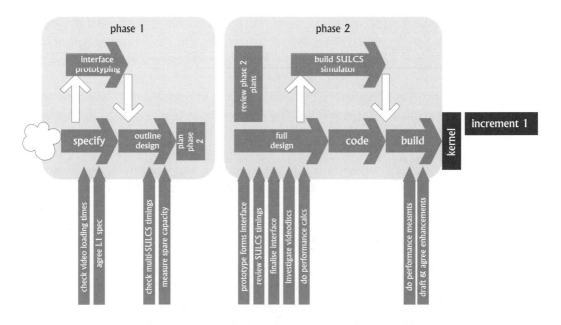

Figure 12-4. Snoozo process model for phases 1 and 2 with process fragments added

3 Quality achievement plan

3.1 Characterisation of system to be developed

The system has two parts: a database-based part which is user-driven from forms and operating on a simple database, and a time-critical real-time part that is event- (e.g. clock-) driven. Some coupling exists. The communications with SULCS take place over a state-driven interface.

There is no element of criticality in the system that requires special software engineering considerations.

3.2 Client expectation or requirements on development

The client expects to be able to maintain the delivered system on their own Beeswax equipment so delivered tools etc. must be based on it. They have said they would buy any licences necessary for their kit.

3.3 Chosen development methods

The target infrastructure of the system is a combination of the BeeOS operating system and its scheduling mechanisms (for the real-time components and overall system scheduling) and the BeeDB database management system (for the database-oriented aspects of the system).

The decomposition criteria will also divide along the line between the real-time components (controlling, for example, the link with SULCS) and the user-driven database-oriented components. For the former, the decomposition will be into BeeOS processes communicating through the supplied BeeOS inter-process communication mechanisms. For the latter, the decomposition will derive principally from the windows presented to the user; a secondary decomposition will cover processes spawned from forms (such as those performing off-line functions, e.g. printing or taking backups). Therefore, our methods should be as follows:

- *User Layer.* For the full specification of the database-based aspects of the system we shall do Chen data modelling to produce a logical ERA model, prepare screen and report layouts, and define screen logic and process descriptions in English. For the definition of the SULCS–ASPIC interface we shall use a state transition model (finite state machine).

- *Architectural Layer.* For the outline design we shall prepare a simple process interaction diagram sufficient for doing timing calculations. For the full design of the overall system we shall use a simple decomposition into concurrent processes and thence a functional decomposition of each process into modules. The process decomposition will be shown in Data Flow Diagrams with the Ward–Mellor extensions for showing process activation logic. A physical ERA model will be derived from the logical model.

- *Implementation Layer.* The code will be written in VB using BeeDB tools wherever possible, with the remainder (principally the real-time parts) being written in C.

3.4 Chosen tool support

We shall use BeeCASE for preparing both logical and physical ERA diagrams and supporting data dictionary. Development will be carried out using BeeDB tools and C. Forms will be tested with the BeeDB Test Manager.

3.5 Chosen target environment

This has already been specified by the client: Beeswax 1904 running BeeOS, BeeDB, etc.

3.6 Consequent activities

Two programming staff will require training in the use of the BeeDB tools: this will mean a two-week course for each (£4000 total), followed by a further two weeks' hands-on familiarisation with the tools.

The system will be developed on a Beeswax on our premises, so an activity is required to transfer the development materials to the client's system where there will be the necessary BeeDB, BeeCASE and C licences (being arranged by the client). Subsequent maintenance will then be done there.

Access to one of our in-house Beeswax systems will be needed, including access to BeeDB and its tools for a team of four, and two BeeCASE seats. Normal in-house support will be used for backup and communications during development.

At some point during phase 2 a dial-up communications link will be required to the client's Beeswax in London. This must be arranged and dates agreed with the in-house support team at the start of phase 2.

4 Quality control plan

4.1 Planned product types

See the table below. Only final and intermediate deliverables from Phase 1 and Phase 2 development are shown; deliverables relating to Phase 3 and beyond are omitted. 'QMx.x' refers to standards in the Corporate Quality Manual.

4.2 Specifications and standards

See the table below.

4.3 Quality control activities

See the table below.

4.4 Consequent activities

An activity will be required to prepare the additional project-specific standard for VB and C components.

5 Quality preservation plan

5.1 Identification control

The standard corporate identification control mechanisms defined in QM9.5 will be used.

5.2 Change control

The standard corporate change control mechanisms defined in QM9.5 will be used. A Change Control Board will be established with representation from the client.

5.3 Configuration control

The standard corporate configuration control mechanisms defined in QM9.5 will be used. Baselines will be determined by the Integration Team Leader.

5.4 Consequent activities

Activities will be required to:

- set up the change management procedures at the start of phase 2
- prepare the project-specific standard for Change Control Forms
- prepare the project-specific standard for Baseline Records
- transfer materials to the client's maintenance environment at the end of phase 2.

[Note how the project-specific standards for Change Control Forms and Baseline Records have themselves been added to the list of product types in the Quality Plan table so that their quality attributes and quality control activities are fully thought through.]

Item	Standard or spec	V&V method	V&V standard	V&V record	V&V approval
User Layer					
System Specification (general)	QM3.1	review	QM2.2	Review Record	Client, Project Manager
– logical ER model	QM3.7	review	QM2.2	Review Record	Project Technical Authority
– Form layouts and logic	QM3.5	review	QM2.2	Review Record	Client, Project Technical Authority
– Functional description in English	QM3.2	review	QM2.2	Review Record	Client, Project Technical Authority
– STD definition of L1	QM3.9	Chow validation suite	QM3.9.1	annotated validation results	Horsefall, Project Technical Authority
Phase 2 system	System Specification	Acceptance Testing based on equivalence partitioning	QM6.5	annotated test output	Client
Acceptance Test Specification	QM6.5 and System Specification (duration etc.)	review against System Specification	QM2.2	Review Record	Client, Project Manager
User Manual	QM3.12	review with client users	QM2.2	Review Record	Client
Training course	QM3.13 and System Specification	review with client management	QM2.2	Review Record	Client

Item	Standard or spec	V&V method	V&V standard	V&V record	V&V approval
Architecture Layer					
Outline design (process interaction diagram)	QM4.3 and System Specification	review	QM2.2	Review Record	Project Technical Authority
Design (general)	QM4.3 and System Specification	review	QM2.2	Review Record	Project Technical Authority
– Ward-Mellor DFD	QM4.2	review and animation	QM2.2	Review Record	Project Technical Authority
– physical ER model	QM4.5 and logical ER model	review	QM2.2	Review Record	Project Technical Authority
– Process Specification	QM4.4 and System Specification	review	QM2.2	Review Record	Project Technical Authority
Specification and design for SULCS Simulator	QM4.3	review against L1	QM2.2	Review Record	Project Technical Authority
Integrated process	Process Specification	dynamic testing	QM6.4	annotated test output	Integration Team Leader
Process Integration Test Specification (per process)	QM6.4	review	QM2.2	Review Record	Integration Team Leader
SULCS Simulator	SULCS Simulator Specification	dynamic testing to level 1	QM6.1	annotated test output	Design Team Leader

Item	Standard or spec	V&V method	V&V standard	V&V record	V&V approval
Implementation Layer					
VB component	VB Component Specification and QM5.8 (VB coding standard)	code inspection	project-specific standard and QM5.1	annotated listing	independent programmer
		dynamic testing to level 2	QM6.2	annotated test output	Design Team Leader
C component	C Component Test Specification and QM5.3 (C coding standard)	code inspection	QM6.1.1	annotated listing	independent programmer
		dynamic testing to level 2a	QM6.1	annotated test output	Design Team Leader
VB Component Test Specification	QM6.2	review	QM2.2	Review Record	VM Team Leader
C Component Test Specification	QM6.1	review	QM2.2	Review Record	C Team Leader

Item	Standard or spec	V&V method	V&V standard	V&V record	V&V approval
Other products					
Change Control Form	QM9.5 and project-specific standard	review	QM2.2	Review Record	Change Control Board
Baseline Record	QM9.5 and project-specific standard	review	QM2.2	Review Record	Integration Team Leader
Project Standard for Change Control Forms	QM0.0 (Standard for standards)	review	QM2.2	Review Record	Quality Manager
Project Standard for Baseline Records	QM0.0	review	QM2.2	Review Record	Quality Manager
Project Plan (phase 1)	QM9.1	review	QM2.2	Review Record	Client, Managing Director
Risk Plan (phase 1)	QM9.1	review	QM2.2	Review Record	Client, Managing Director
Quality Plan (phase 1)	QM9.3	review	QM2.2	Review Record	Client, Managing Director
Project Progress Report	QM9.4	review	QM2.2	Review Record	Managing Director
Purchase Order	QM9.13	informal inspection	–	signature	Project Manager

The Resource Plan

(This section contains an initial WBS derived from the analysis in the Risk Plan, activities from the Quality Plan, and further activities culled from a hypothetical corporate standard *Generic Work Breakdown Structure*.

The two important points to note are:

- while many activities are common to many projects and can therefore be picked from a checklist, Risk and Quality Planning helps you to make them more specific and hence more amenable to accurate estimation

- many key activities are revealed by Risk and Quality Planning, and are unlikely to be picked up from general checklists.)

The Phase 1 Work Breakdown Structure

1000 Project Management (phase 1)

1100	Initiate phase 1
	…
1200	Plan phase 1

    1210   Draft Risk Plan (done)
    1220   Draft Quality Plan (done)
    1230   Draft Resource Plan (being done)
    1240   Review draft plans to provisional status
    1250   Submit provisional plans to client for agreement
    1260   Issue first definitive plans

1300   Prepare firm price for phase 2
    1310   Prepare draft Risk Plan for phase 2
    1320   Prepare draft Quality Plan for phase 2
    1330   Prepare draft Resource Plan for phase 2
    1340   Prepare and submit firm price for phase 2

1400   Monitor and report on project progress
    …

1500   Administer project
    1510   Maintain project accounts
    1520   Maintain project files and backups
    1530   Control project documentation and records
    1540   Prepare Work Package Instructions
    1550   Liaise with hardware suppliers (Horsefall, Beeswax)
    1560   Liaise with client (Snoozo Technical Department)
    1570   Agree training needs with line manager and project team
    1580   Conduct staff training
        1581   Train two programmers in use of BeeDB tools
        1582   Familiarise programmers in BeeDB tools

1600   Close phase 1 of project
    1610   …

2000 Preliminary User Layer

2100   Produce draft ASPIC system specification
    2110   Specify $L1$ interface as FSM with timings
    2120   Review and agree $L1$ specification against standard
            and other quality attributes
    2130   Draft screen and report layouts and logic
    2140   Review layouts against standards
    2150   Review and agree layouts with users
    2160   Prepare overall English functional specification

	2170	Review functional specification with client against standard
	2180	Prepare logical ERA Chen model
	2190	Review and agree ERA model with users
	21A0	Validate ERA model against enhancements
2200	Produce outline design	
	2210	Check video loading timings
	2220	Investigate use of videodiscs
	2230	Investigate multi-SULCS performance
	2240	Establish spare capacity on target machine
	2250	Prepare process interaction diagram
	2260	Carry out timing calculations on spare capacity
	2270	Amend draft ASPIC system specification as necessary
2300	Review draft ASPIC system specification	
2400	Agree ASPIC system specification with client	

The Phase 2 Work Breakdown Structure

3000 Project Management (phase 2)

3100	Initiate phase 2		
	3110	…	
3200	Plan phase 2		
	3210	Revise Risk Plan	
	3220	Prepare provisional Quality Plan	
		3221	Prepare quality achievement strategy
		3222	Prepare quality control strategy
		3223	Prepare quality preservation strategy
		3224	Prepare project standards
			32241 Prepare VB testing standard
			32242 Prepare standard for change control forms
			32243 Prepare standard for baseline records
	3230	Prepare provisional Resource Plan	
		3231	Prepare work breakdown structure
		3232	Prepare activity network
		3233	Deduce staffing and costs
		3234	Choose metrics and indicators
	3240	Agree provisional plans with client	
	3250	Issue first definitive plans	
	3260	Maintain plans thereafter	
3300	Monitor and report on project progress		
	3310	…	
3400	Administer project		
	3410	…	
3500	Liaise with client (Snoozo)		
3600	Train staff		

3610   Agree phase 2 training needs (e.g. via Resource Plan)
3620   Conduct staff training
3700   Install and maintain development environment
3710   Establish dial-up communications to Snoozo
3720   …
3800   Close project (including debriefing)
3810   …

4000 Complete User Layer

4100   Review requirements after phase 1
4110   Prototype forms for user interface
4120   Review SULCS timing characteristics with Horsefall
4200   Specify acceptance criteria
4210   Produce Acceptance Test Specification (ATS)
4220   Review ATS against standard and System Spec with client
4230   Agree ATS with client
4300   Carry out acceptance
4310   Establish test environment
4320   Conduct Acceptance Test of system against ATS
4330   Review results and agree acceptance
4400   Provide supporting material
4410   Provide User Manual
4411   Prepare User Manual for engineers
4412   Review User Manual against standard and with users
4413   Agree User Manual with client
4414   Carry out agreed usability tests on User Manual
4420   Provide training
4421   Prepare and agree engineer training plan
4422   Give engineer training
4423   Check training against learning objectives
4500   Release system
4510   Transfer development materials to client's system
…
45n0   Prepare and agree subsequent phases
45n1   …

5000 Architecture Layer

5100   Prepare architecture
5110   Identify target infrastructure
5120   Prepare and review overall design (DFD and control logic)
5130   Validate process control logic against $L1$ specification
5140   Define physical database structure as ERA model
5150   Validate physical ERA model against logical

5160   Prepare and review process specifications
5170   Check architecture completeness with System Specification
5180   Carry out performance calculations from architecture
5190   Check implications of videodiscs on architecture

5200 Define integration strategy
5210   Prepare Process Integration Test Specification per process
5220   Define development and test tools
    5221   Define SULCS simulator
    5222   Build SULCS simulator
    5223   Validate simulator against *L1*
    5224   Build or procure other test tools

5300 Integrate system
5310   Establish test environment (including SULCS simulator)
5320   Build and test processes against Process Integration Test Specifications
5330   Carry out performance measurements with simulator
5340   Review test results

6000 Implementation Layer

6100 Specify components
6110   Prepare and review real-time component specifications
6120   Prepare and review form specifications
6130   Prepare and review report specifications
6140   Prepare and review physical database definitions

6200 Construct components
6210   Prepare and review real-time (C) components against specifications
6220   Prepare and review forms components (VB) against specifications
6230   Prepare and review reports components (BeeDB Forms) against specifications
6240   Construct and review database tables against physical ER model

6300 Define component tests
6310   Prepare and review real-time component test specifications
6320   Prepare and review forms test specifications
6330   Prepare and review report test specifications

6400 Test components
6410   Test real-time components against specifications
6420   Test forms against specifications
6430   Test reports against specifications

etc

(Notes

- Unless a specific quality control action is noted against a deliverable the production activity is assumed to contain some form of review.

- Much fine detail has been omitted where it does not illustrate the themes of this book.

- The WBS has been constructed initially around the three system models: User Layer, Architectural Layer and Implementation Layer. There is nothing sacred about this.)

HEADLINE

The analysis done in risk and quality planning yields a comprehensive Work Breakdown Structure, and hence provides a sound basis on which to base cost and schedule estimates.

13 Résumé of the planning process and its products

Introduction

We have covered a lot of ground.

En route I have introduced some 'theory' that is designed to make sure that we look at the topics of risk and quality in the most productive way we can. The theory uses concepts that make us look at what is important, in the way that is the most constructive.

I have then applied the theory to the business of planning a project. This has allowed us to construct, piece by piece, a rigorous process for analysing the job in hand and devising, from our analysis, a plan that is as reliable as we can make it.

In this final chapter, I shall now pull together all the separate steps and present them as an apparently seamless process. For my taste, what follows looks almost too mechanical, too much like a cook book recipe. Life is never so simple that we can start at the beginning of such a process and trundle through it slavishly to the end, nor indeed would this ever be a very good idea. For any given situation, the process needs adaptation and thought. Above all, thought.

So, with that warning, here is the complete process and the formats of its two products, the Risk Register and the Risk & Quality Plan. Central to it is of course the big picture, which we saw in Chapter 9 but which bears repeating here as Figure 13-1.

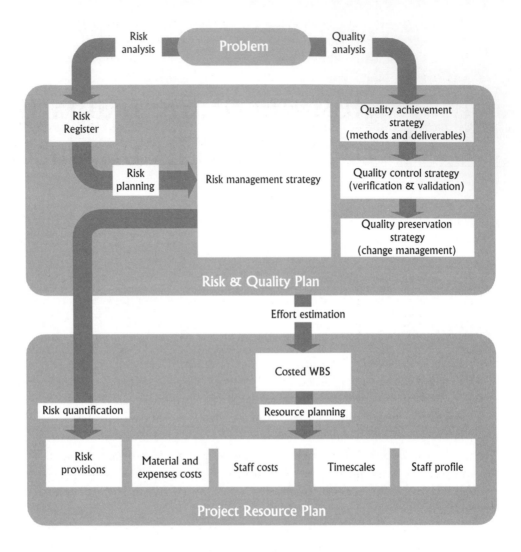

Figure 13-1. The big picture

Risk & Quality Planning summarised

Our starting point is the risk management strategy derived from an analysis of the project risks. A parallel analysis of the system's nature leads us to a sequence of three strategies concerned with the quality of what we shall deliver: the quality achievement strategy, the quality control strategy and the quality preservation strategy. The deductions we make from these strategies yield our Risk & Quality Plan. Together with some effort estimating, this analysis generates everything we need in order to prepare a Resource Plan that covers staffing, costing and scheduling for the project. In the following tables I have summarised the main steps in working through Figure 13-1.

Construct the risk management strategy for the project
R1	Identify the cardinal aims of the project in terms of whole life costs, system goals and side effects. Be clear whether absolute values or variability are the issue.
R2	Use interviews, workshops, past experience and checklists to identify the risks.
R3	Construct a Risk Register that lists all the risks.
R4	Identify the cause–effect relationships between the risks and draw them up as a tree or show them as links in the Risk Register.
R5	For each risk in the Risk Register • decide whether it is due to event uncertainty or estimating uncertainty • make a first estimate of the scale of the risk in terms of its probability and its impact • add this information to the entry in the Risk Register for the risk • use its scale to determine whether you need to take action on a risk or you can leave it on the table for now.
R6	For each risk on which you want to take action • identify one or more risk reduction measures (an information-buying activity, one or more process models, a risk-influencing activity or contractual transfer, a contingency plan or insurance) • determine which (if any) are cost-effective • record the ones you choose to adopt against the risk in the Risk Register • note the switching criteria for any contingency plans.
R7	For each risk • quantify the residual risk that remains after the chosen risk reduction measures, typically indicating a spread of values • record that residual risk and its quantification against the risk in the Risk Register.
R8	Repeat steps R2 to R7 for the opportunities on the project.

Construct the quality achievement strategy for the project

QA1   Characterise the system you are developing in terms of its computational model and criticality. Consider parts of the system separately if they are different.

QA2   Identify any expectations or requirements your client has of the software engineering processes you will use.

QA3   Choose a set of methods that match the computational models from step *QA1* and that together cover the User, Architecture and Implementation Layers of the system. Take into account as appropriate the results of step *QA2* when making your choice.

QA4   Check that the methods you choose have sufficient V&V and correctness potential for the system, especially if there are elements of business or safety criticality in it.

QA5   Give similar consideration to all other major software items that will be built to support the development (eg as risk reduction measures from step *R6*). These might include simulators, test harnesses, prototypes and load generators.

QA6   Identify the activities that arise from the use of the chosen methods. These will be activities that generate different components of the User, Architecture and Implementation Layers of the system (specifications, designs, etc.).

QA7   Given the methods chosen in *QA3*, choose appropriate tools to support them and identify all the activities necessary to acquire, install and use those tools.

QA8   Define the development, target and maintenance environments and identify all the activities necessary to procure, install and support them, as well as activities to manage the movement of material (especially software) between them.

QA9   Record all your decisions in the Quality Achievement part of your Quality Plan.

Construct the quality control strategy for the project

QC1	Given the methods identified in *QA3*, list all the product types that arise from their use.
QC2	For each product type listed in *QC1*, identify where its quality attributes will be defined. This will be either a specification or a standard or both. If necessary, identify activities to prepare any standards that do not yet exist.
QC3	For each product type listed in *QC1*, identify an activity sufficient to test whether the quality attributes for the type are present. Look for reliability and efficiency in the verification and validation techniques you choose by exploiting the verification potential of the production methods you have chosen. Where there is no activity specific to the product type, specify a generic review activity.
QC4	For each quality control activity listed in *QC3*, decide what standard will be used to define its quality. If necessary, identify activities to prepare any standards that do not yet exist.
QC5	For each product type listed in *QC1*, decide what record will be kept of the quality control activity, in particular its inputs (e.g. test specifications and test data) and its outputs (e.g. screen-shots and database listings).
QC6	For each product type listed in *QC1*, decide who must give what sort of approval before an instance is accepted as satisfactory (i.e. of the required quality).
QC7	Record all your decisions in the Quality Control part of your Quality Plan.

Construct the quality preservation strategy for the project

QP1	For each product type listed in *QC1*, define how each instance will be identified (named or labelled) and how its version and state will be defined. Define the procedures and mechanisms that will be used. Identify any activities necessary to set them up.
QP2	For each configuration item type define how changes to it will be controlled. Define the procedures and mechanisms that will be used. Identify any activities necessary to set them up.
QP3	Define how baselines will be defined, produced and controlled. Define the procedures and mechanisms that will be used. Identify any activities necessary to set them up.
QP4	Record all your decisions in the Quality Preservation part of your Quality Plan.

Construct the Resource Plan for the project

RP1	Use the process model risk reduction measures to give the skeleton of your WBS.
RP2	Insert into that skeleton all the information-buying and risk-influencing activities, and any activities required to put contingency plans, contractual transfers and insurance in place.
RP3	Insert, at the appropriate points, each method's production activities as identified in step *QA6*, together with all the support activities identified in steps *QA7* and *QA8*.
RP4	Insert, at the appropriate points, all the quality control activities identified in step *QC3*, together with all the support activities identified in steps *QC2* and *QC4*.
RP5	Insert, at the appropriate points, all the activities identified in steps *QP1* to *QP3* to put your quality preservation strategy in place.
RP6	Add to the WBS any other activities required for the project. (The risk analysis and quality analysis should have generated most, but there may be others required for particular reasons.)
RP7	Estimate the effort requirement of each activity in the WBS, ideally using several approaches including top-down and bottom-up, in order to provide sanity checks on the figures.
RP8	Construct an activity network which • contains all the activities in the WBS • shows all dependencies between activities • shows all external dependencies • allocates resources with the appropriate skills for the appropriate duration to each activity • shows the critical path.
RP9	Deduce the manpower plan (who is required when).
RP10	Identify a small number of important milestones, including project completion, and read off their forecast dates onto a milestone chart.
RP11	Allocate costs to all manpower resources and fixed costs to activities, and read off the forecast total cost for planned activities.
RP12	Examine the quantification of the costs of residual risks in step *R7* and of residual opportunities in step *R8* and sum them and their spreads. Add the forecast total cost for planned activities from step *RP11* to give the total forecast cost of the project and its spread.

The structure of a Risk and Opportunity Register entry

Field	Meaning
risk number	A unique identifier for the risk.
risk description	A brief description of the risk in cause–effect terms.
causes risks	A list of the risks that this one itself causes.
source of uncertainty	An indicator saying whether the risk is caused by event and/or estimating uncertainty.
nature of uncertainty	A description of the event and/or estimating uncertainty that is causing the risk.
probability	An assessment of the likelihood that the risk will materialise.
impact	An assessment of the scale of the impact the risk could have if it materialised.
chosen risk reduction measures	A list of the pre-emptive and/or reactive measures chosen to manage the risk.
risk owner	The name of the person(s) delegated with the management of the risk and its monitoring.
residual risk	The nature of the risk that remains once the chosen risk reduction measures have had their full effect.
best case value	An assessment of the scale of the residual risk in terms of its impact on costs and schedule in the best case.
chosen case value	The value chosen as the costs and/or schedule provision for the residual risk.
worst case value	An assessment of the scale of the residual risk in terms of its impact on costs and schedule in the worst case.

The structure of a Risk & Quality Plan

1 Introduction

2 Risk management plan

2.1 Risks identified

2.2 Chosen risk reduction measures

2.3 Residual risk assessment

3 Quality achievement plan

3.1 Characterisation of system to be developed

3.2 Client expectation or requirements on development

3.3 Chosen development methods

3.4 Chosen tool support

3.5 Chosen target environment

3.6 Consequent activities

4 Quality control plan

4.1 Planned product types

4.2 Specifications and standards

4.3 Quality control activities

4.4 Consequent activities

5 Quality preservation plan

5.1 Identification control

5.2 Change control

5.3 Configuration control

5.4 Consequent activities

Glossary

This section lists the majority of the acronyms, abbreviations and terms that appear in the book and gives their meanings. Further information can be found (where available) by referring to the Index.

ACP	Activity–Channel–Pool. A diagram used in *MASCOT*.
activity network	A network showing all the activities planned for a project, drawn so as to show all their interdependencies.
Architecture Layer	The layer of development products that relate to the architect's or designer's perspective on the system.
attribute	A feature or characteristic. Used in this book in the term *quality attribute*.
base cost	The forecast cost of the planned activities of the project. It is added to the provision for risks and opportunities to give the forecast cost to completion.
binary risk	A risk that either materialises entirely or not at all.
BSI	British Standards Institute – the UK national standardisation body.
cardinal aim	A factor that contributes to the business case for a software system.
CASE	Computer Aided Software Engineering.
CCS	Calculus of Communicating Systems.
CMM	Capability Maturity Model.

change control	That part of change management that ensures that changes to products are appropriately controlled to preserve quality.
COCOMO	Constructive Cost Model.
computational model	Of a method, the types of unit into which it divides the world, and the types of relationships it defines between them.
configuration control	That part of change management that concerns the definition, construction and storage of baselines.
configuration item	Any version of any product that is under identification control.
contingency plan	A plan that will be activated if a risk materialises and that is designed to reduce the impact of the risk.
contractual transfer	Subcontracting a risky activity to someone better able to manage that risk.
CSP	Communicating Sequential Processes.
DBMS	Data Base Management System.
DFD	Data Flow Diagram.
DSDM	Dynamic Systems Development Method.
ELH	Entity Life History.
ER	Entity/Relationship.
ERA	Entity/Relationship/Attribute.
estimating uncertainty	An uncertainty about something in the world, some variability in something in the world.
event uncertainty	Uncertainty due to our lack of concrete information regarding something, as opposed to its intrinsic variability.
FSM	Finite State Machine.
functional quality attributes	Attributes that describe how something (in particular, a piece of software) should behave.
identification control	That part of change management that concerns the naming and versioning of products.
IEC	International Electrotechnical Commission.
IEE	Institution of Electrical Engineers.
IEEE	Institution of Electrical and Electronic Engineers.

Implementation Layer	The layer of development products that relate to the programmer's or implementer's perspective on the system.
IPSE	Integrated Project Support Environment.
ISO	International Organization for Standardization.
ISO 9000-3	The international guideline to the application of *ISO 9001* to software development.
ISO 9001	The international standard for Quality Management Systems.
ITT	Invitation to Tender – also known as *Request for Quotation* or *Request for Proposal.*
JSD	Jackson System Development.
JSP	Jackson Structured Programming.
KLOC	Thousand Lines of Code.
LCSAJ	Linear Code Sequence and Jump, a sub-path in a procedural software component extending from a jump destination to the next 'jump'.
M&E	Materials and Expenses.
MASCOT	Modular Approach to System Construction, Operation and Test.
method	A way of producing a product, combining a notation and syntax, heuristics for generating products in the notation and ways of analysing or verifying the resulting products.
MoD	UK Ministry of Defence.
MTBF	Mean Time Between Failures.
non-functional quality attributes	Attributes that describe how something should be like.
opportunity	Something that would make more likely the achievement of one or more of the cardinal aims of the project.
OS	Operating System.
pre-emptive risk reduction measure	A risk reduction measure that is planned to take effect before the risk materialises.
process model	A model of the development process to be adopted by a project, its basic structure, its skeleton. A strategic

	risk reduction measure that structures the project into phases that are designed to successively reduce risk.
product	Used mainly in this book to refer to anything produced during the development process, as well as the ultimate products of the project (the system, its supporting materials, etc.).
provision	See *risk provision*.
QA	Quality Assurance.
QC	Quality Control.
QMS	Quality Management System. The policy, strategy and mechanisms used by an organisation to manage quality in its products (or services).
quality achievement	That part of quality management that concerns building the required quality into products.
quality attribute	A desired attribute.
quality control	That part of quality management that concerns checking for the required quality attributes in products.
quality factoring	The deduction of the quality attributes of a development product from the quality attributes of the final system.
quality preservation	That part of quality management that concerns ensuring that changes do not jeopardise the quality of completed products.
Quality Plan	A plan implementing the quality management strategy for a project in terms of quality achievement, quality control and quality preservation.
reactive risk reduction measure	A risk reduction measure planned to take effect after a risk materialises.
Resource Plan	The plan comprising a costed Work Breakdown Structure, activity network and financial analysis. Derived principally from the results of risk and quality planning.
review	A general approach to the examination of a product in order to find any faults.
risk	A threat to the achievement of one or more of the cardinal aims of the project.

Risk Plan	A plan implementing the risk management strategy for a project.
risk provision	An amount of money or time set aside against the impact of a risk's materialising.
risk response	A chosen response to a perceived risk, possibly a risk reduction measure, possibly a decision to do nothing or wait and see.
Risk Register	A list of the risks (and opportunities) of the project, including their (cause–effect) relationships, and your analysis of them.
risk reduction measure	Any measure designed to reduce the probability or impact of a risk.
SARA	System Architect's Apprentice.
SEI	Software Engineering Institute (of Carnegie Mellon University).
side effect	Something that will go in the cost–benefit scales when we prepare the business plan for the system. One of the three types of cardinal aim of a system. A side effect an be beneficial or detrimental.
sliding risk	A risk that can have a variable impact.
specification	A definition of the required quality attributes of a product.
SQL	Structured Query Language.
SPC	Statistical Process Control.
SSADM	Structured System Analysis and Design Methodology.
SUT	System/Software Under Test.
standard	A definition of the required quality attributes of a class of products.
system goal	A cardinal aim of a system that is a primary business reason for building it.
TP	Transaction Processing.
UML	Unified Modeling Language.
User Layer	The layer of development products that relate to the user's perspective on the system.
V&V	Verification and Validation.
V&V potential	Of a method, the degree to which its analysis approaches explicitly help us to find all the faults.

validation	The comparison between the actual characteristics of something (e.g. a product of a software project) and the expected characteristics.
VB	Visual Basic.
VDM	Vienna Development Method, a mathematically formal specification method.
verification	The comparison between the actual characteristics of something (e.g. a product of a software project) and the specified characteristics.
WBS	Work Breakdown Structure, a hierarchical decomposition of all the work planned for the project.
whole life costs	The costs of the initial development or procurement of the system, plus the costs of owning the system during its lifetime. One of the three types of cardinal aim of a system.
WLC	See *whole life costs*.
WP	Work Package, an item at any level in the WBS.
Z	A mathematically formal specification method.

Index